CW01261967

William Lockhart

First Fruits of the Oxford Movement

Father William Lockhart, B.A. (Oxon), Priest of the Order of Charity
Born, 22 August 1819; died, 15 May 1892

William Lockhart

First Fruits of the Oxford Movement

*To Liam
with my best wishes
NJ Schofield 18 VII MMXI*

NICHOLAS SCHOFIELD

GRACEWING

First published in 2011

Gracewing
2 Southern Avenue, Leominster
Herefordshire HR6 0QF

All rights reserved. No part of this publication may be reproduced, stored in a retrieval system, or transmitted in any form, or by any means, electronic, mechanical, photocopying, recording or otherwise, without the written permission of the publisher.

© Nicholas Schofield, 2011

Cover photo by Seamus Ryan

The right of Nicholas Schofield to be identified as the author of this work has been asserted in accordance with the Copyright, Designs and Patents Act 1988.

ISBN 978 0 85244 753 6

Typeset by Action Publishing Technology Ltd,
Gloucester GL1 5SR

CONTENTS

List of Illustrations	vi
Abbreviations	vii
Introduction	ix
Prelude: 'That kiss of Orpah'	1
1 'A shadow of the lost Paradise'	4
2 Dreaming Spires	13
3 'The Parting of Friends'	26
4 Martha and Elizabeth3	8
5 Itinerant Missionary	45
6 Kingsland	65
7 Ely Place	91
8 The Apostolate of the Press	109
9 The Rosminian Question	134
10 'That we may persevere to the end'	149
Appendix:	
Cardinal Newman: A Retrospect of Fifty Years, by one of his oldest living disciples	159
Bibliography	171
Index	177

List of Illustrations

Front cover: Portrait of Fr William Lockhart in the presbytery of St Etheldreda's, Ely Place.
Frontispiece: Fr William Lockhart in later life, from Johanna Hastings's *Catholic London Missions*, 1903.
Facing page one: Photograph of the young Fr William Lockhart from *Merry England*, July 1892.

1. Elizbeth Lockhart: photograph from the Franciscan Convent, Braintree.
2. *The Newman-Ooth College*: satirical print.
3. John Henry Newman: lithograph by J. A. Vintner, 1850, after the painting by Maria Giberne.
4. Antonio Rosmini: portrait by Francesco Hayez, 1853.
5. Luigi Gentili.
6. Ratcliffe College: watercolour, anon. c. 1858, from the Rosminian Archive, Stresa.
7. Church of Our Lady and St Joseph, Tottenham Road, Kingsland: postcard of interior c. 1900.
8. Fr William Henry Lewthwaite: photograph from the Rosminian Archive, Stresa.
9. St Etheldreda's, Ely Place: the Chapel exterior engraved by Wallis from a drawing by J. P. Neale in 1813.
10. Henry Cardinal Manning: portrait in the Venerable English College, Rome.
11. Pope Leo XIII: souvenir photograph.
12. Frontispiece from *The Chasuble: its genuine form and size* (1891).

ABBREVIATIONS

AAW   Archives of the Archdiocese of Westminster
ASIC   Archivio Storico dell'Istituto della Carità, Stresa
VEC   Archives of the Venerable English College, Rome

Introduction

On being appointed assistant priest at Our Lady and St Joseph, Kingsland, in the summer of 2006, I was only vaguely aware of the parish's founder, Father William Lockhart. A distant memory of a book hastily read suggested a connection with Blessed John Henry Newman and Littlemore but little else came to mind. I was soon confronted with him, for a striking portrait hung on the wall of the presbytery dining room, right behind the parish priest's usual seat; a picture which is reproduced on the front cover of this book. Lockhart appeared a distinguished gentleman, with a military bearing and a kindly face. Further reading revealed that he was an important figure in the nineteenth-century Church and, on a more personal level, that we were both *alumni* of the same Oxford college. I was intrigued and determined to find out more.

The perfect opportunity appeared when I was asked to research the history of the primary school at Kingsland, which had been established around the same time as the church. The school kindly subsidized a trip to the Rosminian Archive at Stresa, Italy, where I discovered, much to my delight, several boxes of letters from Lockhart to his superiors, giving a vivid description of Catholic life in Victorian London.

When Lockhart died in London in May 1892, *The Tablet* declared that 'perhaps no man, except the Cardinal himself [Manning], had so strong a hold on varying classes and masses of men; and these are now united in a common sorrow over a common and irreparable loss'.[1] A hundred years later, Fr Remo Bessero Belti, in his study of the *Rosminian Question*, called Lockhart 'an outstanding figure in the Church in England during the second half of the nineteenth century'.[2] Likewise, when St

Etheldreda's, Ely Place, was reopened in 1952, following wartime damage, the preacher, Mgr Ronald Knox, said of Lockhart:

> Of all the Oxford converts, he was the first; and if he is remembered for nothing else, he should be remembered for having provoked one of the greatest passages in English literature. It was of him Newman was speaking when he preached his sermon on the Parting of Friends. It was Father Gentili who received him, and before he had been a Catholic a month, he joined the Fathers of Charity. It would be beyond the needs of the present occasion, to speak of what he did for the Church, or for his Institute. For the present occasion, it is enough to remind ourselves that, but for Father Lockhart, you and I would not be here.

In encouraging his listeners to do great things for God, Knox continued: 'don't let us be content to sit open-mouthed in wonder at those giants of yesterday, Father Lockhart and the rest, asking how it was they managed to speed over the mountains, to spurn the hills, in their impetuous apostolate'.[3]

The so-called 'Second Spring' is too often dominated by cardinals and bishops, such as Wiseman, Manning, Newman and Ullathorne. It is the aim of this short work to resurrect the neglected and, luckily for us, comparatively well-documented figure of William Lockhart. Despite many rumours concerning possible preferment, he never wore a mitre and died in harness as Rector of a London parish and Procurator General of his Order. Nevertheless, Lockhart's life straddled the great themes and movements of the times. As a young man he knew both Newman and Manning and was the first to 'cross the Tiber' from Littlemore. Received into the Church by Luigi Gentili, he immediately joined the Institute of Charity, which was instrumental in introducing Italianate customs into the still-cautious English Catholic community. His early years with the Rosminians were spent in Leicestershire, where Ambrose Phillipps de Lisle was sponsoring an ebullient Catholic revival, and in Ireland, where Lockhart was involved in a number of high-profile missions and became something of a celebrity. A brief sojourn in Rome gave the young priest an opportunity to meet with Blessed Antonio Rosmini, whose philosophical works he would translate into English in later life.

Introduction

As a priest, Lockhart is best remembered for founding two important missions in London: Our Lady and St Joseph, Kingsland, and St Etheldreda, Ely Place – the latter having great apologetic significance as one of the only English medieval churches in Catholic hands, stressing continuity with what he called 'the Old Religion'. However Lockhart's dream of establishing a Rosminian house in London, with a large community and an adjacent college, which could act as a centre for preaching and missions, was never realized. For many years he served as the Institute's Procurator General, necessitating long stays in Rome and involving him in the heated polemic between defenders of Rosmini and his (mostly Jesuit) critics. Towards the end of his life, Lockhart was bitterly disappointed by the Holy See's condemnation of forty propositions of the Father Founder.

Alongside these pastoral labours, Lockhart encouraged young writers and publishers, helped run several popular Catholic journals that served to catechize the literate masses, and produced more sophisticated controversial works – his 'generous' views concerning Corporate Reunion on occasion pitting him against the *Dublin Review* and even Manning himself. However, Lockhart enjoyed good relations with the Archbishop, acting as his right-hand man in the Total Abstinence League of the Cross, and even being rumoured as his possible successor.

The story of William Lockhart is also the story of a convert family that gave everything to their new-found faith, including much-needed monetary support. Mrs Lockhart had been a close friend of Archdeacon Manning at Chichester and, as a Catholic, lived beside her son for most of his years at Kingsland – acting almost as a lay patron whose financial resources allowed for the foundation of the mission and the building of the church and schools. Unsurprisingly, the close involvement in her son's pastoral responsibilities inevitably led to some resentment. An attempt at the religious life proved unsuccessful but she poured much energy and money into Catholic publishing. Lockhart's sister, Elizabeth, not only had similar literary concerns but acted as the effective Foundress of three communities: the Anglican Sisters of Wantage, the short-lived Sisters of Charity of the Precious Blood at Greenwich, and the Bayswater Franciscan Sisters of the Immaculate Conception.

Lockhart's life as a Catholic stretched from the days of the Vicars Apostolic to the first weeks of Vaughan's rule at Westminster. In the dedication of his 1882 study of recent converts, E. G. K. Browne described Lockhart as 'One of the First Fruits of the New Spring and One of the Most Indefatigable Collectors of the Sheaves of the New Harvest'.[4] Lockhart called himself 'the first fruits of the Oxford Movement'[5] and, by the time of his death, one of its last survivors. Above all he was strongly influenced by two remarkable men of the nineteenth-century Church, both beatified by Benedict XVI and both viewed with suspicion by many of their contemporaries: Antonio Rosmini and John Henry Newman. Indeed, Rosmini is often seen as a sort of Italian Newman and is widely read today, at least in his native Italy. While Lockhart played a central role in introducing Rosmini to the English-speaking world, his memories of Blessed John Henry are preserved in an article written after the Cardinal's death, which is reproduced here in the *Appendix*.

This is not an academic work and it is certainly not the last word on William Lockhart. More could particularly be written on his literary circle, his work as Procurator of his Order and the impact of his translations of Rosmini. Some of his papers in the Rosminian archive are yet to be sorted and these will undoubtedly add to the picture painted here. There are many people who have made this work possible. First mention should go to Don Alfonso Ceschi, IC, and Br Nigel Cave, IC, for allowing me to access and quote from the Archivio Storico dell'Istituto della Carità (ASIC) at Stresa, including those of the English Province. Br Nigel went beyond the call of duty in providing warm hospitality and a chauffeur service around the Italian Lakes. While reading Lockhart's voluminous correspondence, it was hard to keep one's gaze away from the stunning view of Lake Maggiore which lay beyond the reading room windows. Thanks are also due to Fr David Myers, IC, (Provincial), Fr Antonio Belsito, IC, the late Fr Kit Cunningham, IC, (Lockhart's sometime successor at Ely Place), Fr Philip Scanlan, IC, Fr Terry Watson, IC, and Paul Gillham (who kept me entertained at Domodossola). It was also a privilege to be asked to preach on Lockhart at Ratcliffe in the summer of 2010 as part of the celebrations closing the English Province and opening the new Gentili Province. After the Mass

Introduction

we processed to the little cemetery, where Lockhart and his mother are buried alongside many other distinguished Rosminians, and prayers were said for the repose of their souls.

One of Lockhart's successors at Kingsland, Fr Christopher Colven, gave me the time to visit Stresa and encouraged the project, as did Sean Flood and the school of Our Lady and St Joseph. The late Sr Laura Ingham, MFIC, of the Franciscan Convent at Braintree, provided invaluable information concerning Elizabeth Lockhart, and Sr Francine Shaw, MFIC, was kind enough to share her considerable knowledge of Elizabeth Hayes and the Greenwich and Bayswater convents. Sean Cleary patiently answered my queries about the Rosminians in Cardiff. Mgr Nicholas Hudson kindly allowed me to quote from the archive of the Venerable English College, Rome, while the monks of St Augustine's Abbey, Ramsgate, went out of their way to send me some images of Lockhart from the pages of the *Merry England* journal. Thanks also go to Gerard Boylan, Fr Stewart Foster, Linda Helm, Professor Royden Hunt, Dom Philip Jebb, OSB, Tom Longford, Dr Gerald McEnery, Frank McGrath, Sr Mary Joseph McManamon, OSB, Malcolm Mann, Christine Murphy, Seamus Ryan, Michael and Daniel Scott, Paul Shaw, Una Oligbo, Fr Peter Vellacott, the late Michael Watts and Fr Richard Whinder.

Looking back to his childhood in an Anglican vicarage, Lockhart noted that 'a shadow of the lost Paradise is the innocent child's home, and there is nothing like it on earth'. It is with similar sentiments that I dedicate this book to my mother, Clare. Not only did she prepare the Index for this book but, to paraphrase the words of Lockhart regarding his own mother, she placed me on the right road through her conscientious love of truth.

Fr Nicholas Schofield
Uxbridge
24 May 2011

Notes

1. *Tablet*, 21 May 1892, p. 804.
2. Belti, *Rosminian Question*, p. 68, fn. 1.
3. Knox, *Occasional Sermons*, pp. 323–7.
4. Browne, *The New Spring and the New Harvest* (dedication).
5. *Tablet*, 30 July 1881, p. 180.

William Lockhart

Prelude:

'That kiss of Orpah'

At eleven o'clock on 25 September 1843, a procession emerged from the school at Littlemore, just outside Oxford. The children, wearing frocks and bonnets bought especially for the occasion, and the small group of clergy chanted a psalm as they entered the church, beautifully decorated with dahlias, passion flowers and fuchsias. Every seat was taken and the large congregation necessitated extra chairs to be put out, some of which spilled into the churchyard. And yet, despite the crowds, there was an unusual silence about the gathering. Many looked solemn and preoccupied.

There were several distinguished names in the procession that made its way gravely up the nave. The great Edward Bouverie Pusey, Regius Professor of Hebrew, was there, as was John Brande Morris of Exeter College, William John Copeland of Trinity and Frederick Bowles. However the centre of attention was undoubtedly John Henry Newman, who had shepherded the little flock since 1828 and built both the parish school and church dedicated to St Mary and St Nicholas. More recently he had moved to the hamlet with a group of young men to pray and study, far away from the hothouse politics of the university.

The Communion service now taking place marked the anniversary of the church's consecration but the joy of the occasion was tempered by recent events. Newman had just stood in the pulpit of the university church of St Mary the Virgin for the last time and now he came to this beloved place to preach a farewell sermon.

Sitting in the congregation that day was Edward Bellasis, a notable lawyer, who wrote to his wife: 'the sermon I can never forget, the faltering voice, the long pauses, the perceptible and hardly successful efforts at restraining himself, together with the deep interest of the subject, were almost overpowering'. Newman may have managed to control his emotions, but many others present showed less resolve and Pusey himself 'consecrated the elements in tears, and once or twice became entirely overcome and stopped altogether'. Bellasis was not alone in appreciating the significance of the day: 'the services of the greatest man of our times, the acutest and most laborious and most energetic of the sons of the English Church is lost to us, he retires into lay communion'.[1]

The proximate cause of the emotionally-charged scenes at Littlemore was William Lockhart, a young, rather highly-strung graduate who had joined Newman's community and promised to stay for three years as he worked through his religious doubts to discern a future path. He had lived with them barely a year but had suddenly been reconciled to Rome and was now in the Rosminian novitiate at Loughborough. Newman did not mention this explicitly in his address, but in recounting the Old Testament story of Ruth, it was obvious that Ruth stood for those who had remained faithful to him and Orpah the disloyal Lockhart:

> Orpah kissed Naomi, and went back into the world. There was sorrow in the parting, but Naomi's sorrow was more for Orpah's sake than for her own. Pain there would be, but it was the pain of a wound, not the yearning regret of love. It was the pain we feel when friends disappoint us, and fall in our esteem. That kiss of Orpah was no loving token; it was but the hollow profession of those who use smooth words, that they may part company with us with least trouble and discomfort to themselves.[2]

The young man's 'secession' had provoked uproar and placed Newman in an untenable position, which led to his resignation. However, though it seemed rash at the time, it proved to set a trend. Newman and most of his companions became Catholics over the next few years. Once ordained, Lockhart himself became a figure of some significance for the English Catholic Church and kept in touch with Newman, whom he had once so bitterly disappointed, until the Cardinal's death in 1890. This is his largely forgotten story.

Notes

1. Bellasis, *Memorials*, pp. 59–60.
2. Newman, *Sermons Bearing on the Subjects of the Day,* p. 402.

Chapter I

'A Shadow of the Lost Paradise'

William Lockhart was born on 22 August 1819, the only child of the Rev. Alexander Lockhart and his second wife, Martha Jacob. Though born in Surrey and spending most of his priestly life in London, Lockhart considered himself a Scotsman and was proud of his family name. One of his earliest-known ancestors was Stephen, Laird of Loch Ard, who had married an O'Neill princess in the eleventh century. Lockhart delighted in this distant Irish connection, though confessing that 'had my ancestress been a dairymaid I would have told my dear Irish-men that I was proud of that old tie with their sweet Erin; but her being an O'Neill would make it pompous'.[1]

After the death of Robert Bruce in 1329, the King's heart was embalmed and taken on a crusading campaign in southern Spain by Sir James Douglas. After the latter's death in battle against the Moors of Granada, the heart became the responsibility of Sir Simon Locard of Lee, who brought it back to Scotland's Melrose Abbey.[2] Around this time the spelling of the family name changed to Lockheart or Lockhart and a heart within a lock was included in the arms of the family with the motto *Corda Serrata Pando*, 'I open locked hearts'.

According to legend, Sir Simon not only brought back from Spain the heart of the Bruce but also a celebrated amulet, known as the 'Lee Penny'. This later formed the basis of Sir Walter Scott's novel, *The Talisman* (1832). As the great novelist explained:

> [Sir Simon Lockhart] made prisoner in battle an Emir of considerable wealth and consequence. The aged mother of the captive came to the Christian camp, to redeem her son from his state of captivity. Lockhart

'A shadow of the lost Paradise'

is said to have fixed the price at which his prisoner should ransom himself; and the lady, pulling out a large embroidered purse, proceeded to tell down the ransom, like a mother who pays little respect to gold in comparison of her son's liberty. In this operation, a pebble inserted in a coin, some say of the Lower Empire, fell out of the purse, and the Saracen matron testified so much haste to recover it as gave the Scottish knight a high idea of its value, when compared with gold or silver. 'I will not consent,' he said, 'to grant your son's liberty, unless that amulet be added to his ransom.' The lady not only consented to this, but explained to Sir Simon Lockhart the mode in which the talisman was to be used, and the uses to which it might be put. The water in which it was dipped operated as a styptic, as a febrifuge, and possessed other properties as a medical talisman. Sir Simon Lockhart, after much experience of the wonders which it wrought, brought it to his own country, and left it to his heirs, by whom, and by Clydesdale in general, it was, and is still, distinguished by the name of the Lee-penny, from the name of his native seat of Lee.

The most remarkable part of its history, perhaps, was that it so especially escaped condemnation when the Church of Scotland chose to impeach many other cures which savoured of the miraculous, as occasioned by sorcery, and censured the appeal to them, 'excepting only that to the amulet, called the Lee-penny, to which it had pleased God to annex certain healing virtues which the Church did not presume to condemn'.

By the time of Scott, the powers of this mysterious amulet were 'chiefly restricted to the cure of persons bitten by mad dogs'.[3] The 'penny' (a red gemstone set in a groat from the reign of Edward I) is still treasured by the family and kept in an ornate snuffbox given to Sir James Lockhart by the Empress Maria Theresa.

In the seventeenth and eighteenth centuries, the Lockhart family was strongly Jacobite. George Lockhart of Carnwath was involved in the 1715 rebellion and went on to act as a go-between for the exiled Stuarts and the Scottish Jacobites. His brother, Philip, was captured with the Jacobites at Preston and, despite having resigned his commission, was court-martialled for desertion and subsequently shot. Fr Lockhart inherited these sympathies for the Stuarts and once upbraided a friend for referring to Prince Charles Edward as the 'Young Pretender'.

Lockhart's great-grandfather was the lawyer Alexander Lockhart, Lord Covington, whom Boswell considered a prodigy in his profession, and the priest's grandfather was a Rear-Admiral, also called William. Lockhart's father, Alexander, has been described as 'a high churchman of the Scotch Episcopalian school'[4] and being 'of an old-fashioned type, more of a squire than a parson' and 'a member of the Brunswick Club, then patronised by the Duke of York as the sole hope of the old conservative Protestant party'.[5] He had studied at St Mary's College, Oxford, and married Miss Carr-Newnes, by whom he had a daughter on 10 August 1811, Mary Elizabeth Crawford Lockhart.

Like many clergyman of the time, he was a local magistrate and held a number of benefices: Langford, Bampton, Warlingham and Chelsham, and Stone with Bishopstone. The latter seems to have been at the instigation of a close friend, Richard Plantagenet, later second Duke of Buckingham and Chandos.

A double tragedy struck in the winter of 1813. At Christmas, the news reached the Lockhart household that Alexander's brother, William, had died of wounds received at the battle of Vittoria. At this time Mrs Lockhart was also seriously ill and she died shortly afterwards. With a young daughter to care for and his responsibilities as a clergyman, it was understandable that Alexander should eventually seek a new wife. One day he was visiting Westminster Abbey and was introduced to Martha Jacob – an encounter that, according to family tradition, occurred at the romantic setting of Poets' Corner. The widower was already acquainted with Martha's father, William Jacob, a merchant and former Member of Parliament for Westbury and then Rye, and her brother, Edward, an up-and-coming barrister. Soon afterwards the couple married and in August 1819 William was born.

Through his mother, William Lockhart could claim descent from Samuel Stuckey of Langport, founder of Stuckey's Bank, and distant cousins included Walter Bagehot, the influential editor of *The Economist*, and Vincent Stuckey Reynolds of Cannonsgrove, Somerset, who married the niece of Benjamin Disraeli's mother. Indeed, in the 1880s, one of Lockhart's lodgers at Ely Place, Wilfrid Meynell, made a 'pilgrimage' to a local office of solicitors where Disraeli had started his career. The young journalist recalled that 'Father Lockhart, laughing at my boyish enthusiasm, remarked that one of the members of the firm was his mother's relation or connexion'.[6]

The Lockhart family settled at the spacious rectory at Hartwell, near Stone, where Alexander was Vicar from 1823. The church of the Assumption at Hartwell was one of the country's first Gothic Revival churches, designed by Henry Keene, based on the chapterhouse at York Minster and completed in 1756. It stood in the grounds of Hartwell House, the home of the Lee family which, between 1809 and 1814, housed Louis XVIII's court-in-exile. One day, during this period, little Elizabeth and her French nurse met the Duchess of Angoulême, daughter of Louis XVI and Marie-Antoinette, while walking in the park. On asking whose child Elizabeth was, the Duchess showed much astonishment – and disapproval – that her father was a clergyman. 'All that Father Lockhart remembered his father saying of the French exiles,' we are told, 'was that they did not like English fish, which they thought devoid of taste'.[7]

Looking back at his childhood, William Lockhart described himself as 'an idle little vagabond, never thinking of anything but my amusements – my pony and my dogs'. He was born into a life of privilege and in later life remembered visits to the local gentry, especially the home of the dukes of Buckingham at Lilies, Weedon, near Aylesbury.

Even in his youth he had a keen religious sense and occasionally experienced what he described as 'special communications from on high,' which 'stand out in relief, like nothing else that has fixed itself in my memory'.

> They came distinctly, and consciously, from without, each like a flash of light, leaving an indelible impression in my soul. There was nothing to lead up to them in my reasonings or states of feeling. They were not logical inferences from any known premisses, for the premisses were wanting, so far as my consciousness goes. I can only think of them as intuitions of faith, special supernatural visitations, or the action of angelic guardians, which are always present, seldom noted. Afterwards, too, their influence seems to have passed away, without any moral effect, leaving me just as thoughtless as before.

One such 'communication from on high' occurred when he was aged seven or eight at Hartwell:

> I was standing, by myself, at my father's study window, a ground-floor room looking out into the garden. I remember the scene exactly;

the green turf, the flower-beds, the high laurel boundary hedge, the church wall beyond, with the lofty dark cedar-trees, in the garden an ancient cypress-tree, near the house, standing tall as a poplar; I have never seen one like it in England. It was always teeming with little wrens, and was full of their nests. Suddenly, I felt the conscious feeling of existence, of 'I am'. I remember this first fresh feeling of conscious existence of being; nay, it has never left me. I said to myself, 'I am, things are, God is'. It was the feeling and the thought of *being* and of *cause*. It brought with it a sense of awe, of sadness, of responsibility. I suppose that consciousness and conscience were born within me. I think this never left me.

Although the young William often found himself in trouble, 'from that time, I was sensitive to right and wrong. I felt grieved with myself when I had gone against obedience to my parents, and could get no peace till I had told it to them'. He had a terror of flocks of rooks that could be seen in the Hartwell sky: 'I had heard a text of Scripture about the ravens that would pick out the eyes of wicked children, and I thought the rooks were ravens, and that they would come some day and take me'. He sometimes imagined God to 'have a long spear with which He killed wicked people and put them I know not where, but I thought the entrance was under a great stone in the neighbouring churchyard'.[8]

The world of Catholicism that would later play such a central role in his life was fleetingly glimpsed through an aunt, Isabella, a Catholic convert who had married the secretary to the Neapolitan Legation in London, the Marquess Antonio Riario Sforza. William sometimes stayed with his aunt in Belgrave Square, London, and in September 1831 attended the Coronation of King William IV as a member of the Neapolitan legation, an occasion that gave him a first taste of splendid ceremonial:

> a magnificent altar, with candlesticks of gold, and covered with gold plate, and the Archbishop and others vested in gorgeous copes: but I thought of it only as a part of the grand pageant of a coronation, like the peers and peeresses, in their magnificent crimson and ermine robes, putting on their coronets when the Archbishop placed the crown on the head of the youthful sovereign.[9]

The Marquess later became Ambassador to Florence and then

Spain and, in later life, Lockhart made much use of the Italian side of the family, especially when he worked as Procurator General of his Order in Rome.

His early religious instruction was centred around the Bible – his father on one occasion making him learn a chapter in *Proverbs* on obedience and avoiding evil ways – and the Church Catechism, but he later recalled how he had no notion of the Trinity or Incarnation and 'therefore also of the nature of Baptism and of the Lord's Supper; and I had not the dimmest notion of the Real Presence of Christ in the Lord's Supper'. Indeed, 'there was an engraving hanging in our dining-room, taken from a painting by one of the old masters, of the Annunciation, the Blessed Virgin and the Angel Gabriel, but I do not remember ever to have had any religious idea connected with it, such as would be in the mind of any Catholic child'. He attributed any early feelings of piety to 'nothing but Natural Religion'.

William was close to his father and in later years treasured his Latin edition of the *Imitation of Christ*, published at Antwerp in 1664 and marked with pencil annotations.

> My father was a good man. How happy my days were with him! I was always his companion in his rides, on my pony, by his side, holding his horse when he went into the cottages to visit the sick and dying. It was happiness, because it was the sense of home: a shadow of the lost Paradise is the innocent child's home, and there is nothing like it on earth.[10]

This 'Paradise' was shattered on 7 February 1832 when his father died at Ampthill, Bedfordshire. He was buried under the chancel at Stone.

William received his education at Bedford Grammar School where, he later admitted, the *Eton Latin Grammar* was only mastered thanks to the frequent birchings, and through private tutors, including the curate at Waddesdon, Frederick Cox, who used the cane to drum into the young lad's mind Greek verbs and multiplication tables. A few months before his death, Lockhart recalled that 'he preferred spending the two hours after supper reading novels to the labour of preparing his lessons and, when morning came, and he was found not to know his lessons, he accepted the inevitable punishment as an alternative of his own choice'.[11]

Lockhart undoubtedly included the novels of Sir Walter Scott among his nocturnal reading sessions, especially since a distant cousin, John Gibson Lockhart, was Scott's son-in-law and celebrated biographer. Writing in 1886, Fr Lockhart argued that 'perhaps most of those who have become Catholic during the last fifty years can trace the attractions of Divine Grace, through the Providence of God, in the pure literature which came into their hands in their early youth'. For Lockhart, Scott was the chief exponent of this 'pure literature':

> the immense popularity of his works is a sign that they supplied a want. It was a high, noble, religious, and moral sentiment which these works have done more to foster or create among us than perhaps all the directly religious books that had been published for centuries. They purified the ideas of the young, especially on the subject of love, raising the minds of young men to a pure, noble, chivalrous feeling towards women, and raising the minds of young women to look for this sentiment in young men. These works teach the spirit of the Christian gentleman, loyalty to king and country, a great respect for religion and for truth and honourable dealing.[12]

Newman himself praised Scott for preparing 'men for some closer and more practical approximation to Catholic truth' and it is clear that Romanticism, with its idealization of history and its stress on beauty and imagination, helped create the right atmosphere for the Oxford Movement and the discovery of Catholic tradition.

Another key influence was the young man's first experience of overseas travel. At the age of nineteen, he toured the Rhineland with his maternal grandfather, William Jacob, who was himself a seasoned traveler and who Lockhart was said to greatly resemble in later life. Jacob's *Travels in the South of Spain* (1811) had been favourably reviewed at the time of publication and the Government had sent him to Germany, Poland and Russia to investigate agriculture and the corn trade in the 1820s. The subsequent reports were highly influential and helped prepare the way for the eventual repeal of the Corn Laws in 1846.

Lockhart used the opportunity to visit the Catholic churches of Belgium and Germany, 'with the feeling that I did not know what to make of it, and that, in what they were doing, I had no part or lot; much as one might feel if one entered a Turkish mosque or a Buddhist temple'. He was astonished by 'the people in their thousands at Antwerp, and afterwards at Aix-la-Chapelle and at Cologne cathedrals, at five o'clock in the morning, on weekdays'. One Sunday morning he observed Mass at Baden-Baden and saw for the first time 'a Catholic altar and priests clad in sacred vestments, like the Jewish priesthood of old of which I had seen pictures'.

> As I gazed upon the spectacle, with the eyes of the body only, suddenly I saw clouds of incense rising up from the altar. Then all that vast assembly fell upon their knees, the music ceased, there was dead silence throughout the church, broken only by the sound of the wind outside, by the tinkling of silver bells at the altar, and the solemn booming of the great church bell. I never before had felt what worship was. I could not keep from falling on my knees with that vast multitude, and a feeling came over me which I still feel, and which I now know is the feeling which faith gives of the Real Presence of Christ in the Blessed Sacrament ...
>
> As I knelt in the church, I felt thrilled through and through, under a sense of the presence of God; and words of Holy Scripture flashed into my mind almost as if a living voice had spoken them, 'Truly, God is in this place, and I knew it not'. I think my feeling was rather akin to that of the patriarchs of old, of Abraham, Jacob and Moses, when they bowed themselves to the earth under an overwhelming sense of what we may call a localized presence of God, guaranteed by the visible manifestation of angels.

Lockhart counted this experience as one of his defining 'communications from on high' – 'supernatural, not to say miraculous' – and he regarded his visit to Catholic Europe as 'a preparation for faith'.[13]

Notes

1. Hirst, 'Necrology: Father Lockhart' in *Ratcliffian*, p. 344.
2. A leaden casket containing the remains of a human heart was found during an archaeological excavation at Melrose Abbey in 1996.
3. Scott, *The Talisman*, pp. ix–x.
4. Gillow, *Bibliographical Dictionary of English Catholics*, vol. iv, p. 298.

5. Hirst, 'Necrology', p. 318.
6. Meynell, 'Further Reminiscences of Father Lockhart', p. 160.
7. Hirst, 'Necrology', p. 318.
8. Ibid., pp. 319–21.
9. Ibid., p. 322. Hirst says that Lockhart confused Victoria's Coronation with that of William IV, hence the reference to the 'youthful sovereign'.
10. Ibid., p. 320.
11. Ibid., p. 323.
12. Lockhart, *Life of Rosmini*, vol. ii, p. 97.
13. Hirst, 'Necrology', pp. 321–2.

Chapter II
Dreaming Spires

The bereaved family eventually moved from Buckinghamshire to 'Rocklands' in East Hill, Hastings, and on 17 May 1838, Lockhart was matriculated into Exeter College, the fourth oldest college in Oxford. Mark Pattison of Lincoln College described the college at the time as 'genteel but unintellectual'[1] and Lockhart considered his first year wasted since he entered a circle of 'idle, hunting, boating men' who lived on the same staircase. He consequently spent far too much time 'skiffing on the river in a pair-oared boat' and showing off his top boots.[2] A friend testified that

> Lockhart was exceedingly particular about his scholastic toggery ... He was considered one of the best dressed men in Oxford. His fine figure and lovely countenance made him more conspicuous even than his quiet gentlemanly dress. There was only one greater 'glass of fashion' than he, and that was our late Dominican Father Trenow, of St John's – no. xi., in our St John's boat ... [Lockhart] had a big loathing for untidy undergraduates. Fr John Wynne of All Souls', now S.J.; Fr Anderdon, S.J. of University; and George Bagot of Exeter College, all followed suit. At Lockhart's wine parties, in the room with the oriel window, against Exeter College gateway, all were remarkable for being 'correct' men.[3]

By the time Lockhart went up to university, the Oxford Movement was five years old. For Newman, the Movement started with John Keble's 'National Apostasy' sermon in July 1833, attacking the Irish Bishopric's Bill, which reduced the number of dioceses, as unwanted government interference in ecclesiastical matters. The series of ninety 'Tracts for Our Times' was sparked off, produced by young dons such as Newman (who wrote about a third of them), Froude, Palmer and Pusey. It constituted a rediscovery of patristic theology, the reality of sacramental grace and the beauty of holiness in the Church of England, as well as fighting for its independence in matters spiritual from the State.

At first, Lockhart was 'resolved to keep clear of Tractarianism' and did not think much of the 'Catholicising school at Oxford',[4] even though these influences lay beneath his very nose at Exeter. The new Rector, Joseph Loscombe Richards, was the only Oxford head of house with Tractarian sympathies, and the Dean and Professor of Moral Philosophy, William Sewell, was also supportive. A fellow student at the college, two years Lockhart's senior, was John Dobre Dalgairns, who would follow Newman to Littlemore and then the Oratory. Another future convert was the College's lecturer in Hebrew and Syriac, John Brande Morris, who lived above Lockhart in the tower, earning him the nickname 'Symeon Stylites'. He was not an ideal neighbour, apparently having 'a noisy and odious turning machine' in his room, and was excluded from Lockhart's select parties 'on account of his *air farouche*, and his unpresentable appearance'.[5] Morris was obsessed with fasting, bringing the subject frequently into his sermons and following it rigorously during Lent. Indeed, when Dalgairns imitated his example during Holy Week 1840, he was found by his scout collapsed on the floor, having not eaten for 36 hours. Morris became a Catholic in 1846 but died in comparative obscurity in 1880 as chaplain to the Sœurs de Miséricorde in Hammersmith. He remained an eccentric to the last and on one occasion even claimed in *Notes and Queries* that the mythical phoenix really did exist.

Surrounded by these influences, it proved impossible for Lockhart to maintain his disinterestedness in religious affairs. The 'Catholicising' forces continued while on vacation at his mother's new home in Chichester – the 'Pallant', an elegant Queen Anne town-house built in 1712 that today houses a collection of modern art. Mrs Lockhart and her daughter keenly read the *Tracts for the Times* and regularly attended the choral services at the cathedral. A University friend who visited William in Chichester recalled the family's 'progress towards Catholicism, through their High Church teaching and proclivities'. Keble's

Christian Year was treated almost as a sacred text and 'each Sunday we had what was called the Sunday Puzzle, viz., to find out the meaning of Keble's ode for that day'. They took fasting seriously and Mrs Lockhart even wrote to Frederick Oakeley, then presiding over the fashionable Margaret Street chapel, for his advice. He sent her a copy of a Pastoral Letter recently produced by Bishop Griffiths, the (Catholic) Vicar Apostolic of the London District, which proposed a Lenten diet of 'cheese, butter, dripping and lard'. The young Lockhart began to disapprove of 'self-indulgence in Protestant clergy' and was scandalized when he called on the incumbent of All Saints', Hastings, and caught him 'in the act of dipping a splendid ripe strawberry, with a silver tablespoon full of cream and sugar, and of thus imbibing celestial mouthfuls of the mixture'. On leaving, Lockhart exclaimed, 'what an unchastised-looking man!'[6]

When Henry Edward Manning, the recently widowed Rector of Lavington, was appointed Archdeacon of Chichester in 1841, he became a frequent visitor at the 'Pallant'. Indeed, Mrs Lockhart's sisters commented that 'we do not think it right that a young and attractive widow should go to live so near an engaging widower'.[7] With his encouragement, Martha and Elizabeth, together with a third lady, Mary Reid, opened a small school for poor children. Lockhart vividly remembered his first sighting of the Archdeacon:

> His grand head, bald even then, his dignified figure in his long white surplice, occupying the Archdeacon's stall in the Cathedral; his face was to me some first dim revelation of the meaning of the *supernatural in man*. I have never forgotten it, I see him as vividly now in my mind's eye as when I first beheld him. I think it was the beginning of reflected thought in my soul. Somehow, by one of those mysterious links of thought which come from God's Providential guidance, I at once connected his face with those of the old Churchmen of Catholic times that I had seen in stained glass windows, and in the portraits of the whole line of Catholic Bishops painted in long order on walls of the South Transept of the Cathedral.[8]

Around this time, Lockhart read the *Remains of the late Reverend Richard Hurrell Froude* (1838), jointly edited by Newman and Keble, which vigorously attacked English Protestantism and opened to the young man 'entirely a new view of Christianity'.

He had had little experience of Catholics and, though he had 'papist' cousins, he assumed that 'their goodness had kept them from being idolaters, and that some day they would become good Protestants like the rest of us'. However, the posthumous writings of Froude made him realize that Catholics were Christian and, indeed, that Catholicism was 'the old Christianity of England'.[9] Frederick William Faber's *Sights and Thoughts in Foreign Churches and among Foreign Peoples* (1842) would have a similar effect.

Lockhart gradually fell away from the 'idle, boating, hunting' set at his college and came under the influence of John Henry Newman. Lockhart's first encounter with this future cardinal, albeit at a distance, remained indelibly etched on the memory:

> I saw him first on a certain day which I vividly remember. I was walking down High Street – it was between All Souls' and Queen's College. He was crossing, I think, to Oriel. My companion seized my arm, whispering to me, 'Look, look there, that is Newman!' I looked, and there I saw him passing along in his characteristic way, walking fast, without any dignity of gait, but earnest, like one who had a purpose; yet so humble and self-forgetting in every portion of his external appearance, that you would not have thought him, at first sight, a man remarkable for anything. It was only when you came to know him that you recognised or began to recognise what he was.[10]

Along with many other students, he attended Newman's sermons at the University church, where he had been Vicar since 1828:

> The effect of his teaching on us young men was to turn our souls, as it were, inside out; in measure and degree it was like what he says in the *Dream of Gerontius* of the soul after death presented before God.
>
> > Who draws the soul from out its case
> > And burns away its stains.
>
> God the Creator was the first theme he taught us, and it contained the premisses of all that followed. We never could be again the same as before, whether we 'obeyed the heavenly vision' or neglected it. We

had gained some notion that there were false forms of Christianity to be avoided. Socinianism was one; Roman Catholicism was another; and this had been impressed upon us very strongly. But the Church of England, which we supposed was much the same in doctrine with the other Protestant Churches, we did not doubt was the old and true religion. The next truth which we learned from the tenor of all his teaching was, that God who is so near us, that 'in Him we live and move and are,' who is the ultimate hidden force and First Cause beneath the phenomena of the visible universe, and of our own spiritual consciousness and conscience, our Moral Governor, might be expected beforehand to have given a religion to man by supernatural revelation. He had done so. We accepted the Christianity of the Church of England as the original Revelation. Being now convinced of the duties we owed to God and to Revelation, we set to work to practise the duties it taught – to repent of our sins and amend our lives, to pray very earnestly, and to frequent the Communion celebrated every Sunday morning early in the chancel of St Mary's.[11]

Lockhart later stated that Newman 'impressed me in these ways more perhaps than any but one other man has impressed me – the great master of thought under whom I passed when I left Newman; another of the greatest minds of the age – Antonio Rosmini, the Founder of the Order to which I have the honour to belong'.[12]

Newman's sermons were a revelation, even though it seemed extraordinary that 'a few words, read very quietly from a manuscript, without any rhetorical effort, could have so penetrated our souls'.[13] Lockhart in particular noted the 'moral revolution' that Newman's words caused. While daughters of the country gentry and clergy were generally brought up to be 'models of English gentlewomen', the sons were often corrupted by the time they reached early adulthood. Indeed, 'there was a kind of tacit understanding ... that it would not do to be too hard on the young; that we must keep our blind eye on the doings of our young sons, that "youths must sow their wild oats".' They would eventually learn from their mistakes and develop into 'grave and reverend seniors', like their fathers. For Lockhart, this was the atmosphere of early Victorian Oxford, a result of 'Protestant culture' and the lack of examens of conscience and sacramental confession. Amidst the immorality, the preaching of Newman instilled 'an intuitive perception of moral obligation'.[14]

Lockhart's peers also provided a strongly Catholicizing influence. Chief among them was Johnstone Horace Grant, who had started his Oxford studies at St John's in 1837. Lockhart and Grant got into trouble with the University 'police' (proctors) for visiting the Catholic chapel of St Clement's; they were summoned to the rooms of John Bloxam of Magdalen, who in later years remembered 'the consternation that fell on their faces and their trembling attitudes'. Indeed, it seems that they faced possible rustication had their conduct not otherwise been irreproachable. During the Michaelmas term, 1840, the two friends were followed by 'bull dogs' (proctors) as they caught the train to London one day and got off at Reading to see Pugin's new church in the old Abbey grounds. This led to another reprimand.[15]

Following his friend's death over half a century later, Grant recalled two sketches made by Lockhart in a blotting book around 1840, during a vacation in Chichester, showing the west end and sanctuary of an idealized ritualistic church. Lockhart and Grant dreamed that they would set up their churches in such a way once they became vicars. Grant recounted an alarming incident in Chichester Cathedral, which the two students loved to explore:

> [From the triforium] we looked down into the depths of the nave, when suddenly Lockhart, who was in advance of me, distinctly said: *Eripe me Domine ab homine malo!* When we got back to the Pallant and into my room, I asked him what had caused him to utter that ejaculation. 'Well, Grant, I will tell you. I felt dizzy, and had the strongest temptation to throw myself down into the nave, and so end all doubts'. I requested him then to kneel down with me. He did so. I took out *The Garden of the Soul*, opened it at the long Litanies of the Saints, and began.[16]

It is unclear how serious an episode this was. Grant may well have been making their youthful religious doubts into a Victorian melodrama but it was undoubtedly also an early indication of Lockhart's somewhat nervous and impulsive temperament, which necessitated periods of recuperation amidst his many pastoral and literary duties.

On another occasion, Grant showed Lockhart some letters received from a family friend, the Jesuit Xavier Biden, and these had a great effect. Lockhart passed them to Pusey and returned one of them to Grant with the words, '*That* letter has done *for me*'.[17]

Another close companion was Edward Douglas of Christ Church, a cousin of the Marquis of Queensbury. Lockhart seems to have known him prior to University and occasionally visited his mother's house in Sevenoaks. Douglas would become a Catholic in Rome in 1842. Originally ordained for the Franciscans, he later entered the Redemptorists and worked in Rome as Provincial and Rector of Sant' Alfonso. The two friends often met during Lockhart's frequent stays in the Eternal City and at their last meeting, in February 1892, Lockhart reminded Douglas of a ball they had both attended at Sevenoaks as students and the 'large flowered waistcoat' that the future Redemptorist had daringly sported on that occasion.[18]

Other associates included William Henry Anderdon of University College, Manning's nephew, who became a Catholic in 1850 and joined the Jesuits; James Robert Hope-Scott, Fellow of Merton and a key promoter of the Tractarian cause, who later married Charlotte Lockhart, daughter of Scott's biographer; and Charles Robert Scott-Murray, then at Christ Church. Lockhart was also acquainted with John Ruskin of Christ Church, whom he met in Douglas' rooms. Lockhart later reflected that the earliest Oxford converts – Grant, Douglas, Scott-Murray and himself – shared 'Jacobite and Scotch Episcopalian stocks'. He conjectured that 'not being so rooted as Englishmen are, in favour of everything English, left us freer to criticize and condemn Church of England Christianity'.[19]

As Lockhart's studies at Oxford continued, 'doubts had begun to arise in my mind whether I ought not to become a Roman Catholic at once, for I could not see how the Church of England could still be a part of that Church from which it had separated'.[20] During one vacation, Mrs Lockhart advised him to visit Manning at Lavington. 'Early one morning, therefore,' writes Hirst, 'he mounted the large horse his mother kept for her country carriage, and rode from Chichester over the Sussex Downs, a distance of perhaps eight or ten miles'.[21] The young student was overawed by the Archdeacon and found he could not organize his thoughts clearly beneath his penetrating gaze. Manning advised him to continue his studies, seek ordination in the Church of England

and work amongst the poor in one of the growing cities. In this he would be able to imitate the work of Dean Hook of St Saviour's, Leeds. 'Just at this point,' Lockhart reminisced,

> a visitor arrived, one of name and position in the political world and a member of Parliament, so I had no more conversation with the Archdeacon. I dined with him – a very frugal meal – cold boiled beef. I remember it was hard. I remember nothing else except that he seemed to be without servant, for an untidy old woman was doing duty in the kitchen. Seeing he was engaged with his visitor, I retired to my room, and I heard them talking in the room below me – the library – until the small hours after midnight. Early the next day I rode back over the hills to my home, and my friends were greatly comforted by my comparatively composed state of mind.[22]

For the time being, Lockhart's doubts were eased. The visit to Lavington 'woke up in me the hope that, after all, England was part of the Universal Church – of the Church of St Augustine, and of the old Fathers and Schoolmen, of the great Saints and founders of the Cathedrals and Monasteries'.

One of Lockhart's main concerns in his search for the truth was the question of the forgiveness of post-baptismal sins and the necessity of confession.

> An important matter to us was the teaching of Dr Pusey on *Baptism* and on *Post-Baptismal Sin*. From hearing these doctrines, most of us came to hold that, as a fact, we had been made 'temples of God in baptism'. What was our present condition, if by sin perhaps from early youth or even from childhood, we had driven out the Spirit of God and had become a dwelling place of evil spirits? I do not know what to say about others; for myself no words can express the dark terror of my soul. But the Anglican doctrine, clear as it is about baptism, could tell us no remedy for sin committed after baptism.
>
> It was for me most providential that I happened at this critical moment to come across a Roman Catholic book, Milner's *End of Controversy*. I read it eagerly, for I was in sore distress. I saw at once, first, that I had been misled and mistaken as to the tenets of the Roman Catholics – that they believed in One God and in Jesus Christ as their only Redeemer and source of Grace; I saw that they taught that, in Baptism, we are made Temples of God, that sin deserves everlasting punishment, but that if we sin God has provided 'a second

plank after shipwreck,' equivalent, if repentance is deep, to a second Baptism – the Holy Sacrament of Penance – Confession and Absolution.

This was the first time I had ever heard of this Sacrament. It was Milner who sent me to the Anglican Prayer-book for the same doctrine of Confession and Priestly Absolution, and then I saw it clearly laid down in the 'Ordination Service of Priests' and in the 'Office for the Visitation of the Sick'. I afterwards read the same doctrine in the works of Jeremy Taylor, and of other Anglican Divines. I was immensely relieved, and began to practise confession...[23]

On one occasion Lockhart asked a High Churchman in Chichester to hear his confession. The minister was somewhat taken aback and, after asking advice from his wife, declared that he could only do so with the express permission of the Archdeacon.[24] Lockhart later mused:

What then was to be thought of a Church which had neglected for 300 years an essential Sacrament in which it professed in words to believe – what confidence could one have that in other weighty matters it had not neglected its trust? This led me to see for the first time the meaning of the words in the Creed 'I believe in One, Holy, Catholic, and Apostolic Church'. I saw that the Roman Catholic Church was by far the largest portion of the Church of the Creed. I saw too that England was, up to the time of Henry VIII, a visible part of that Church. I supposed it was so still, or ought to be.[25]

During his final year at Oxford Lockhart worked hard 'for the first time in my life'. This new seriousness did not prevent him from attending the annual Scotch dinner for St Andrew's Day, held in the Union rooms. It was a happy evening of whisky, Jacobite songs, toasts to Charles I, Archbishop Laud and 'Bonnie Prince Charlie', and a menu of oyster soup, haggis and 'cockie-leeky'. He and Grant went in plain evening dress although the other guests were 'in kilt, spurs, and as many cairngorms as they could stick on'. They had been invited by Scott-Murray, who 'with silk gown and velvet cap, announced each toast or sentiment, in turn, from a paper'. Grant recalled,

Lockhart had inscribed his name for [a toast to] 'The Scotch Episcopal Church'. There was a dead silence, because it was evident that many at table were of Presbyterian families. Scott-Murray asked therefore: 'Mr Lockhart, how would you desire that this toast should be drunk?' Lockhart showed then his ready wit, his adroitness, collectedness, and gentlemanly appreciation of the position by saying: 'Since the Episcopal Church of Scotland is a Church in affliction and obloquy, I propose that the health be drunk with dumb cheers'. So the difficulty was eased off, and we all reseated ourselves with contentment and satisfaction.

Afterward the dinner, having 'imbided a good deal of Scotch whisky and not a few "Willie-waughs",[26] as they say', Lockhart walked round the University Parks to sober up and declared: 'I am in a state now in which I might be drawn into any wickedness. I shall go to confession to William Sewell, of Exeter, tomorrow, and make some atonement, if I can'. The following morning he went to see the said Senior Tutor and Professor of Moral Philosophy, who refused and offered the student a dose of Epsom salts instead of absolution. Lockhart commented, 'I came away from that ass at once. I asked my father for bread, and he gave me a stone. I asked for fish, – he gave me a scorpion'. Grant felt that his friend was 'far gone and he meant business' in regard to Rome. Shortly afterwards, Grant himself became a Catholic at Bruges:

> I had worked out the problem for myself, and had already put up a large Madonna and Child in my room window, in painted glass, – a picture now in Stonyhurst College, near the Church, of Rafael's [sic] Sistine Madonna. This was my open and first profession of Faith in St John's, Oxford. I was denounced to Dr Winter, the President, for it, and then the end came. All was easy: I took leave of Lancelot Sharpe, my tutor; of James Hessey, my coach in Logic (since Archdeacon of Middlesex, and once my father's Curate at Kentish Town); and last of all, I took leave of Wilson, the Bursar of St John's. I took my name off the books, and he, with true gentlemanly courtesy, wrote me a cheque for £60 – guineas – my caution money, and with this small sum, I began Catholic life, and passed over to Bruges and to Tronchiennes, after receiving four Sacraments in one day: Public Baptism (conditional), then Absolution, then Holy Communion, and Confirmation from Bishop Boone of Bruges.[27]

He went on to enter the Society of Jesus, taking the name Ignatius.

Around this time, Newman's *Tract 90* (February 1841) was causing a great sensation by its claim that the Thirty-Nine Articles were 'patient but not ambitious of a Catholic interpretation' and that a narrowly Protestant reading of them would 'run the risk of subjecting persons, whom we should least like to lose or distress, to the temptation of joining the Church of Rome, or to the necessity of withdrawing from the Church established, or to the misery of subscribing with doubt and hesitation'.[28] The subsequent row led to the discontinuation of the influential *Tracts for Our Times* but, as Lockhart commented, 'on us young men *Tract 90* had the effect of strengthening greatly our growing convictions that Rome was right and the Church of England wrong'.[29]

The furore caused by *Tract 90* led Newman to retire to Littlemore in April 1842. As Vicar of St Mary's, Newman had had pastoral care for the little hamlet since 1828 and opened a new church for the villagers in 1836 and a little school two years later. He dreamed of founding a 'monastery' there, large enough for his extensive library, and had bought land for this purpose in May 1840. However, his hurried retreat from Oxford in 1842 led him to set up home in the 'Cottages', former stables in College Lane. His sister Harriet noted that it had

> a dozen windows – one storey. Inside it is very pretty and neat – just my fancy. I do not wonder at John's present enthusiasm. There are 4 or 5 sets of rooms – sitting and bedroom – all on the ground floor – the door opening into the verandah which runs all along, a length of the diagonal of Oriel quad. The kitchen is in the middle – a pretty little garden before the verandah. At right angles is the library, a large pretty room with a nice roof, the sides covered with books. Inside, another small book room and above a spare bedroom.[30]

Newman settled down to work on the Church Fathers and the *Lives of the English Saints*. However, it would prove to be no rural idyll. Newman was, after all, a celebrity and his life was considered public property. The setting up of what appeared to be an Anglo-Catholic monastery led to varying rumours. In his *Apologia*, Newman complained that

> one day when I entered my house, I found a flight of Undergraduates inside. Heads of Houses, as mounted patrols, walked their

horses round these poor cottages. Doctors of Divinity dived into the hidden recesses of that private tenement uninvited, and drew domestic conclusions from what they saw there. I had thought that an Englishman's house was his castle, but the newspapers thought otherwise.[31]

As Newman was settling into Littlemore, Lockhart gained his B.A. Due to the Test Acts, which were not repealed until 1871, those taking public degrees had to subscribe to the Thirty-Nine Articles. 'This I felt I could never do again, yet I must do it if I took Orders in the Church of England'.[32] Indeed for this reason he never took his M.A. and, as a Catholic writer, proudly signed himself 'William Lockhart, B.A. (Oxon)'.

In 1842 Manning was chosen as one of the Select Preachers at Oxford University and Lockhart made an appointment to meet him at Merton College. They proceeded to the beautiful fourteenth-century chapel where the Archdeacon locked the door and heard the young man's confession at the Communion rails. At this meeting, which would be their last as Anglicans, Manning advised Lockhart to accept Newman's recent invitation to join his embryonic community at Littlemore, an offer that had been made at the request of a friend. Johnstone Grant had recently converted to Rome and everyone expected Lockhart to follow immediately; the invitation to Littlemore was an attempt to keep him within the Church of England and prevent further scandal.

Notes

1. Pattison, *Memoirs*, p. 24.
2. Hirst, 'Necrology', p. 326.
3. Ibid., p. 324 (quoting Fr Grant, SJ).
4. Lockhart, 'Some Personal Reminiscences of Cardinal Manning', p. 372.
5. Hirst, 'Necrology', p. 324.
6. Hirst, *Biography of Father Lockhart*, pp. 28–30. The University friend who visited Lockhart was Johnstone Horace Grant.
7. Hirst, 'Necrology', p. 326.
8. Lockhart, 'Some Personal Reminiscences of Cardinal Manning', pp. 372–3.
9. Ibid., p. 373.
10. Lockhart, *Cardinal Newman*, p. 1. He elsewhere noted that Newman moved 'like a man walking fast in slippers, and not lifting his heel' (p. 23).
11. Ibid., pp. 5–6.

12. Ibid., p. 4.
13. Ibid., p. 24.
14. Ibid., pp. 25–6.
15. Hirst, 'Necrology', p. 328.
16. Ibid., p. 324.
17. Ibid., p. 324.
18. Ibid., p. 323.
19. Lockhart, *Cardinal Newman*, pp. 50–1.
20. Ibid., p. 8.
21. Hirst, 'Necrology', p. 326.
22. Ibid., p. 327.
23. Lockhart, *Cardinal Newman*, pp. 6–7.
24. Lockhart, 'Some Personal Reminiscences of Cardinal Manning', p. 374.
25. Lockhart, *Cardinal Newman*, p. 8.
26. Quoting from *Auld Lang Syne* – meaning a goodwill drink.
27. Hirst, *Necrology*, p. 325.
28. Blehl, *Pilgrim Journey*, p. 271.
29. Lockhart, *Cardinal Newman*, p. 10.
30. Mozley, *Newman Family Letters*, p. 122.
31. Newman, *Apologia*, p. 172.
32. Lockhart, 'Some Personal Reminiscences of Cardinal Manning', p. 374.

Chapter III

'The Parting of Friends'

Littlemore is so often associated with Newman's subsequent conversion but the future Cardinal viewed it originally as a place of retreat, where he could lead a more regular life, concentrate on prayer and study, spend more time working in the parish and, as he explained to the local bishop, help keep 'a certain class of minds firm in their allegiance to our Church'.[1] He referred to Littlemore as 'my Torres Vedras', referring to the forts secretly built by Wellington to defend Lisbon during the Peninsular War, and hoped that 'some day we might advance again within the Anglican Church, as we had been forced to retire'.[2]

Although Lockhart had long been an admirer, Newman was not personally acquainted with him until the young man arrived at Littlemore in July 1842.[3] It is interesting that Newman's first three companions were all graduates of Exeter: not only Lockhart but Dalgairns (the first to join) and Frederick S. Bowles, an Anglican clergyman who later followed his master to the Birmingham Oratory. Lockhart recalled that

> We spent our time at Littlemore in study, prayer and fasting. We rose at midnight to recite the Breviary Office, consoling ourselves with the thought that we were united in prayer with united Christendom, and were using the very words used by the Saints of all ages. We fasted according to the practice recommended in Holy Scripture, and practised in the most austere religious orders of Eastern and Western Christendom. We never broke our fast, except on Sundays and the Great Festivals, before twelve o'clock, and not until five o'clock in the Advent and Lenten seasons.
> We regularly practised confession, and went to Communion, I think, daily, at the Village Church.[4] At dinner we met together, and

after some spiritual reading at table, we enjoyed conversation with Newman. He spoke freely on all subjects that came up, but I think controversial topics were tacitly avoided. He was most scrupulous not to suggest doubts as to the position of the Church of England to those who had them not.[5]

Newman encouraged his disciples to study:

It was his wish to give us some direct object of study (partly to keep us quiet) in his splendid library, in which were all the finest editions of the Greek and Latin Fathers, and School-men, all the best works on scripture and theology, general literature, prose and poetry, and a complete set of Bollandist *Acta Sanctorum*, so far as they had been printed. He had a project of bringing out *Lives of the English Saints*, and a translation of Fleury's *Ecclesiastical History*. I was set to work on the history of the Arian period, with a view to undertaking the translation of a volume.[6]

The edition of Fleury was published in 1842, together with a preface by Newman which was later printed separately as *An Essay on the Miracles Recorded in the Ecclesiastical History of the Early Ages* (1843). Lockhart also helped in the village school and was assigned the task of writing a life of St Gilbert of Sempringham for the English Saints series. Newman hoped this project would cool down the ecclesiastical passions of his young followers, bringing them, as he later explained to Keble, 'from doctrine to history, from speculation to fact; again, as giving them an interest in the English soil and English Church, and keeping them from seeking sympathy in Rome as she is'.[7] Lockhart threw himself into the task with great enthusiasm and seems to have been taken by the saints of 'Catholic' England – the family wealth that he brought with him allowed him to commission Hardman of Birmingham to produce a chalice for Littlemore, based on one recently found during excavations in the tomb of St Richard at Chichester. The chalice later followed Lockhart to Ratcliffe.

Lockhart's recollections of Littlemore reveal something of Newman's warmth and humanity:

Newman would never let us treat him as a superior, but placed himself on a perfect level with the youngest of us. I remember that he insisted on our never calling him Mr Newman, according to the custom of Oxford when addressing Fellows and Tutors of Colleges. He would have had us call him simply Newman.

    Newman was an excellent violin player, and he would sometimes bring his violin into the library after dinner and entertain us with exquisite sonatas of Beethoven. It is said that a well-known Protestant controversialist – Canon Hugh McNeill of Liverpool – a great speaker on anti-Popery platforms, once advised himself to challenge Newman to a public disputation. The great man's answer was like himself. He wrote saying that Canon McNeill's well-known talent as a finished orator would make such a public controversy an unfair trial of strength between them, because he himself was no orator. He had had in fact no practice in public speaking. His friends however told him that he was no mean performer on the violin, and if he agreed to meet Canon McNeill, he would only make one condition, that the Canon should open the meeting, and say all he had to say, after which he (Mr Newman) would conclude with a tune on the violin. The public would then be able to judge which was the best man.[8]

Despite the privileges of life at Littlemore, Lockhart was soon plagued by fresh doubts about the claims of the Church of England and the issue of confession. He spoke to Newman:

> I doubted the orders, and still more the jurisdiction of the Church of England, and could feel no certainty of absolution. If I remember clearly I said to Newman, 'But are you sure you can give absolution?' to which I think his reply was, 'Why ask me? – ask Pusey.' He came to me a little later and said, 'I see you are in such a state that your being here would not fulfil the end of the place. You must agree to stay here three years, or go at once.' I said, 'I do not see how I can promise to stay three years. Unless I am convinced that I am safe in staying I cannot do it. And if I do not feel that I know enough to make my submission to Rome, when so many better and more learned men do not see their way to do so.'

Newman suggested that he go and speak to William George Ward, Fellow of Balliol and editor of the Tractarian journal, the *British Critic*. The two men had a three hour conversation walking around the University Parks, convincing Lockhart that:

> I knew enough of myself to know that I ought to distrust my own judgment; that I knew little of religion and practised less, in fact that

my conscience was not in such a state that I could have any confidence that my intellect would not be warped in any judgment so momentous, involving all manner of moral and intellectual questions, etc. He had just brought out [some articles in the British Critic] in which ... he lays great stress on the necessity of conscience being clear in order to make a right intellectual judgment on religious questions. In the end I went back to Newman and told him (as I learned afterwards to his surprise) that I had made up my mind to stay three years before taking any step Romewards.[9]

On one occasion, Lockhart remembered looking down on Oxford from Littlemore and wondered about

the meaning of those old towers and spires, of all the towers and spires that cut the horizon in every wide extent of open country in England? The answer came: they mark where a church lies hid, and every church of olden time was built as a tabernacle of the Blessed Sacrament, because they believed that Christ was in the Blessed Sacrament and that Christ is the Incarnate God.[10]

Despite his promise to stay at Littlemore for three years, everything changed when Lockhart met the fiery Italian missionary, Luigi Gentili of the Institute of Charity, on 19 October 1842 in Ward's rooms.

Luigi Gentili and the Institute of Charity

Luigi Gentili, a Roman by birth, was one of the most colourful figures of nineteenth-century English Catholicism, called by one biographer 'Sower of the Second Spring', but overshadowed somewhat by the Passionist missionary, Dominic Barberi, who has been raised to the altars of the Church.

Gentili's first contact with the English was in Rome, where he spent several years teaching Italian to visitors and conducting them around the Forum, the catacombs and the other tourist sites. He also cultivated friendships at the highest levels of Roman society, being granted the Order of the Golden Spur by Duke Sforza Cesarini, and buying a vineyard on Monte Mario so that he could boast of having an 'estate'. He hoped to turn it into an English-style experimental farm.

Gentili was something of a gallant, who had on one occasion declined the invitation to take part in a duel, and he fell passionately in love with the English-born Anna de Mendoza y Rios, then staying in Rome. One of her guardians was Bishop Peter Baines, then the Coadjutor to the Vicar Apostolic of the Western District, who was recuperating in Rome and who made sure the young Italian's advances did not proceed very far. In the words of the Rosminian historian Claude Leetham, 'the hand that struck the blow to Gentili's pride was destined to be the instrument of providing Gentili a few years later with the opportunity of fulfilling his apostolic mission in England'.[11]

Gentili's romantic disappointment matured into a spiritual conversion; he left High Society behind him and met Antonio Rosmini Serbati, the Tyrolese Count who had become a priest and prolific philosopher. With the encouragement of St Maddalena di Canossa, Rosmini founded the Institute of Charity (commonly called the 'Rosminians') in 1828 at the mountain-top sanctuary of Domodossola. The purpose of the Institute was perfect charity, which meant, in Rosmini's mind, perfect justice. This was fulfilled in an almost limitless number of ways, dictated by local needs and clearly seen in the variety of the Institute's subsequent activities in Great Britain: the preaching of missions and retreats, the running of schools and colleges (such as Ratcliffe and the Market Weighton Reformatory), the publishing of Catholic literature and the pastoral care of parishes.

Impressed by Rosmini and his vision, Luigi Gentili joined the Institute the year after its foundation and was ordained in 1830. His conversion was complete. Indeed, Lockhart later recalled that 'when the English newspapers sometimes mentioned his [Gentili's] name as "a remarkable preacher among the Roman Catholics", I remember a relative of mine, a Protestant, much used to Roman society, saying, "Can this be that Luigi Gentili with whom we used to sing duets in Rome?"'[12]

Disappointed in his love for an English lady, Gentili felt inspired to devote his life to preaching the Faith in England and becoming a second St Augustine of Canterbury. With this in mind, he undertook studies at the Irish College, then situated on the Via degli Ibernesi, and was thus able to improve his English. His love for England was something he shared with Rosmini, who admired the English parliamentary tradition and the work of English philosophers, and once wrote that 'for the restoration of this once an *Island of Saints* to the bosom of the Church, I would willingly shed my blood'.[13]

While at the Irish College, Gentili met Ambrose Phillipps, a zealous convert who dreamed of creating a Catholic Utopia in the neighbourhood of his Leicestershire estate, Grace Dieu.[14] Phillipps hoped that Gentili would return with him to the Midlands, but around the same time Bishop Baines requested that the Italian teach at Prior Park, near Bath, which was being established as a College and Seminary for the Western District, and perhaps ultimately as a Catholic University.

Gentili eventually set out for England in May 1835, together with Fathers Belisy and Rey. They not only received the blessings of Rosmini's friend and admirer, Pope Gregory XVI, but actually received an impromptu visit from the Pontiff on board ship, for the papal court happened to be passing through the port of Civita Vecchia as they were setting sail. Arriving at Prior Park, Gentili started work as professor of philosophy, but his principal importance was in introducing the practices of continental Catholicism to the Western District. Thanks to Gentili, the boys were soon vested in cassock and surplice, then unheard of in England; the ceremonial and chanting were firmly modelled on the Roman usage; and during Passiontide 1836 he preached one of the first public Retreats after the Jesuit manner in the country. The Fathers also assisted in Catholicizing the buildings at Prior Park. According to Bishop Ullathorne, Gentili often wandered about the house

> in distress of mind, saying that he verily believed that 'the devil was in the place'. I have heard an amusing story from eyewitnesses of his having set the boys to pull down the statues of pagan gods from the central mansion to the wings, then erected into two Colleges ... [Fr Gentili] had got a rope round Hercules and the boys were put to the other end of it, and he directed them: 'When I say the third time come down, you great monster, all of you pull together!' He had given the signal once, and twice, when Dr Baines put his head out of a window and stopped the destruction. It is a literal fact that after the great flight of steps were constructed up to the portico, a feature which spoiled the architect's design, and pulled down the elevation of the

whole facade to the eye, these pagan gods were taken down from their elevated position, manipulated with canvas and plaster, and made to represent two rows of saints, standing on the two sides of this broad flight of steps; and that Hercules with a tiara, a plaster cope and a triple cross in his hand in place of his concealed club, did duty for St Gregory the Great.[15]

Relations between Baines and the Institute disintegrated when two of the bishop's students, Moses Furlong and Peter Hutton, decided to join the novitiate. Rosmini sent reinforcements, including Gian Battista Pagani (later English Provincial and then Rosmini's immediate successor as Father General), Angelo Maria Rinolfi (another future Provincial) and Fortunatus Signini (who would work alongside Lockhart in London). However, the Fathers left Prior Park and began work in the Central District, with the support of the forward-thinking Vicar Apostolic, Thomas Walsh. They opened a house at Loughborough (1841) and taught at Old Oscott (now Maryvale). Gentili was sent as chaplain to Phillipps at Grace Dieu, which acted as a base, to preach in the locality. Lockhart later wrote that 'from Grace Dieu as a centre, Father Gentili, with the zeal of a St Francis de Sales, in all weathers, on foot from the moment he had finished Mass till a very late hour at night, penetrated into all the villages for many miles round, and made acquaintance with the people'.[16]

'One of the First Fruits of the Oxford Movement'[17]

It was while ministering in the Midlands that Gentili visited Oxford, accompanied by Phillipps, in October 1842. The priest's cassock, crucifix and Roman collar caused a sensation and Emily Bowles, a keen Tractarian, later revealed that it was Gentili's courage in openly wearing the soutane that first made her consider becoming a Catholic. Gentili met many of the leading figures of the Oxford Movement including Newman, who asked for advice on giving missions, and Pusey, with whom he had a lively discussion on transubstantiation.

Lockhart himself was so impressed that he wrote to Gentili the following year, on 30 March 1843, signing himself 'A. R. Z.' and using the cryptic address of the 'Post Office, Oxford'. The letter was full of youthful fervour:

> Reverend Sir, From the character of your order of Charity I venture tho' anonymously to ask a favour of you – which is that you would inform me how and where I could procure a hair shirt with perfect security of secrecy. I have strong reasons for wishing to make trial of one, but am deterred from doing what I believe will be acceptable to God, for fear of its being known. This is my case, and if you can help me I am sure you will. If you could also give me some advice upon the subject of corporal mortifications, you would add to the favour.[18]

It seems that Gentili had given him a copy of Rosmini's *Maxims*, which had been translated into English and distributed among many of the Tractarians. Lockhart had first seen this several years before through a friend, William White, who later became British Ambassador at Constantinople, but now he was able to read the book with greater concentration.

In a second letter to Gentili, written on 12 July 1843, Lockhart apologized for his earlier query since 'it would be impossible for you to give me salutary advice without being my confessor'. Lockhart had approached Newman over the matter and had been forbidden to undertake extra mortifications on account of his fragile health. The young man continued:

> I heard from Pugin that you are to build a house of your Order [at Ratcliffe], which gives us all pleasure at Oxford. Mr Newman was much pleased, as he always is at hearing any progress you are making. I have a great wish to know the rules and intention of your Order. Perhaps if I am able to come to Loughborough some time, you will explain it to me, as I believe it is not printed.[19]

The opportunity came in the summer of 1843, when Lockhart spent some weeks away with his mother and sister in Norfolk. His intention was then to make a brief tour of the sites in Lincolnshire connected with St Gilbert of Sempringham, whose life he was writing for the Oxford series. The young man took the chance to visit Gentili at Loughborough, where the Rosminians had been running a mission and novitiate for the past two years.

John Rouse Bloxam, Newman's former curate at Littlemore and a Fellow of Magdalen, recalled:

> I was traveling in Leicestershire about the end of August, when I met Lockhart in a train on his way to pay a visit to the Brothers of Charity at Loughborough. The next day was a rainy day, and the thought occurred to me that he would not be able to see the sights in the neighbourhood, and his mind would be upon the [visit?]. However I thought no more about it. When I returned to Oxford I met Dalgairns and asked him if Lockhart had come back. He gave me a look which I at once understood.[20]

When Lockhart arrived at Loughborough, events progressed with unexpected speed. He had not intended to stay long but met Lady Mary Arundell, a wealthy convert who had married Lord Arundell of Wardour and had become acquainted with Rosmini during their tour of Italy. She invited the young man to dinner, for she was the daughter of the Duke of Buckingham, a close friend of Lockhart's father, and the Catholic Baroness Nugent. She would become a great supporter of Lockhart, up until her untimely death in 1845, and confided to him that she had embraced the Faith because of the example of her mother and 'that through a chink in the door of her Oratory, which was always locked, and was an object of the greatest mystery to the children and servants, she had seen her elevated from the ground in prayer'.[21]

Lady Arundell's invitation to dinner that summer day in 1843 provided the opportunity for the inevitable to happen. Pagani reported to Rosmini that:

> Don Luigi with his gentle attractive ways, began little by little to win the soul of the good young man. Dinner over, Don Luigi persuaded him to go and visit the Trappist monastery [at Mount St Bernard] and the Church at Shepshed the next day; he consented. During his visits of these places, Don Luigi proposed to him to stay at Loughborough and make a retreat. He accepted this proposal also, and he is now received into the Catholic Church by Don Luigi in our chapel at Loughborough.[22]

Lockhart was received into the Church on 26 August 1843. Just three days later he was admitted into the Rosminian novitiate. Lockhart wrote to his friend Grant from Loughborough on the Feast of St Rose of Lima:

> My heart is so full and so heavy with writing and receiving painful letters that I cannot write more than just enough to tell you that I have become a Catholic. Thank God for this, and for the vocation which I believe He has given me to the Order of Charity. I was brought here to Dr Gentili at Loughboro' in a wonderful way, and have just finished my Retreat. Of course I shall get no credit with any of my dear, dear friends whom I have left at Oxford and Littlemore. But I know I cared too much for their good opinion, and it would be strange indeed if I had not something painful to bear in exchange for all these blessings. Thank you and all your community for their prayers, and please to combine to pray for all at Oxford and for my mother and sister. I will write again when I can, but at present I seem to have all my feelings blunted, and to be like a lump of cold boiled veal.[23]

Since Lockhart was a disciple of Newman, his 'secession' was widely reported and soon became a *cause célèbre*. Edward Churton, a member of the 'Hackney Phalanx' and a critic of Romanizing tendencies within the Church of England, referred to the 'defection of that rogue, Lockhart; who has played the *Monastery* a thorough Jesuitical trick, and left N[ewman] to bear the obloquy'.[24] John Duke Coleridge of Balliol, a future Lord Chief Justice, wrote to a friend on 11 September 1843:

> I grieve to see an Exeter man of the name of Lockhardt [sic] and one of the 'mynckerie' at Littlemore has seceded. It is not a thing to be surprised at nor, I think, very much vexed at, except as far as it concerns Newman himself. There is a man who has lived a great deal with him gone – which would seem to show, either that he is a more dangerous man than most people (I, for one) believed, or that he can't keep these 'myncks' of his in proper order.[25]

The Rector of Exeter College, Joseph Loscombe Richards, wrote to Newman:

> I am indeed shocked and grieved to hear of the step which Lockhart has taken. At the same time I am not altogether surprised at it. I never

could feel confidence in him. There was a great deal of vanity in his character and I think a want of ingenuousness. He made the mistake which many young men make in the present day of beginning at the wrong end. He took up religious controversy before he had realized religion as a practical matter, and he saw and felt, or affected to feel, difficulties in the position of the Anglican Church before he knew what the Church offered or had attempted to act up to her system. However, I do not wish to speak unkindly of him – or at all, except as a warning to other young men.[26]

Newman was always highly sensitive about his friendships and felt severely let down by the young Lockhart, whom he considered a protégé and who had promised to stay at Littlemore for three years. 'You may fancy how sick it makes me,' he wrote to Keble.[27] In a letter to Gentili, Newman confessed that 'what pains me is Mr Lockhart's conduct, in that he has broken an engagement to me – and taken me by surprise. It seems he was writing to you, while I thought he was putting himself under my guidance'.[28]

The scandal of Lockhart's departure and Newman's apparent lack of control over his 'myncks' led to his resignation as Vicar of St Mary's on 18 September 1843. Seven days later he preached his last sermon as an Anglican at Littlemore, entitled 'The Parting of Friends'. The occasion was made doubly poignant by the fact it was the anniversary of the consecration of the church at Littlemore, which Newman had built and which was associated with many happy memories.

Lockhart's entrance into the Institute of Charity displeased Nicholas Wiseman, who was at the time Coadjutor of the Central District[29] and President of Oscott. The English Provincial of the Institute, Fr Pagani, was with Wiseman when the news of Lockhart's conversion arrived, and the bishop was 'depressed and very disappointed and he did not fail to express his great displeasure, and he began complaining'. As Pagani explained to Rosmini, 'he fears that these Oxford men who become Catholics may want to join us rather than take up an ecclesiastical career under the bishop. Such opposition does not arise from a special dislike of our Institute, but rather from the very great desire that the bishop and his friends have of having subject to themselves all the best converts to the Catholic Church'. Wiseman was

'The Parting of Friends' 37

adamant 'as to men of value, and especially if they are men of means, as in the case of Lockhart, he cannot endure that they should place themselves under any direction but his own'.[30]

Notes

1. Blehl, *Pilgrim Journey*, p. 303.
2. Newman, *Apologia*, p. 148.
3. Newman, LD IX, p. 484.
4. Elsewhere Lockhart says that they went to Communion only on Sundays.
5. Lockhart, *Cardinal Newman*, pp. 10–11.
6. Ibid., pp. 11–12.
7. Gilley, *Newman and His Age*, p. 217.
8. Lockhart, *Cardinal Newman*, pp. 12–13.
9. Ward, *Ward and Oxford Movement*, p. 210.
10. Lockhart, 'On the Road to Rome', p. 415.
11. Leetham, *Luigi Gentili*, p. 12.
12. Lockhart, *Life of Rosmini*, ii, p. 87.
13. Ibid., ii, p. 86.
14. He changed his name in 1862 to Ambrose Phillipps de Lisle but, for the sake of consistency, will be referred to as 'Phillipps'.
15. Ullathorne, *The Devil is a Jackass*, pp. 285–6.
16. Lockhart, *Life of Rosmini*, ii, p. 101.
17. *Tablet*, 30 July 1881, p. 180.
18. Gwynn, *Father Luigi Gentili*, p. 179.
19. Leetham, *Luigi Gentili*, p. 174.
20. Middleton, *Newman at Oxford*, pp. 211–12.
21. Lockhart, *Life of Rosmini*, vol. ii, p. 126.
22. Leetham, *Luigi Gentili*, p. 177.
23. *Tablet*, 9 July 1892, p. 66.
24. Turner, *John Henry Newman*, p. 459.
25. Coleridge, *Life and Correspondence of Lord Coleridge*, vol. i, pp. 138–9.
26. Newman, LD IX, p. 502.
27. Ibid., p. 472.
28. Ibid., p. 475.
29. As the Midland District had become in 1840.
30. Leetham, *Luigi Gentili*, pp. 177–8.

Chapter IV

Martha and Elizabeth

It is worth pausing the narrative for a moment to consider the journey Romewards of Lockhart's mother, Martha, and half-sister, Elizabeth. Unsurprisingly, the family was initially badly shaken by William's dramatic conversion. Only his maternal grandfather, William Jacob, showed a more relaxed approach: 'Well!,' he said, 'young men do take odd courses nowadays! He might have taken to the turf!' On the other hand, his eccentric great-aunts, Miss Henderson and Mrs Curran, who lived in a villa on the Forth and, refusing to travel by train, came down to London each year in an old yellow carriage, feared 'for his damnation in the world to come, and the loss of beauty, happiness, family, in this, all owing to the unaccountable madness of becoming a Catholic'. They did not want Lockhart to visit them in Scotland, for they imagined him to be barefooted and tonsured like the monks they had seen years previously on their European travels.[1]

Martha Lockhart herself appeared mystified at her son's antics. She told Newman that 'he seemed to think and represented to us that you had given him leave to go to Loughborough or we should have remonstrated on the imprudence of the step'. However, she admitted that 'Willie's state of mind for several months at intervals has been so painful that I feared his body or mind could have sunk under his struggles'.[2]

As time went on – and the likes of Newman were received into the Church – Mrs Lockhart herself was gradually approaching the threshold of Rome, which led to a sharp exchange with Manning, who was still committed to the established Church. She asked him, 'Mr Archdeacon, are you quite sure of the validity of

Anglican orders?' Manning curtly replied, 'You are a good deal too like your dear son.' Indeed, on hearing of William's conversion, Manning told her, 'I would rather follow a friend to the grave than hear he had taken such a step' and advised her to cut all relations, 'as she valued her salvation'.[3]

However, she did not follow this advice. William visited Chichester whenever the opportunity arose and at the beginning of 1845 Mrs Lockhart reported to Newman that

> all his natural cheerfulness is restored and he is as merry as a boy, not at all like the melancholy notion gained from novels and tales of a gloomy monk; and more interested in us and all our doings than he has been for years, and loving us better than he ever did ... He has never been so much to me in his life before.[4]

One of Mrs Lockhart's final difficulties was the undoubted fact that sanctity could be found in the Anglican Communion. William forwarded her letter outlining this query to Newman, who by now had himself become a Catholic and replied:

> What great joy your letter which I received yesterday from your son, gave me! – Not that I dare build upon it what it does not say, and what is still in the hands of God, but it really does seem as if William's prayers and your own earnestness and goodness were bringing you safe into the one fold of Christ. May it be so, and my help such as it is, shall not be wanting while we anxiously and eagerly wait for the blessed issue of God's dealings with you.[5]

On 9 July she was received into the Church by Fr Pagani at the convent chapel of Loughborough in the presence of the Sisters of Providence and her delighted son. She remained there for three weeks, to continue her religious instruction, and visited Ratcliffe. On 16 July, mother and son paid a visit to Newman, who was then at Oscott. Mrs Lockhart occupied herself with literary work in these early years as a Catholic and translated from the Italian two devotional works that had been written by Pagani: *The Anima Divota; or, Devout Soul* (1848) and *Anima Amanta; or, the Soul-Loving God* (1849).

'The Debora of the Tractarian Movement'

In the meantime, Elizabeth remained loyal to the Church of England, despite contrary rumours that circulated around the High Church circles in Sussex. She found Newman's *University Sermons* particularly helpful in answering some of her queries and continued to enjoy the guidance of Manning and the friendship of Keble, Pusey and Dyson. Indeed, on account of her High Church credentials, the memorialist of Robert Aston Coffin, future bishop of Southwark, called her the 'Debora of the Tractarian Movement'. At the end of 1845, while still Vicar of St Mary Magdalen's in Oxford, Coffin took a month's leave to discern his future as an Anglican. One of the friends he wished to consult was Manning and, arriving at Chichester, he first approached Elizabeth to see if the Archdeacon was available. However, he seems to have suffered from last minute nerves:

> Miss Lockhart answered that that very day he [Manning] was to be her guest. Mr Coffin therefore confided to her the object of his visit, and begged her to put to the Archdeacon the following question: Whether he who believes all the dogmas of the Roman Catholic Church may still remain in the Establishment or go over to Rome? The answer which Miss Lockhart communicated on the part of the Archdeacon was: Who believes all the dogmas of the Catholic Church ought to become a Catholic.[6]

After her mother's conversion, there was an estrangement between them. On 6 August 1846 Manning met Mrs Lockhart for the first time since her conversion. He noted in his diary that it was a 'most painful interview':

> I avoided all discussion, and said all I wished was to say nothing inconsistent with sincerity and charity. She said of her daughter, 'It is not you, but she will not live with me'. What strikes me is –
> 1. Her inability to realize the effect of what she has done on others – Keble, her father, Miss Lockhart.
> 2. Her want of consideration and tenderness for Miss Lockhart.
> 3. Her great want of gentleness and meekness. Surely the greater truth the greater charity. The true Church ought to teach the Sermon on the Mount.
> 4. Her reckless, cruel, assaulting way of speaking and acting.[7]

Aware of Elizabeth's talents and estrangement from her immediate family, Manning recommended her to William John Butler, who was hoping to establish a Sisterhood at Wantage. The establishment of Anglican convents was one of the notable fruits of the Oxford Movement. Owen Chadwick has called the trend 'astonishing and almost unique among the Protestant churches'.[8] The first of these Sisterhoods was established at Park Village West, near London's Regent's Park, in March 1845. Designed as a memorial to Robert Southey, the late poet laureate who had favoured the foundation of such communities, and supported by the likes of Gladstone and Pusey, the Sisters did valuable pastoral work in the Euston Road area, running a school and orphanage.

When twenty-eight-year-old Butler was appointed Rector of the Oxfordshire market town of Wantage in 1847, he set about forming a similar community of women to provide education in the area. The following year, Manning sent Elizabeth Lockhart to him in the hope that she could form the backbone of the new community and, in doing so, would be kept away from Rome. Although already in her late thirties, she had considered the religious life for some time and several years earlier had been introduced to Pusey as a possible aspirant for a community. She stayed at Wantage during Lent 1848 and talked at length with Butler about his vision of a teaching Sisterhood. After Easter, two cottages in Wallingford Street were taken to form an embryonic convent, although they moved to a larger cottage several months later. Elizabeth was named the first Mother Superior and was joined in May by Mary Reid, a close friend from Chichester who had been involved in the Lockharts' small school. Although in poor health, she took charge of domestic affairs at the new convent and was admired for her cheerful kindliness.

As soon as the community was founded, the work of teaching began, with assistance from Mrs Butler and a number of guests who stayed with the community for a brief time to share in their work. The Sisters started reciting the Sarum Office, which had been translated by the future Jesuit Albany Christie and bound in parchment. A young pupil teacher remembered their first oratory as being 'an attic with a sloping roof and roughly boarded floor, the only furniture being two long desks with sloping sides made of bare deal, at which we stood to say the office'.[9]

Although the convent was Butler's brainchild, Manning acted as spiritual director and visited several times a year. In August 1848 the Archdeacon reported:

> Miss Lockhart is established in an old small house, with a very pretty strip of garden at the back, most private and quiet. She has two companions with her, and her work is to be found about five hours a day in the school. The rest of her time is ordered on a very even and good rule of employments and devotion. The vicar is the visitor and guardian of the house, and is most worthy and fit in every way for this Office.[10]

Whereas Butler's stress was on education, Elizabeth increasingly felt called to undertake rescue work with former prostitutes and unmarried mothers. It is normally thought that Manning was responsible for planting this idea in his spiritual daughter's mind and she may have been further inspired by an article by the vicar of Tidenham (John Armstrong), published in the *Church Quarterly* of September 1848, which underlined the inadequate provision for the care of 'fallen women' within the Church of England, especially when compared to the Catholic Church. In face of the determination of the Archdeacon and the Reverend Mother, Butler was unable to resist the new direction that his community was taking, despite his misgivings.

Plans were drawn up for 'St Mary's Home for Penitents'. Although at first Manning suggested this should be located in London, a Queen Anne house opposite the convent was soon procured. Elizabeth had been asked to help nurse her octogenarian step-grandfather, William Jacob, and one of his daughters at their residence of 31 Cadogan Place and her sojourn in London allowed her to meet with Manning to discuss their plans for Wantage. The opening of St Mary's Home was delayed until 2 February 1850, normally considered the foundation date of the Sisterhood of St Mary the Virgin. By the time of the inauguration of Elizabeth's new establishment, several 'fallen' women had already asked to be admitted and the parish curate was deputed to act as chaplain.

Despite the success of these new initiatives, tensions remained at Wantage and there was the perceived threat of Romanizing influences. Within a year of Elizabeth's arrival at Wantage, the life of the community grew increasingly monastic in its tone. Silence was observed for longer periods and Elizabeth began to wear a sort of religious habit rather than the inconspicuous black dresses and muslin caps favoured by Butler.[11] Despite the earlier shock of his conversion, she remained in contact with her brother, who visited Wantage in March 1849 and possibly on other occasions. Butler noted with a sense of relief that when the Rosminian dropped into the Vicarage he spoke wisely and without controversy.

In 1850 the Gorham Judgment produced a storm in the Church of England, when the Privy Council Judicial Committee reinstated George Cornelius Gorham to the living of Bramford Speke, despite having been removed by the bishop of Exeter on account of his heterodox views on baptismal regeneration. Many were horrified by this blatant interference of the civil authorities in the realm of doctrine, including Manning himself, who addressed a letter to the bishop of Chichester on 'The Appellate Jurisdiction of the Crown in Spiritual Matters'. He did not submit to Rome until the following year, but in the meantime watched many of his friends and penitents cross over the Tiber, including Charles William Laprimaudaye (his former curate), Henry Wilberforce, Thomas William Allies, William Maskell, William Dodsworth, and Lord and Lady Feilding.

On 17 April Butler heard from Manning that Elizabeth's conscience was much troubled over the matter. Less than two months later, on 12 June, she announced that she was to leave the Church of England. Butler wrote in his journal:

> This is a heavy blow but not unexpected. Of course there was the strong influence of a mother and brother gone and the weak support of her spiritual adviser was little able to withstand their weight. So she yielded. She has been a great help to us in every way, setting before the people the sight of one seeking to fulfill our Lord's Counsels of Perfection, and in every way being well calculated to touch the hearts of rough thoughtless people like ours. May He who sends this grief give us strength to bear it, and save our parish from injury. It seems right to endeavour to carry on the work at a risk. The Penitents have made decided progress and it would not be right to cast them again on the world. There is every disposition on the part of Miss L. and the Archdeacon to help us in this; and I have therefore placed all arrangements in the Bishop's hands.[12]

Elizabeth remained in Wantage for a short time sorting out her affairs but nothing could deaden the blow of her departure. Her trusty companion, Mary Reid, also decided to leave, as did some of the penitent women, who were shaken by the Mother Superior's decision. Another Sister, Harriet Day, was strongly tempted to follow the Romewards tide but Butler invited her to spend some time with his family at the Vicarage and persuaded her to remain at Wantage. Butler was unsure of the future of his Sisterhood now that he had lost Manning's spiritual direction and Elizabeth's leadership and financial backing, although she agreed to pay the rent on convent property until the following year. The Wantage Sisterhood survived these early ruptures and became one of the most important religious communities in the Anglican Communion. Elizabeth Lockhart, meanwhile, settled into her new life as a Catholic and occupied herself with much reading and study as she discerned her future path.

Notes

1. Hirst, 'Necrology', p. 19.
2. Newman, LD IX, p. 500.
3. Lockhart, 'Some Personal Reminiscences of Cardinal Manning', p. 378.
4. Leetham, *Luigi Gentili*, p. 179.
5. Newman, LD XI, p. 184 (Newman to Mrs Lockhart, 26 June 1846).
6. Purcell, *Cardinal Manning*, vol. ii, p. 78.
7. Ibid., vol. i, pp. 448–9.
8. Chadwick, *The Victorian Church*, vol. i, p. 505.
9. Anon., *Butler of Wantage*, p. 36.
10. Purcell, *Cardinal Manning*, vol. i, p. 491.
11. Out of doors the Sisters wore black straw poke bonnets and black shawls, although on one occasion Miss Lockhart was spotted wearing a tartan shawl on a school treat.
12. Anon., *Butler of Wantage*, p. 39.

Chapter V

Itinerant Missionary

First Years in the Institute of Charity

As a Rosminian novice, Lockhart found himself in northern Leicestershire, which was witnessing a remarkable Catholic revival thanks largely to the patronage and vision of Ambrose Phillipps. He had founded the Trappist monastery at Mount St Bernard in 1835 and a mission at Whitwick two years later. Thereced was a thriving chapel at Grace Dieu, where he was particularly proud of the singing of Gregorian chant, and hoped that it could be a base for an Italian missionary. Having failed to tempt the Passionist Dominic Barberi, he invited Luigi Gentili, whom he had met in Rome. The Rosminian arrived in June 1840 and began evangelizing the villages of Shepshed, Hathern, Belton and Osgathorpe.

After two months in the novitiate at Loughborough, Lockhart's health broke down, due to the stress of recent events and also, we are told, the 'self-inflicted penances, which, unknown to his director, he had indiscreetly indulged in during the first fervour of his life as a Catholic'.[1] The young novice recuperated with the Italian branch of his family who, as Catholics, were still on friendly terms with him and hoped to ensure his quick promotion up the ecclesiastical ladder. The brother of his aunt's husband was Cardinal Tommaso Riario Sforza, Camerlengo, Proto-Deacon of the Sacred College and Prefect of the Sacred Congregation of Good Government. It seems that he insisted Lockhart should leave the Rosminians at once and accept an inter-nunziatura, which might eventually bring him a mitre or even a red hat. This was indeed a possibility, for Sisto, the Cardinal's nephew, had just been appointed Archbishop of Naples and was raised to the sacred purple the following year. To the consternation of his family, however, Lockhart chose to remain in obscurity in England with the Institute, although his Italian connections proved particularly useful in later life when he would spend part of the year in Rome on Rosminian business.

The period was an eventful time for the English Rosminians. Writing in 1886, Lockhart claimed that the years 1843 and 1844 saw the Institute 'introducing into England four works of piety and charity, till then unpractised, but now forming an integral part of Parochial administration'. The Fathers started preaching missions, the first one being given by Gentili and Furlong at Loughborough and resulting in sixty-three conversions. The experiment was repeated at Shepshed and Whitwick, where a Calvary was erected on a hill, the landscape reminding Lockhart of Rosmini's native Tyrol, and then throughout the country. A mission preached at Coventry involved what was said to be the first Marian procession in England since the Reformation. Such was the demand for their preaching, that Rosmini suggested the opening of a college to train missionaries for the English-speaking world.

The other new 'works of piety' were the *Quarant' ore* (Forty Hours Exposition of the Blessed Sacrament), May devotions in honour of Our Lady, and the Renewal of Baptismal Vows, usually made at the end of a mission.[2]

In 1843 two Italian members of the female branch of the Rosminian family, the Sisters of Providence, arrived in the Midlands at the invitation of Lady Mary Arundell. In her widowhood, Lady Arundell had moved to Loughborough to assist the Institute and gave hospitality to the Sisters at her home on Wood Street. Despite their lack of English, they soon took charge of a school for Infants and Girls that Lady Arundell had started. Lockhart wrote that

> great was the astonishment, which I can testify as an eye-witness, of the good town's-folk of Loughborough when, on the first Sunday after their arrival, these Sisters appeared in the street on their return from Mass at the parish Chapel, wearing their Religious habit. It was the first time such a sight had been seen in the Midlands, and all

turned out to see them, following them on both sides of the street; but they meant wonder only and no harm, and the wonder soon passed away.[3]

Around this time, Ratcliffe was chosen as the location of the Institute's new novitiate and college and Pugin provided the designs, Gentili even insisting on a tower which could, he thought, be utilized for astronomical observations. The building of the house caused some ill-feeling locally and Mr Nettleton, a Protestant preacher, even knelt near the building site and prayed that God would send down fire from heaven to destroy the Romish encampment. A few years later he converted to Catholicism, after claiming to see an angel hovering above the tabernacle in the completed chapel.

Lockhart proved to be quite a catch for the Institute – not only because of his connections with Newman and the Oxford men, but because of the money he brought with him. The building of the college was made possible partly by the security provided by the £20,000 that Lockhart brought to the Institute. £1,000 quickly went towards the building of the first part of the complex, and soon after its opening Fr Hutton wrote to Rosmini that 'Lockhart's money would enable a new wing to be built immediately'.[4]

In the summer and autumn of 1844, Lockhart spent most of the week at Ratcliffe with Brother James Bowen preparing and painting the chapel furnishings, returning to Loughborough by foot for Sunday. The local roads were limited so that the members of the Institute who came to visit the building site 'in their cassocks and broad-brimmed foreign clerical hats ... had to make the approach from Syston ankle-deep in mud'.[5] The college was ready to be opened on 21 November 1844 and when Lockhart visited it in his later years, he liked to look at the tall trees along the old laurel path and 'recall to mind how, after planting them, he and Brother Akeroyd had gone straddlewise over every one of them, up and down the rows, in order that they might say so, *ad futurum rei memoriam*'.[6]

In the meantime Lockhart was prepared for the Rosminian vocation, which involved not only the pastoral care of parishes but the preaching of missions. Lockhart's voice was considered rather weak when he entered the novitiate, but Furlong 'taught him to strengthen it by reading aloud every day, and to perfect his delivery by special and unwearied attention to the effective employment of marked labial action'. In later years he would be noted for 'his clear musical voice, and the delicate accuracy and distinctness of his pronunciation,' which 'kept spell-bound the ear'.[7]

Lockhart was professed at Ratcliffe on 8 September 1845 and a few months later, on 19 December, ordained subdeacon at Oscott. He received several visits from Oxford friends who had eventually followed in his footsteps Romewards. Dalgairns was at Ratcliffe from 30 October to 3 November 1845, together with Bowles. Newman himself was received into Holy Mother Church on 9 October 1845 and visited Ratcliffe the following Epiphany, in the company of Ambrose St John. Pagani later wrote to Newman: 'What an edifying sight to see Mr Newman receiving Holy Communion kneeling on the floor with our lay brothers and behind our clerics, among whom was Lockhart, once his disciple and spiritual son!'[8] Lockhart was ordained deacon at Oscott on 5 June 1846 and raised to the Sacred Priesthood by Bishop Walsh in the little oratory at Ratcliffe on 19 December the same year.

The early days of Lockhart's priesthood were spent at Ratcliffe, where he preached at the opening of the new chapel on 1 June 1847,

> in which he undertook to show the necessity of external worship in the true Church of God, drawing his arguments principally from the nature of man as composed of body and soul, and from the sublime mysteries of our holy religion which regard the sacred humanity of Jesus Christ; depicting, also, in glowing colours the transcendent superiority of the Sacrifice of the New Law over all the Ancient Rites, and how that it was this great and adorable mystery that had called into existence all that was truly excellent in Christian art.[9]

Ratcliffe would grow into a successful College, 'intended for the service of those who desire a liberal education for their sons, but one less expensive than that of the larger Colleges'.[10] When a sudden decline in the number of students led to talk of closure in 1852, Lockhart strongly opposed the idea and offered his services if they were needed. Rosmini himself encouraged the Fathers to persevere and, under the long Presidency of Peter Hutton, the school went from strength to strength.

Lockhart also helped conduct missions in the neighbouring towns of Melton Mowbray and Loughborough. On 5 June 1847, he was sent to work at Shepshed, which had been first visited by Gentili in 1840 and formally taken over by the Institute in 1845. Under the patronage of Ambrose Phillipps, a church had been built by Pugin in 1841 and dedicated to St Winefride. It was the architect's first experiment in natural architecture, constructed in local stone and merging in with the surrounding rubble walls. Together with the school buildings at Whitwick (also designed by Pugin), St Winefride's was an attempt by Phillipps to provide spiritual nourishment amidst increasing rural poverty in the face of the depression that hit both agriculture and the domestic industries. Chartism had raised its head in the locality and Gentili had been shocked by the conditions of the poor. He wrote to Rosmini in January 1841: 'Not to be able to help these poor people is for me a great trial. Many cannot come to the chapel to be received or to receive the Sacraments or hear Mass, because they have no shoes, no hats, no decent clothing, as they are in rags and half-naked'.[11]

Gentili's missionary efforts were greatly helped by his compassion for the local population, who felt alienated from the 'respectable' Church of England – indeed, unlike the vicar, Gentili made a point of not charging for baptisms. His technique of evangelization was based on house visiting and talking to people in the roads and lanes. By May 1841 he had succeeded in converting 320 people from Shepshed (out of a population of roughly 5,000), 100 from Belton (out of 2,000) and nearly 100 from Osgathorpe (out of 800).

Lockhart continued Gentili's custom of visiting the local villages and preaching in the open air, starting with a spiritual exhortation and then launching into controversy. The young priest became a familiar figure in the country lanes, accompanied by Brother Simone from the Tyrol, who carried all the books that were needed in a black bag, and wearing the distinctive cassock and *feriola*.[12]

Lockhart also spent a brief period stationed at St Marie's, Rugby, which the Institute took over in September 1849. A beautiful church, designed by Pugin, had been built by Captain Washington Hibbert, who converted to Catholicism after the building had been erected. He also opened schools and presented the Rosminians with land for a new novitiate ('St Marie's College') since Ratcliffe was now concentrating on its secular students. Mrs Hibbert, who was a member of the old Catholic family of the Tichbournes of Tichbourne and the mother (through her first marriage) of the seventeenth earl of Shrewsbury, sponsored the building of a convent for the Rosminian Sisters nearby. Rugby thus became an important centre for the Institute. Lockhart wrote that 'the whole group of buildings, all in the purest style of Gothic architecture, the college, schools, and church, with its graceful tower and spire, form a most beautiful picture. From the tower the Angelus and musical chimes ring out three times each day'.[13]

The first Rosminian Rector of Rugby, to whom Lockhart acted as assistant, was Pierlugi Bertetti, a former Canon of Tortona Cathedral and Rector of the diocesan seminary. He had already made a name for himself as a theologian when he entered the Institute in 1847 and Rosmini relied greatly on his expertise, writing to him in Rugby at the end of 1849 to resolve some philosophical questions. Bertetti also had a deep appreciation of the Founder's works, which he first encountered while a seminarian at Turin, and 'there would be frequent correspondence between the two, and perfect understanding'.[14] Given this close relationship, together with his administrative and diplomatic skills, it is little surprise that he left Rugby in January 1851 to become the Institute's Procurator in Rome, while Rosmini's works were being examined by the authorities, and ten years later he was elected Father General. Lockhart undoubtedly benefitted from his time at Rugby and grew in his understanding of the Rosminian corpus, which in later life he would begin to translate into English.

Crowded Churches and Confessionals

From 1851 Lockhart acted as a full time missionary, as did many of the Rosminians, travelling around the United Kingdom preaching the Gospel and winning converts to the Faith. In March

1851, for example, he was at St Joseph's, Liverpool, 'a parish almost exclusively inhabited by the poor – labourers, artisans and small tradesmen'. Lockhart was impressed by their piety – 'the bell need only be rung and in a few moments the church will be filled from the immediate neighbourhood' – and by the priest, Fr Carter, who had just moved from a country parish, situated 'amidst green meadows watered by a beautiful salmon stream, surrounded by a zealous congregation of old Catholics', to a densely populated part of Liverpool, where his two predecessors had died of cholera. The Institute had preached a mission at St Joseph's in 1849 and Lockhart noted two years later that 'a great number of those who were reconciled with God during the last retreat died during the cholera which visited Liverpool soon after'. Such recent history gave increased urgency to the mission and helped ensure its success.

Having completed their duties at St Joseph's, the missioners met the brother of Bishop Baines, 'a farmer of the old school', who picked them up in his cart and drove them 'at a brisk pace over the rough paved country roads and sandy lanes' to his house near Ince Blundell. Lockhart thought the family 'an excellent specimen of the Lancashire Catholic Yeomanry' and was especially taken by the ladies who, 'if they had been Protestants of the same class would have sat up like ladies with gloves on and condescended to do nothing more than play an air on the piano', but who instead earnestly served the 'poor priests' at table. 'We returned to Liverpool', continued Lockhart in his mission diary, 'all the better for our excursion which blew away the remains of the thick atmosphere in which we had been living in crowded churches and confessionals for the last fortnight.'[15]

Bringing Back the Irish 'Jumpers'

Lockhart was also involved in a number of missions in Ireland, then recovering from the tragedy of the Great Famine. His Irish experiences, which have been called 'perhaps the most important and fruitful of his priestly career,'[16] were not simply an attempt to catechize the Irish poor. It has been said that 'one of the main concerns of the [Irish] Catholic hierarchy in the 1850s was the threat of proselytism and the decade was dominated by the struggle between Protestants and Catholics for the souls of the Irish population'.[17] The early nineteenth century had seen a growth in proselytizing activities organized by Protestant evangelists. The Famine was seen as an opportunity to intensify these efforts and was interpreted as a punishment for centuries of Romish superstition. Organizations appeared, such as the 'Society for the Irish Church Missions to Roman Catholics'; founded in 1849, within five years it had set up 125 mission stations, especially in the west of Ireland. Charity was combined with proselytizing, as 'sums of money without end were poured into Ireland, and ship-loads of cast-off clothes, and sacks of stirabout, were sent from England, in order to bring the light of the Gospel to that benighted Popish country'.[18] Bibles and tracts were distributed and the starving were offered soup if they agreed to convert. Those who apostasized became known as 'soupers' or 'jumpers' and were often ostracized by the rest of the community.

The missions preached by Lockhart and his companions were thus an attempt to counter this proselytism and demonstrate the health of Irish Catholicism. They met with considerable success. The Belfast mission of April 1851 was considered a high point; when Lockhart and Rinolfi boarded the ship for the return voyage to Liverpool, hundreds came to the quay to see them off and even kiss and touch their garments as they passed. Indeed, during Benediction on the last evening of the mission, 'the people within and without the churches saw a bright meteor pass over the town which seemed to many a heavenly token. The simple people believed it to be an angel'.[19]

A Belfast newspaper described the structure of a typical day:

> Each morning, after an early Mass, one of the preachers addresses the people; and, each evening, both gentlemen deliver discourses. These are directed with a view to the full inculcation of the broad principles of charity and moral rectitude; but as the special object of the Mission is to give an opportunity to the Roman Catholics to perform one of the sacraments of that Church – the sacrament of penance – the exhortations of the clergy are directed in a special manner to an explanation of the conditions laid down by the Church as necessary for the proper realization of the sacrament. The mere matter of preaching is a very subordinate portion of the duties of the Missioners. It is in the confes-

sionals their labours are onerous, – indeed, remarkably severe. From so early an hour as six in the morning till ten at night they are engaged in them, except a very brief portion allotted for meals, and the periods occupied by the lectures.[20]

Often the crowds were too large for the church building and the mission was moved into the open air. On the last day of the 1853 mission at Headford in County Galway, an altar was erected in the ruins of the church dedicated to the seventh-century monk, St Fursey. The Dublin *Freeman's Journal* reported that 'the effect produced on the people by the Very Rev. Father Lockhart's sermon, standing in the ruins of that memorial both of past sanctity and spoliation, was thrilling'. Emotions were heightened even further when the Archbishop of Tuam arrived, with mitre and crozier, to give an address in Gaelic.[21]

At Partry in County Mayo, there was a Mass 'in the open air, at an altar formed of stones and turf ... on the mountain side – when the very rocks rang again, as the whole multitude recited together the Apostles' Creed and renewed their baptismal vows'.[22] *The Tablet* reported this mission to be 'a splendid triumph' and 'a most humiliating exposure of the feebleness of the miserable "Jumpers".' This was especially the case since Thomas Plunket, second Baron Plunket and Protestant Bishop of Tuam, Killaly and Achonry, owned a lodge in nearby Tourmakeady, where he apparently spent 'a considerable part of the summer in the Episcopal avocations of fishing and grouse-shooting'. The bishop was a keen supporter of the Irish Church Mission Society and not only built a chapel near his lodge in 1852 but 'established a system of distribution of Jumper soup and Bibles' in order 'to rob the poor people of the Faith'. *The Tablet* delighted in the fact that on the last Sunday of the mission, large crowds gathered to hear Lockhart preach in the open air while only 34 individuals gathered in the bishop's chapel. Around the same time, Lockhart and Rinolfi visited Fairhall, where they also had to abandon the packed church for a spacious field and reported that there was 'scarcely a trace of Jumperism'.[23]

Lockhart was something of a curiosity to the Irish congregations as an Oxford convert and his name attracted widespread attention. At St Audeon's in Dublin, where Gentili had been buried in 1848,

> a particular attraction was given to this Mission by the fact of Father Lockhart being an Oxford convert. It was a great subject of joy to the Catholics to see such a man in the midst of them. Apart from that consolation which Catholics experience in the good and happiness of others, they could not help rejoicing in hearing one who had come out from the camp, as it were, of the enemy, bearing witness to the truth and sanctity of their religion; and whenever the good Father alluded to his own conversion, and to its motives, a low murmur of joy and of gratitude was to be heard through the whole mass of the devout faithful people.[24]

Indeed, at Boyle, County Roscommon in June 1853,

> towards the hour on which the public car was to arrive, by which Father Lockhart was to come from Galway, a great many of the people went out from town to meet him, and as soon as they saw him, they raised their voices to welcome him, and accompanied him thus into the town, where, as it was market day, there were thousands of people from all the neighbourhood, and all gathered around him, giving him a thousand welcomes; he could scarcely, even with the assistance of the clergy, make his way through the crowd to the Parish Priest's house, and when at last he had reached it, the devout multitude would not disperse, but remained in the street till the Father said to them a few words from the window and gave them his blessing, hoping to see them all, as well as their neighbours, on the morrow, when he would speak to them of the reasons of his conversion to the Catholic Faith.[25]

The missions were not popular with the local Protestant community and anti-Catholic placards and pamphlets were frequently produced. At Clifden, in Galway, we are told that

> one day, one of the parsons went to the chapel, whilst the priests were hearing confessions, and the people were at their devotions before the Blessed Sacrament, exposed for the *Quarant'ore*, and asked to see Father Lockhart, in order to dispute with him. Father Lockhart met him with dignified ridicule, and the poor man might have paid dear for his rashness and irreverent conduct in the chapel, at the hands of

the people who crowded around him, had not Father Lockhart prevented them from rushing upon him.[26]

Outrageous claims were made about the content of the mission. It was claimed, for example, that Lockhart had said that both his parents were damned and in hell and that he was glad of it. The Rosminian pointed out that his mother was happily still alive and currently living in a Greenwich convent and that his father had died, he hoped, in a state of invincible ignorance.[27]

A Meeting with Rosmini

Throughout Lockhart's life, the active apostolate was interrupted by periods of poor health and nervous exhaustion – a weakness that had presented itself at Oxford as he was struggling with his Anglican difficulties. In a letter to Rinolfi in April 1853, Rosmini himself underlined the need of rest for 'our two zealous workers Furlong and Lockhart' and suggested that 'after three weeks of work, or a month at the most, there should be a period of a week or ten days of complete rest before they undertake another mission'. Moreover, 'there should be one day of rest every week' and 'they must absolutely cut down their hours in the confessional so as to leave themselves with at least seven hours' sleep'. The Founder firmly believed that 'special care has to be taken of those who are not so strong'.[28]

Despite such precautions, the strenuous preaching tours of Ireland and elsewhere led to a physical and nervous breakdown, and in the autumn of 1853 Lockhart recuperated in Rome. He went by way of Paris to Marseilles, where he picked up a steamboat to Genoa, Leghorn and Civita Vecchia. The final stage of the journey was by carriage to Rome, where he arrived on 4 November. He later recalled that 'it was the hottest weather I ever remember'.[29] His travelling companions included two future Archbishops of Westminster, Manning and Vaughan, together with Robert Whitty (Wiseman's Vicar General), and Manning's nephew and niece. The two future Cardinals were studying at the Accademia degli Nobili Ecclesiastici, where Vaughan served Manning's Mass almost daily. Manning later described his Roman years (1851–4) as 'a time of great peace but of great trial. I found myself at forty-two among youths; and a stranger among foreigners – I had broken almost every old relation in the world, and was beginning life over again.'[30] Little surprise, then, that he often met Lockhart for walks around the Eternal City, a favourite haunt being the gardens of the Villa Ludovisi, to which Manning had a key. The two converts were able to strengthen their relationship, despite earlier disagreements, and this would bear much fruit in later years.

John Gibson Lockhart, who had just resigned the editorship of *The Quarterly Review*, also spent the winter of 1853–4 in Rome. Despite being in poor health, he made the most of opportunities offered by the great city. At the Palazzo Doria he 'saw some splendid beauties, and more red stockings than perhaps I shall ever see again' and thought Wiseman's English sermons 'a good contrast to the donkeys of our Anglican Chapel'.[31] His letters give a rare insight into the life of Fr Lockhart at the time. He found his cousin to be 'a fine, handsome, amiable young man' and was impressed that he had 'given up a fair fortune to be a monk of some new Order'.[32] When the Scottish Catholic philanthropist, Robert Monteith, and his family caught 'Roman fever' (malaria), he wrote that Lockhart 'sees them hourly, and lets me know daily ... One little girl died on Saturday, and I greatly fear my next intelligence may be the death of another of them, with that of poor R. Monteith himself'. He continued: 'this William Lockhart came over with Manning, and will return with him. He is very near to the Lees, and I knew his father well in early life. He seems a most amiable young man, and is very kind to me, as, indeed, sundry of his cloth here are'.[33] Indeed, he thought Vaughan was 'another handsome, elegant, good-natured, young English gentleman, gone the way of Newman' and judged Manning's gestures to be 'the most graceful I ever saw in a pulpit performer'.[34] He sometimes met the latter for solo dinners. On one occasion, 'I asked him to invite Vaughan or W. Lockhart, both of whom I am as fond of as he is, but he preferred a two-handed talk for once'.[35]

William Lockhart was not purely a man of leisure for he was assigned once again to assist Bertetti, who, as already mentioned, was now acting as Rosmini's agent in Rome. These were critical years for the Institute since the works of the Father

Founder were being examined by the Holy See. Rosmini had been encouraged by the Popes not only in his vision for the Institute, which was approved by Gregory XVI in 1838, but also in his philosophical writings. Pius VIII had told him in May 1829,

> It is the will of God that you should occupy yourself in writing books; this is your vocation. The Church at present has great need of writers – I mean of sound and reliable writers, of whom we have a notable shortage. To exert a useful influence on men there is no other means nowadays than to convince them with reason, and so lead them to religion. Take it for certain, then, that you can render a much greater benefit to your neighbor by occupying yourself in writing than by undertaking any other work of the sacred ministry.[36]

His early writings were received with great enthusiasm and many of the northern Italian dioceses introduced the *Nuovo Saggio sull'origine delle idée* (New Essay on the Origin of Ideas, 1830) to the seminary curriculum.

However, opposition to Rosmini's writings grew and was especially prevalent within the Society of Jesus. Following the publication of his *Trattato della coscienza morale* (Treatise on Moral Conscience) in 1840, an anonymous critic using the pen name 'Eusebio Cristiano' produced *Some affirmations of Antonio Rosmini*, setting forth the perceived errors of his writings and comparing him to the likes of Luther, Calvin and Jansenius. The point of issue was Rosmini's writings on original sin, the doctrine of justification and the distinction between 'sin' and 'guilt,' and Cristiano's accusations were furthered by three other publications in 1841. Rumours abounded that Rosmini was about to be condemned by the Holy See and Fr Giuseppe Rovazen, the Assistant to the General of the Society of Jesus, published a letter in the paper *L'Ami de la Religion* in February 1843 that drew parallels with the case of Lammenais, the French priest condemned in 1834. The following month Gregory XVI, who had approved the Institute and called Rosmini 'a man of eminent intellect, adorned with noble qualities of soul,' imposed 'an absolute silence on both parties' and asked Rosmini not to publish further works. He also called the Jesuit General in for an explanation. Meanwhile Rosmini withdrew copies of the second part of his *Ideas of Sin and Guilt* from the booksellers. Cardinal Castracane told Rosmini that the papal decision was

> a complete victory for you and your Institute, while at the same time it banishes the suspicions of false teachings imputed to your writings, gives the lie to the rumours spread about imminent condemnations, and opens the way to a growth in the number of subjects and houses of your Institute.

Wiseman, then Rector of the English College, Rome, also congratulated him 'on the ending of the mistaken attacks on your doctrines, which have been put to the test and fully vindicated'.[37]

In 1846 Gregory XVI died and was succeeded by Pius IX. Rosmini initially continued to enjoy papal favour and the new Pontiff promised him both the red hat and the prestigious position of Secretary of State. Intrigue and opposition increased against him, however, and in June 1849 two of his books were placed on the Index: *La costituzione civile seconda la giustizia sociale* (The Constitution according to Social Justice) and the well-known *Delle cinque piaghe della Santa Chiesa* (The Five Wounds of the Holy Church). Of course, it was not the first time a future saint had works censored, Rosmini finding himself in company with the likes of St Ignatius Loyola and St Teresa of Avila. The decision of the Holy Office only encouraged further attacks on 'Rosminianism'. An anonymous pamphlet was distributed among the Italian bishops, known as the *Postille* (Comments), declaring Rosmini's writings to be 'false, erroneous, heretical, contrary to Catholic doctrine, ... offensive to pious ears, blasphemous, seditious, subversive of the ecclesiastical hierarchy, dangerous to souls'. In 1850 two volumes of *Lettere* were published, calling Rosmini 'a Jansenist fox, an insinuator of wicked doctrines, [and] a teacher of hellish ideas'.[38]

The Pope decided to inaugurate a formal examination of Rosmini's writings and in March 1851 renewed his predecessor's precept of silence 'on both parties'. Pagani, the English Provincial, had addressed a petition to the Holy Father that January, asking 'that your Holiness will deign to use his authority so that the fury of this persecution may cease, ... so that the Institute and its members – who glory in being devoted sons of the Holy See, ready to give their lives for it – may not be forced to become victims of a faction'. Some of the English Rosminians had indeed been 'denounced as being imbued with the same errors, and as stubborn defenders of pernicious doctrines'.[39]

Urged by his supporters, Rosmini asked Bertetti to represent him in Rome. The Pope proceeded with great caution and prudence and the whole process took several years, during which time Rosmini and his Institute remained under a dark cloud. When Lockhart arrived in Rome, he soon found himself immersed in this polemic and helped Bertetti the best he could. Lockhart liked to tell the story of two unexpected visitors he received during this period:

> One day, I think in April [1854], I was sitting in my room in the Via del Gesu, when I heard a knock at the door, and on going to open it, I introduced two Fathers, whom I knew at once as Jesuits. At that time the Jesuits were again in Rome after the restoration of the Pope, and still wore that well-known venerable habit now never seen in Italy. The senior introduced himself as Father Etheridge, a much respected English Jesuit, at this time Father-Assistant to the newly-elected General ... After the usual friendly salutations and conversations on general topics, Father Etheridge said: 'Reverend Father, you are perhaps surprised at my visit, as we are personally strangers'. I replied, of course, that 'good Father Etheridge could be no stranger to me, and that I was always glad to meet any of the Society, for which I had always felt the greatest respect and affection'. He continued: 'I have come, sent expressly by my Father General, to say to you, and through you to your Superiors of the Institute of Charity, that the Father General regrets the opposition to your venerated Founder, Rosmini, and he wishes it to be understood that this is not the work of the Society of Jesus, but of a School of opinion in the Society'. I expressed my satisfaction at this assurance, which I promised to convey to my General, Father Rosmini.[40]

The Pope had already heard the mostly favourable opinions of six consultors and now passed Rosmini's writings to two new examiners, Fr Caiazza (an Augustinian) and Fr Trullet (a Conventual Franciscan). The former decided that Rosmini's works 'were worthy of being acclaimed, not prohibited' and the latter confessed in March 1854 that in reading them, 'I found myself faced with a world of thought incomparably grander, more noble and more beautiful ... than these material and corporeal heavens of ours'.[41] The final verdict of the Congregation was conveyed verbally to Bertetti on 10 August 1854 and is referred to as *Dimittantur opera*:

> The Sacred Congregation of the Index decrees that all the works of Antonio Rosmini-Serbati which were recently submitted to examination are to be exonerated, and that the fact that this examination has taken place must in no way be allowed to detract from the good name of either the author or the religious society founded by him, or from the praise due to his life and singular good services towards the Church. And so that no further dissensions or accusations (new or old) shall arise and be spread about, by order of the Holy Father silence is for the third time enjoined on both parties.[42]

Bishop Ullathorne, one of Rosmini's sternest critics in the English hierarchy, later suggested that the works

> only escaped censure by a fluke. Dr Bertetti, who represented the author, adduced a letter by Benedict XIV, written after the revision of the writings of Cardinal Noris, in which the Pontiff said that where an author had done distinguished service to the Church less grave errors in his writings were not to be censured. On this precedent the works were acquitted.[43]

The result was technically a triumph for Rosmini but the Holy See decided to be prudent in its approach so as not to offend the Jesuits, regarded as the great champions of orthodoxy. Thus, rather than a public absolution or 'dismissal' (*Dimittantur*) from the accusations, the decision was communicated privately to those involved and was not published until 1876. It spoke only in general terms and so 'it was very natural that those who did not know but only conjectured (for beyond the fact of the acquittal of the works, all else was a secret of the Congregation), "should make open secrets" according to their inclination'.[44]

Lockhart was not to witness the promulgation of *Dimittantur*, for his health had fully recovered and he returned to England in May 1854 to take up a new posting in London. He stayed at Stresa on his way home and thus had the chance to spend some time with Rosmini. In his biography of the Founder, Lockhart looked back on these happy days. He joined Rosmini for his afternoon walks along the vine-clad path bordering Lake Maggiore and was particularly impressed by Rosmini's practice of assembling the community after the evening Rosary to read a few verses from the Gospel and suggest three points for the morning's meditation:

> Rosmini's grand figure, half-a-dozen disciples round their great master, all dimly seen by the light of his shaded lamp ... the scene was enough to impress me with a life-long conviction of the importance of daily meditation and of the great advantage, as a general rule, of regularly preparing for it over-night.[45]

Lockhart no doubt spoke to Rosmini about the English Mission. Years later he observed that many of Rosmini's finest men had been sent to England:

> How full was the mind and heart of Rosmini with the thought of England as he sent forth these men, who were after his own heart, and with whom he had taken sweet counsel as they walked together along the borders of the Lake! They had gone to exchange the lovely scenes of Italian sky, lake, mountain, and luxurious foliage, for the cloud-shrouded land, and the smoke and fog of its huge cities of ceaseless din and labour. Rosmini's heart went with them in their 'pilgrimage of Grace'. His last words to me when I saw him for the last time as we parted in the Quay at Stresa were 'I hope perhaps next year to visit England.' This was in May 1854. In little more than a year he was gone for ever from this world in body; but, as we firmly believe, the impediment of the body being removed, he is with his children, in spirit, wherever they go, and guides them, under God, and guards them in all their ways.[46]

The Greenwich Convent

Meanwhile both Elizabeth and Martha Lockhart also considered following the Rosminian vocation. Together with a group of other convert ladies, they stayed as guests with the Sisters of Providence at Loughborough in 1852. Shortly afterwards, Elizabeth moved to a large house in Greenwich, at 66 Crooms Hill, which became the Convent of Our Lady and was later expanded by the purchase of neighbouring properties.

Elizabeth's vision was to continue her Wantage apostolate by opening a home for penitent women, as well as a hostel for convert ladies who invariably faced rejection from family and friends. The Sisters also taught the poor in the Girls' School and supervised the Infants' School attached to the local church of Our Lady, Star of the Sea. The community tried to unite the Greenwich house formally with the Rosminian family and this was considered by the Provincial, Fr Pagani, and even Rosmini himself, who asked that the Greenwich Sisters should first complete their novitiate at Loughborough. Three members of the community duly travelled there in October 1853, although disagreements soon emerged. One of the new novices later wrote:

> I was deeply prejudiced against the convent, having been told of odd things commanded by the Superiors and done by the Sisters; some persons alleging that the Sisters were foolish and silly, that there was no order or regularity in the house, and that their methods of carrying on the works of charity did not at all represent the Founders' views on the subject.[47]

During their stay at Loughborough, Lockhart visited to preach the annual ladies' retreat and undoubtedly used the opportunity to see his sister. However, the decision was duly made by the Greenwich Sisters in late September 1854 to discontinue the novitiate at Loughborough and to form their own Institute, the 'Sisters of Charity of the Precious Blood'. Mother Mary Agnes Amherst, the Superior at Loughborough, wrote that some of the Greenwich novices left 'in the greatest distress and grief' since 'they do not wish to be separated from us' and in fact two of their number finally decided to leave Greenwich and formally enter the Rosminians.[48]

Alongside their charitable works, the Greenwich Sisters busied themselves with the writing of articles and the translation of devotional literature, which was seen as an apostolate in its own right and a way of countering the spiritual problems facing Victorian society. In 1856, for example, the 'Sisters of the Convent of Our Lady at Greenwich' translated from the Italian *An Outline of the Life of the Very Rev. Antonio Rosmini, Founder of the Institute of Charity*, with the editorial help of Fr Lockhart. According to Gillow, much of this short work was translated by Mrs Lockhart.

By 1857 there were eleven professed Sisters and five postulants. As with any community, there were many comings and goings. Mrs Lockhart (Sr Mary Monica) left the Convent due to weak health, though 'she often spent some time as a guest at Loughborough, remaining a devoted friend of the Sisters'.[49] Many members of the Greenwich community came from well-connected and wealthy backgrounds and it is interesting that, although the experiment was short-lived, a number of its members went on to establish their own religious communities. Not only was there Elizabeth Lockhart who, as we shall see, moved to west London in 1857 and started the Bayswater Franciscan Sisters of the Immaculate Conception, but also Elizabeth Hayes, who had been made Superior of the School Sisters at Wantage in 1855 and sought refuge in Greenwich after her conversion the following year. Eventually settling the other side of the Atlantic, she founded the Franciscan Missionary Sisters of the Immaculate Conception in 1873. Another of the convert ladies of Greenwich was Catherine Anne Bathurst, the granddaughter of Henry Bathurst, Bishop of Norwich and, on her mother's side, Andrew Thomas Stuart, first Earl Castle Stewart. As Mother Catherine Philip she is remembered as foundress and first Mother General of the Dominican Congregation of the Holy Rosary, founded in Ghent in 1871 and based for many years at Harrow-on-the-Hill.[50]

Notes

1. Hirst, 'Necrology', pp. 328–9.
2. Lockhart, *Life of Rosmini*, vol. ii, pp. 104–8.
3. Ibid., ii, p. 127.
4. Leethan, *Ratcliffe College*, p. 15.
5. Hirst, *Brief Memoir of Fr Hutton*, p. 21.
6. Hirst, 'Necrology', p. 330.
7. Ibid., p. 340.
8. Newman, LD XI, 87 fn.
9. *Tablet*, 12 June 1847, p. 374.
10. Lockhart, *Life of Rosmini*, vol. ii, p. 110 fn.
11. Leetham, *Luigi Gentili*, p. 138.
12. These were not openly worn outside the church compound after the 'Papal Aggression' controversy, following the Restoration of the Hierarchy in 1850.
13. Lockhart, *Life of Rosmini*, vol. ii, p. 111.

14. Mariani, *Rosminian Generals and Bishops*, p. 33.
15. ASIC Lockhart's Mission Diary, March and April 1851.
16. Hirst, 'Necrology', p. 331.
17. Kinealy and Mac Atasney, *The Hidden Famine*, p. 137.
18. Rinolfi, *Missions in Ireland*, p. iv.
19. ASIC Lockhart's Mission Diary, April 1851.
20. Rinolfi, *Missions in Ireland*, p. 43.
21. *Tablet*, 28 May 1853, p. 341 (quoting the *Freeman's Journal*). The Rosminians often asked the local clergy to supplement the mission with sermons in the Irish tongue.
22. Lockhart, *Popular Lectures on the Catholic Religion*, p. 6.
23. *Tablet*, 7 May 1853, pp. 295–6
24. Rinolfi, *Missions in Ireland*, p. 40.
25. Ibid., pp. 149–50.
26. Ibid., p. 89.
27. Ibid., p. 90.
28. Rosmini, *Counsels to Religious Superiors*, p. 167.
29. Lockhart, 'Some Personal Reminiscences of Cardinal Manning', p. 379.
30. Purcell, *Cardinal Manning*, vol. ii, p. 19.
31. Lang, *Life & Letters of John Gibson Lockhart*, vol. ii, p. 375.
32. Ibid., p. 383.
33. Ibid., pp. 380–1.
34. Ibid., p. 376.
35. Ibid., p. 385.
36. Belti, *The Rosminian Question*, pp. 2–3.
37. Ibid., pp. 19–20.
38. Ibid., p. 27.
39. Ibid., pp. 38–9.
40. Lockhart, *Life of Rosmini*, vol. ii, p. 314.
41. Belti, *The Rosminian Question*, p. 44.
42. Ibid., pp. 52–3.
43. AAW/Ma 2/36/222 (Ullathorne to Manning, Easter Sunday 1888).
44. *Dublin Review*, January 1887, p. 85.
45. Lockhart, *Life of Rosmini*, vol. ii, p. 194.
46. Ibid., p. 22.
47. Anon., *Life of Mother Mary Amherst*, p. 149.
48. Ibid., p. 165.
49. Ibid., p. 165 fn.
50. In 1929 this Congregation was united with the Congregation of St Catherine of Siena (Stone).

Chapter VI

Kingsland

The first Archbishop of Westminster, Cardinal Nicholas Wiseman, was initially friendly towards Rosmini and had visited him at Stresa in July 1842. The work of the Institute also fitted in with his vision of an energetic Ultramontane Catholicism and the perceived need, which he had foreseen since the mid-1830s, for clergy who could travel from place to place giving systematic courses of instructions and missions. However, in light of the censuring of two of Rosmini's works and the increasing opposition to his teachings, Wiseman forbade members of the Institute to preach in his diocese because, as Rosmini himself put it, 'they had as their Superior a man who had books on the Index'.[1] The English Provincial, Fr Pagani, wrote to Rosmini in 1851 that 'since [Wiseman's] return from Rome and his elevation to the cardinalate, he has openly become a powerful enemy of ours, and that he uses his influence (which is very great) to block out our every advance ... The suspicions which he spreads about us are thoroughly dishonourable and slanderous when found in one who has a Catholic heart'. In a conversation at the home of Scott-Murray, the Cardinal had apparently declared that 'he had received a special commission from Rome to keep a vigilant eye on us, so as to know what we do, and what we teach and preach, with a view to delating this information there'. Wiseman predicted that Rosmini would be removed as Superior and that the Institute would be reformed and 'would not (in his opinion) be allowed to go on in its present state – with a sphere of activity so broad that it was bound to produce great confusion'.[2]

Eventually the Cardinal's attitude softened, especially in the lead-up to *Dimittantur*, and negotiations were made to present the

Institute with a base in London. In an undated letter of 1853 or 1854, Lockhart reported to the Provincial that 'I was at the Cardinal's place last night where I found him particularly friendly and agreeable. There is no doubt that a great change has taken place in his feelings towards us'.[3]

Various options were considered for the new Rosminian mission in London, including the combining of the missions of Baldwin Gardens and Saffron Hill, where there was a large Italian community. Finally, in May 1854, Lockhart moved to Kingsland in north London, an area carved out of the existing missions of Moorfields and Hackney. Kingsland is not a name in common use in the twenty-first century but, as the name suggests, the area had been used as the king's hunting land and was said to have been particularly favoured by Henry VIII. The tradition that he used the hunting lodge to secretly meet Anne Boleyn is continued in modern road names such as 'King Henry's Walk' and 'Boleyn Road'. By the eighteenth century, much of Kingsland was sold to private individuals and leased to watercress growers, brickmakers and claypit owners, while in the nineteenth century it saw a population boom and the coming of the railways.

Lockhart took up residence at 83 (later renumbered 164) Culford Road. This was made possible thanks to the generosity of Thomas Kelly, a well-to-do Irish builder in the locality, who owned the property. At first, the drawing room and back parlour of his house, divided by folding doors, served as the chapel, and two rooms were provided for Lockhart. Manning, already a rising star in the diocese, celebrated the first Mass in the presence of a dozen people. Lockhart soon organized a choir which 'performs the music of Mass and Benediction very respectably'.[4] By Christmas 1854 the congregation overflowed onto the pavement and the chapel was soon transferred to the storage sheds behind the house, which could seat about 75.

At the end of 1854, while Lockhart was busy setting up the mission, he was summoned to the deathbed of his cousin John Gibson Lockhart at Abbotsford. His daughter – and Walter Scott's granddaughter – Charlotte had recently been received into the Church, as had her new husband, James Hope-Scott, a university friend of Lockhart's. The dying man welcomed the priest's presence, despite their ecclesial differences, and allowed him to read passages from *The Garden of the Soul* in his final days.[5] He died on 25 November 1854, and was buried at Dryburgh Abbey, beside Scott.

Back at Kingsland, appeals were made for funds and in October 1855 a paper-staining factory was purchased, situated in Tottenham Road behind Mr Kelly's house and yard, together with the corner house on Culford Road. Thus, the mission was no longer reliant on Kelly's good will, and work was begun on converting the factory building into a two-storey complex, with schools on the ground floor and a church above.

Why was Kingsland chosen as the location of the new Rosminian mission? On the surface, it seems another example of ensuring sacramental provision for a populous area, where the nearest church was a fair walk away. Cardinal Wiseman wrote about the rapid growth of the Church in north London in a Pastoral Letter of 1856:

> It is yearly happening that a district springs up and becomes densely peopled, where before was only a thin and scattered population. The few Catholics among it were amply provided for in the next mission, by whose priests they were attended. But the encrease [sic] of numbers now requires a new foundation, a decent chapel, a residence for a priest, a school, and then maintenance, however slender, for priest and teacher.
>
> This, dearly beloved, is no fanciful picture of our ever growing wants. The two missions of Clerkenwell and Islington arose within the limits of a mission in the city, by the spread of the population towards the north, and the formation of new suburban districts ... Two priests had to be stationed at each. Within the last few years two new missions arose from the first of these, requiring three additional priests: making five where two had sufficed before. Then lately it has been found necessary to subdivide the second of the districts mentioned. A new and flourishing mission has been started in Kingsland, conducted by two Fathers of Charity, and a large building has been transformed into a most becoming temporary chapel, with ample schools. And already this new mission is preparing the way for further extension, by the purchase of schools at some little distance.[6]

Lockhart wrote to the Cardinal soon afterwards, saying that 'we are much pleased here at the mention of St Joseph's, which will also aid me much in the begging which I must now begin to cover the expenses of our new establishment'.[7]

There was, however, another motive in the establishment of the Kingsland mission. The nearby Anglican parish of St Mary's, Stoke Newington, had seen a clash between Low and High Church factions, the latter being led by a prominent local doctor, Robert Brett, who started a Sunday School and evening lectures to deter people from attending dissenting chapels. The Rector, Archdale Wilson Tayler, was sympathetic to Brett's ideas and tried to introduce various Tractarian practices. However, the Dean of St Paul's stepped in and ordered Tayler to return to the Prayer Book services and wear the preaching gown rather than the 'Romish' stole. However, he was soon joined by a like-minded curate, Thomas Alder Pope, originally from Prince Edward Island and a graduate of Jesus College, Cambridge. He was also Tayler's son-in-law, later described as 'a distinguished classical and mathematical scholar, and in his earlier days he and Manning were deemed the two most finished speakers in the Anglican communion'.[8] With Pope's help, a chapel-of-ease, dedicated to St Matthias, was founded in 1849 and a splendid gothic church, designed by William Butterfield, completed four years later. St Matthias would become a well-known High Church centre in north London. Indeed, in 1850 Thomas Pope's effigy was burned during the hysteria surrounding the 'Papal Aggression' by those who objected to his High Church ways. His name, of course, made him an obvious target. In 1853 Pope was received into the Catholic Church by the Archbishop of Rouen. At the same time his curate, John George McLeod, and a group of parishioners also followed his example.[9] The Catholic mission of Kingsland could thus serve this group of converts, as well as the many Irish in the area.

The first Mass in the converted factory was said on 29 June 1856 and it was solemnly opened at Michaelmas by Bishop Richard Butler Roskell of Nottingham. Cardinal Wiseman preached and Fr Faber provided a specially written hymn to St Joseph that enjoyed considerable popularity for many years: *There are many saints above*. The new church was spacious and practical, with a flat roof and small windows running along the sides. Two areas were screened off on either side of the sanctuary, which were used as the sacristy and organ chamber, and the two side altars (dedicated to Our Lady and St Joseph respectively) were set forward of these enclosures. There was a reredos behind the High Altar, with an image of Christ holding the Blessed Sacrament and flanked by the two great Doctors, St Augustine and St Thomas, and stained-glass windows were soon added.

In 1859 Mrs Lockhart paid for a 'steep open roof', designed by Edward Welby Pugin, and 'stone mullions with tracery in the window spaces'. The same year a house was bought next to the presbytery and joined to it. The whole property was now raised by a storey, the walls refaced to give it an 'ecclesiastical character' and 'an internal communication, with adjacent parlours, was made to the church'.[10] Mrs Lockhart is said to have had an annual income of £500 in the 1860s[11] and continued to support the expansion of the parish, as well as the College at Ratcliffe and the Loughborough convent. In 1863 Lockhart offered to obtain the freehold of the parish property through money from an uncle's will.[12]

The presence of a new Catholic church in north London was not universally welcomed by the local community. Lockhart began a series of popular controversial lectures, based on the principle 'Hear what we have to say for ourselves – you have heard plenty against us'. A local Protestant distributed an *Answer* to Lockhart's lectures, which criticized the priest's 'proselytising' activities in Islington and Kingsland and attacked some of his premises. Moreover, as Lockhart later related in a pamphlet version of his talks:

> no sooner had I begun this course of lectures ... than I received a challenge to a controversial discussion, in which, before a select and equal number of Protestants and Roman Catholics, I was to be put, as it were, on trial. I declined this on the ground that I thought it no amendment on my own plan, as I found the course I had adopted answered well the purpose I had in view ... On my declining this discussion, I found the walls of the neighbourhood placarded with an announcement of the fact; by which it was sought to produce the impression that I was ashamed or afraid of bringing the doctrines of my Church to test.

However, Lockhart did not believe that public controversial discussions were appropriate or effective – 'in every instance on record, both parties have claimed the victory', he wrote, and 'a fool can ask more questions in half an hour than a wise man can answer in a week.' He confessed that

> I will never have anything to do with public controversial discussions – first, because I am neither a walking dictionary, nor a polyglot, nor an encyclopedia of universal knowledge; and, secondly, though, on the spur of the moment, I might be able to render a plausible answer to an opponent, yet I would wish to give something more – a reply which should be solid, exhaustive, and unanswerable.

Lockhart's way of conducting controversy was through the pen, based on prayer, reflection and research in his own library or in that of the British Museum.[13]

Lockhart was assisted at Kingsland by a number of Rosminian confreres: Henry Clark, Richard Richardson, John Bailey, Joseph Ackeroyd, Joseph Gagliardi and Fortunatus Signini. Gagliardi seems to have been something of an absent-minded professor: 'the poor man was never intended by his Creator for a Missionary Parish', Lockhart wrote, and 'if he is sent on a sick call he loses his way or leaves out some sacrament or the sick person cannot understand him and then Richardson has to go to the place'.[14] Signini, who was the nephew of Pagani, had been in England since 1845 and had previously been Private Secretary to Rosmini – in later life he helped Lockhart in translating the Rosminian corpus into English. In his *Life* of the Founder, Lockhart included a chapter of 'Anecdotes and Reminiscences of Rosmini by Father Signini (AD 1835–45)'. Other priests served the parish briefly, including the Polish Henry Lipowski, who left for Hong King in 1862 as chaplain to the Catholic soldiers stationed in the colony.

The longest-serving assistant was William Henry Lewthwaite, who worked at Kingsland for twenty years, with the exception of a brief period at Ratcliffe in 1867, and followed Lockhart to Ely Place. Lewthwaite was a graduate of Trinity College, Cambridge and a founding member of the Cambridge Camden (or Ecclesiological) Society, founded by students to promote the study of gothic architecture and ecclesiastical antiquities. At the Society's first meeting in November 1839, Lewthwaite read a paper on the sculptures of Adel church in Yorkshire, where his father was Rector. In 1842, shortly after his ordination in the Church of England, Lewthwaite was appointed to St Luke's, Clifford, which had been built by the patron, George Lane-Fox of Bramham Park, partly as a response to a recently established 'popish' mission in the village. Despite the Protestant sympathies of the lay patron, Lewthwaite quickly Catholicized many elements of parochial life, hearing confessions of his flock, keeping rigorous fasts and building an arch over the village well, with an inscription referring to the baptismal waters of St Luke's being drawn from there. He also built a small convent in the Gothic style for a group of pious ladies and the orphans they cared for, funded from his own money.

He became friendly with Dr Walter Farquhar Hook, the High Church Vicar of Leeds, and ministered during the cholera epidemic of 1848–9, which claimed over 2,000 lives in the town. He also belonged to Hook's Leeds Rubric Club, which discussed liturgical matters and encouraged strict conformity with the Church's ceremonial, and acted as secretary of the Yorkshire Architectural Society. Lewthwaite was received into the Church at St Anne's, Leeds, on 3 April 1851, and the following year entered the Institute of Charity. On his conversion, Lewthwaite presented his convent at Clifford to Bishop Briggs of Beverley and on 24 September 1851 it was opened as the Convent of SS Stephen and John, run by the Rosminian Sisters of Providence. After a short course of studies, he was ordained in September 1854 and arrived at Kingsland in the spring of 1855. He worked effectively as Lockhart's assistant, taking charge of the Hoxton area in the early years and acting as the mission's procurator, having 'a good deal to do with the collection of funds, the management of the schools, with the young men's recreation club attached to the clergy house, as well as with the boarding establishment ... for young men'.[15]

Correspondence with the Provincial reveals occasional tensions between Lockhart and Lewthwaite. The latter was, after all, two years older than Lockhart and a man with great pastoral experience and scholarly interests. His memorialist later noted 'a seemingly rough exterior, and somewhat hasty manner', although the poor of Kingsland often said that 'a shake of his hand was worth a shilling'.[16]

At Christmas 1856 a house on Culford Road was rented by Mrs Lockhart and Miss Athy, who had also belonged to the Sisters of Charity of the Precious Blood at Greenwich. She was later joined by her sister and mother. They wore habits and hoped to establish a convent at Kingsland. In the meantime they opened a Private School for middle-class children, although ill health forced Mrs Lockhart to stop the following year. The widow of the Rector of Stoke Newington, Mrs Tayler, also helped in the teaching.

In 1862 Fr Joseph Costa (known for his later ministry in America) arrived at Kingsland and was impressed by the 'kindness and loving manner' of Fathers Lockhart and Lewthwaite.[17] However, by October he described himself in a letter to Fr Bertetti as being 'never so unhappy and discontented as at present'. This was the result, it seems, of Mrs Lockhart and her two companions, who helped with the housekeeping in the presbytery and took on something of an advisory role. Costa resented their arrogance and the way they acted like the Superior in a religious house, even to the extent of opening Lockhart's personal mail.[18]

Lockhart was aware of Costa's complaints and told the Provincial that he had

> taken a very censorious view of the relation in which I stand to my Mother as her confessor and also as confessor to my friends Mrs and the two Miss Athy – he thinks it probable that the Sacraments are hereby profaned and sacrilege committed ... He is also scandalized because I often take some meal at my Mother's house ... He says I am under the governance of women.[19]

Given that Mrs Lockhart was the mother of the Rector and the principal benefactress of the mission, perhaps her attitude was understandable.

The Parish Schools

Education was a key concern and, as with many other Catholic missions, there were separate schools for boys, girls and infants, together with a private school for middle-class children, initiated by Mrs Lockhart. Each establishment took up a room either below the church or in one of the parish houses. The Headmaster of the middle-class boys was the Liverpudlian Joseph Atkinson, who, as we will see later, combined his teaching duties with the editing of a popular magazine, *Catholic Opinion*, which was purchased by Mrs Lockhart in 1867. Atkinson left Kingsland in 1869 and joined the Rosminians.

In 1865 the female branch of the Institute of Charity, the Sisters of Providence, arrived in Kingsland to take care of the Girls' and Infants' schools and set up a Private School for 'young ladies'. In his letters to Stresa, Lockhart frequently complained that the Sisters refused Government inspection (which was required) and were reluctant to teach boys under the age of seven. 'If the Nuns do not take them', he wrote, 'they will have to go to Protestant schools and their condition will in some cases be worse than before'.[20] He criticized their 'want of elasticity' and 'morbid prudishness in regard of the relation of the sexes, so at least it seems to us of these northern climates, though I doubt not experience has shown that such precautions are necessary in southern climates where the human temperament is more excitable'.[21] Indeed, he threatened to get rid of the Sisters and replace them with a more compliant congregation, such as the *Filles de la Croix* from Belgium, who had previously shown an interest in working at Kingsland.

The school year was punctuated by a number of special events. Each summer there was an excursion to a nearby attraction. On 15 July 1857, for example, the schools at Kingsland and Hoxton (both under the Institute of Charity) spent the day at Rye House. There were also school plays; indeed, St Joseph's seems to have had a thriving theatrical tradition. On 9 March 1862, Lockhart wrote that Cardinal Wisemen 'did us the honour of dining with us and attending the dramatic entertainment by the boys of our Collegiate School. On the last day of the Carnival he attended again the performance of his own drama founded on the life of S Alexius and expressed himself greatly pleased.' The following year the *Church Notice Book* advertised a school play, written by Fr Lewthwaite, that 'embodies various historical facts connected with the Conversion of England to Christianity in the sixth century and shows the hold of the Catholic Faith in Ireland, at the time the first missions to England were desolated by the Pelagian heresy'.[22]

The school had a strong relationship with the parish, the children participating at Masses, processions and other festive occasions. In 1864 a Children's Mass was started every Sunday at half past nine, during which 'the children will occupy the front seats and sing during Mass'. The parish notice went on to say that 'children will not be admitted to the other Masses without a note from the clergy'.[23]

St Joseph's Institute

The Fathers set up a hostel for young men in the presbytery on Culford Road, which was called St Joseph's Home or Institute. The boarders each had a room and took their meals with the clergy. The aim was 'to afford them a safe home from the dangers of London Life'. In the evenings they were encouraged either to stay in the house or 'should they desire relaxation, there is on the premises a Catholic club, where, safe from the temptations and allurements of London gaiety, they may enjoy a game at cards or billiards, or an agreeable chat in good Catholic society'. The conduct of the boarders was encouraged by 'genial influence' rather than 'disciplinary restraint',[24] although there were clear expectations – residents should return to the house before eleven at night, come to dinner 'properly attired', and 'should take a sitting in the Church; and the cultivation of good Catholic practices such as hearing daily Mass and assisting at Rosary is what the Fathers earnestly desire to see in the household'.[25]

In 1867 the boarders even included Mr Ryder, nephew of Manning. Lockhart declared in a letter of 1862:

> I think the house for pensioners a very important work of charity in our neighbourhood ... The Cardinal and many leading priests and laymen speak of our 'Home for Young Men' in the highest terms as a great *desiderato* which has been so far realized. Among other advantages they form the Choir of the Church. I think it likely that from time to time we shall find vocations amongst them.[26]

Their participation in the parish choir meant that Lockhart could follow the Archbishop's wishes and get rid of women singers, a policy which 'the people did not like at first, but are now getting to like it'. Lockhart was able to send to the mother house 'the first of a series of pure Gregorian Masses which are being brought out under my direction with the approval of the Bishops – they may like to try them at Stresa'.[27] The first Synod of Westminster (1852) had promoted 'grave and devotional' music and encouraged the teaching of music to children 'in order to exclude women singers, especially those who sing for hire. Thus, by degrees, will be brought about, what we so much desire to be accomplished, that the whole congregation will join with one voice and heart in the psalmody'.[28] The fourth Synod (1873) specifically named the ancient Gregorian Chant as worthy of restoration in parishes,[29] and Lockhart's 'pure Gregorian Masses' anticipated this.

Despite their usefulness, it was far from ideal to have young men living in the same house as the clergy. Lockhart told Fr Bertetti in 1861 that 'present arrangements, though only transitory, [are] not pleasant for any of our Fathers who may be staying with us, nor for ourselves if we had a regular community as I hope before long may be the case'.[30] As time went on, he became increasingly frustrated about the lack of a regular religious house and the presence not only of lodgers but female servants. He sometimes doubted the effectiveness of the hostel, for 'as long as we have mountains of female flesh in all directions about the house, absolutely nothing can be done'.[31] Lewthwaite even compared life in the presbytery to that of 'a large, badly ordered public Hotel' and complained that the young men often stayed in bed on Sunday morning.[32]

Hoxton and Clapton

The Fathers of Charity had pastoral oversight of a substantial area of north-east London, which has since been divided into separate parishes. In a letter to Wiseman in August 1857, Lockhart revealed that 'he considered Hoxton together with Kingsland and Stoke Newington covered too large a space to be worked from one centre except as a temporary expedient'.[33]

Lewthwaite at first had particular responsibility for the Catholics of Hoxton. As early as January 1856 a small school was founded in rented rooms on Pimlico Walk and later that year he celebrated Mass for the first time in a room in Wenlock Street, on which occasion Dr Gilbert 'showed very great patience and kind diligence in extracting [an altar stone] very firmly fixed in the *mensa* of a side altar of the Pro-Cathedral'.[34] Lockhart appealed for funding to purchase 'a handsome and commodious school, lately occupied by the Methodists, at a cost of £400',[35] although the scheme was later abandoned due to a lack of funds and the faithful had to make do with a Sunday Mass and an evening service in the week, together with the hearing of confessions.

In 1864 Hoxton was placed into the hands of the Irish Augustinians (the English Province was not founded until 1977) and St Monica's Priory on Hoxton Square became the first Augustinian house in England since the Reformation. At the time of the laying of the foundation stone, much was made of

> a rather curious coincidence that the old house now inhabited by the Fathers was formerly a favourite place of resort of King Charles II. The Merry Monarch had, we believe, a residence not far distant [York House] between which and the house in question a subterranean passage communicated. The passage, or at least some traces of it, are said to be still discernible.[36]

Provision for the Catholics of Clapton began through the charitable enterprise of Miss Elizabeth Harrison of 19 King Edward's Street, Hackney. Miss Harrison was well known for her good works and had already founded St John's Hospice at Hackney for four poor people. In 1859 she bought land at Clapton with the intention of setting up a home for the elderly. The foundation stone was laid by Cardinal Wiseman on 24 September 1861, after which the Cardinal had dinner at Miss Harrison's.[37] The whole enterprise was funded by the estates of Miss Harrison's late brother, Robert (d.1852) and his wife Charlotte Scholastica (d.1858). To honour her memory, the institution was called 'St Scholastica's Retreat'. Although the buildings, designed by Edward Welby Pugin, were not completed until 1874, the first inmates were accepted in 1862. The first of these was Marianne Oxley, aged 65, who, according to the register, was 'formerly named Hogsflesh, but good reasons were given for the change of name, which was simply a matter of family agreement.'

The Retreat's purpose reveals something of the Victorian obsession with decorum and social status. According to the *Catholic Directory* of 1863, St Scholastica's had been established 'for the benefit of the poor and reduced Catholics, of either sex, of the age of sixty years and upwards, who belong, or have belonged, to the ranks of the gentry, or of the professional or wholesale commercial class'.[38] To be eligible to apply for an apartment, a person had to have an annual income of less than £60 plus property up to the value of £100. Each resident had a carpeted sitting room, bedroom, kitchen, pantry-scullery and provision for accommodating a servant. Indeed, 'although the employment of servants as a general rule shall be at the option of the Inmates, yet batchelors or single gentlemen shall not be their own servants'. Moreover, 'the Inmates shall at all times maintain a respectable and becoming decency of attire. They shall also be cleanly and orderly in the care of their rooms, and shall not convert the front to a bedroom'. The inmates were given an annual allowance of £40, or, if they already had private means, an allowance of not more than £40 to make up the total income to £60. Thanks to the Retreat, the members of the gentry and professional classes in reduced circumstances could maintain their dignity and live the life to which they were accustomed.

Although little is known about Miss Harrison, she was evidently a strong character with a good head for business. This led to frictions with the Fathers of Charity at Kingsland, under whose spiritual care the Retreat was placed. Lockhart wrote to Pagani that

> in order to provide for the spiritual welfare of the inmates of the alms-house, she offers to purchase and make over to our Order sufficient freehold land for a Church and Religious house, on condition of undertaking to say Mass on all Sundays and Holidays for the inmates in the domestic chapel, until a church shall be built, when the alms people shall have a right to free seats in the church.[39]

Pugin's original design for St Scholastica's envisaged the Retreat to form two sides of a square, the other two sides being provided by a church and the London Road (as it was then called). It seems that Lockhart made a verbal promise to Miss Harrison that such an edifice would be built, but there was a problem in funding. In February 1867, shortly before her death, she wrote to Archbishop Manning:

> Firstly. I am not able to help the Fathers of Charity with any pecuniary assistance in building their church. Secondly. In any Church that the Fathers may of themselves build accommodation must be provided free of expense for the inmates of the Retreat, according to the Deed of Covenant between the Fathers and myself. Thirdly. The Fathers are bound by word to me to build a Church in the Gothic style of architecture to harmonise with the building erected, and moreover to build in such direction that the Church shall form the third side of a square, the public road completing the quadrangle.

In the meantime, the Common Hall, which was used as the Retreat's library, was fitted up as a chapel for Mass on Sundays and holy days and Lewthwaite celebrated the first Mass on Rosary Sunday 1862. Eventually, one of the Fathers of Charity moved to Clapton as Warden and was able to celebrate daily Mass. However, the Fathers were keen to pull out of Clapton and hand over the responsibility, and Lockhart hoped to build up the mission and make it self-supporting during his time there. In 1864 it was handed to the Augustinians in Hoxton, but they did not enjoy a satisfactory relationship with Miss Harrison and it was given back to the Rosminians two years later. It was at this stage that Lockhart himself moved to Clapton, along with his mother, and during their two-year residency benefited from its elevated and healthy position. In 1868, a diocesan priest was sent there by Manning – Raymund Stanfield, who in later life did much to arrange the Westminster Diocesan Archive and, as a result, was made a Canon. He remained in Clapton until 1873, when poor health required him to winter in Algiers.[40]

The Quest for a Regular Life

Lockhart was not content with merely parochial affairs; he envisaged a large Rosminian house with a proper religious life, a large community and an elite College. In his letters to superiors, he repeatedly emphasized

> the importance of making Kingsland, as being in London and so being more before the public, a Normal house, bringing together some of our best men for preaching in London and other places, making the parochial mission one, but not the only object of the establishment.[41]

He reported in November 1861 that:

> Our mission and schools are going on satisfactorily. We are always receiving some converts and our congregation is in other ways always on the increase. The Diocesan inspector most highly extolled the state of our girls' school at both his last visits ... The superior boys school under Atkinson is progressing very satisfactorily and will I hope always form a nursery for Ratcliffe – twelve of our former pupils are there at present.[42]

In 1861, Lockhart discussed with Cardinal Wiseman and the Vicar General, Dr Whitty, the possibility of the Institute taking over the recently established Italian mission in Clerkenwell from the Pallottine Fathers, an option that had been raised back in 1854, before the establishment of the Kingsland mission. On 27 July 1861 he wrote to Bertetti:

> I have seen the land purchased for the Italian Church. There is room for a Church nearly 200 feet in length by 60 in width but I should not propose to build one quite so large. Besides there is room for a large community house capable of holding 20 or 30 priests and religious and room also for parochial schools for boys and girls. The principal entrance of the Church would front one of the largest streets in London which they are about to commence. The ground is on the top of a hill so that the drainage would be good, and the air as good as it can be in London. It is within a stone's throw of the railway which is to run chiefly underground to connect all the different Termini. The ground cost about £6000 and they could sell it tomorrow for £8000 or

more. The Cardinal and Vicar General tell me that they believe there are about £3000 in hand for building. The Cardinal is most enthusiastic about this matter and only wants your sanction, in order to write to the Pope and the Propaganda to get the transfer of the property made and the rescript now held by the other Congregation cancelled and another made in favour of our Society.[43]

Lockhart stated that parochial ministry had precedence over that of preaching missions:

I see we are weak and I would not propose to undertake any new or rather additional work but rather to transfer priests from a less permanent, less urgent and less important work of charity to one which is in all these respects of a higher grade. I would for the present give up undertaking the preaching of missions and transfer the priests hitherto engaged to the parochial charge ... I hear complaints in many quarters that our best preachers have preached so often that they only repeat themselves and that some others make a very poor hand of the work.[44]

The Italian Church project was still being entertained in the summer of 1862. The Pallottines showed no wish to leave the mission, although, in Lockhart's opinion, they 'have quite lost the confidence of everyone'.[45] The Cardinal considered merging the Italian Chaplaincy with the mission of Baldwin Gardens (with an Irish congregation of some 3,000), turning the chapel into a school.

Lockhart's letters first mention the idea of leaving Kingsland for a 'more suitable' part of London in 1863 and it seems that Manning, in his early months at Westminster, suggested an alternative site in the West End. In a letter written from Clapton to Bertetti dated 7 May 1864, Lockhart stated that such a location would be more suited for the highly-educated Gagliardi and even called the people of Kingsland 'half-educated'. Mrs Lockhart added a note at the bottom of the letter, pleading that her son be relieved of his responsibilities at Kingsland due to his weak health. Furthermore:

William has told you that I am willing to take a house at the West End of London and to assist in the foundation of a new mission which he is anxious about and I hope you will consent to his making the trial. Many of my Son's friends in London of the higher classes of society think it of great importance that the Institute should be represented amongst the more educated classes and that Father Lockhart is peculiarly suited to act upon such.[46]

As Fr Costa had previously discovered, Mrs Lockhart was a powerful force in Kingsland and acted as both the Rector's proud mother and the mission's lay patron.

Three days later, Lockhart stressed that 'nothing is more needed than good preachers in London. Faber is dead and there is no-one of much name but Manning – as for the Jesuits they are preaching only to the ladies!'[47] The Rosminians could make a valuable contribution to the Church in London.

This eagerness to leave the East End for the West is more forcefully expressed in a letter of 1 March 1864, written during his sojourn at Clapton:

> Clapton is six miles to the East of any spot in which the Jesuits would consider it worth their while to open a church!! i.e. six miles from all persons of influence. Hence though it is true that East End souls have cost exactly the same price as those of the West End, yet if we have to choose I suppose we should not select the East End of London as the one permanent seat of the Institute in the chief city of the British Empire![48]

Soon after his appointment as Archbishop of Westminster, Manning told Lockhart that he wished the Fathers to establish a 'school for boarders and day scholars similar to St Charles School [Bayswater]'.[49] Lockhart considered Clapton to be a suitable and healthy location for this project. He proposed that the extension of the Ratcliffe buildings, which was then starting, should be delayed so that the Institute could 'have time to deliberate on the whole merits of the case of Clapton versus Ratcliffe'. When a Belgian priest later showed interest in buying Ratcliffe and opening a Catholic Lunatic Asylum there, Lockhart recommended that the Institute should accept the offer and transfer the College to the Kingsland mission.[50]

Kingsland – A Centre of Catholicism in North London

By 1872, Lockhart was disillusioned with his lot – 'we are doing nothing more than the work of secular priests. No wonder no one joins us'.[51] Despite these reservations, however, Kingsland had become an important centre of Catholicism in north London. A letter of 1870, begging for an extra priest, gives some idea of parochial life on Sunday:

> Confession from 7.30, two Masses, a short sermon at the first and a regular sermon at High Mass at 11. If Lewthwaite is unwell I have to sing the Mass and preach as well. I have to give Catechism and Benediction at 3 o'clock and to preach again in the evening and sing Vespers and Benediction.[52]

There were occasional special services, such as Mass in the Greek Rite offered by a visiting priest from Syria in June 1864,[53] and organizations such as the Association of Constant Homage to St Joseph, indulgenced by the Pope in 1856.[54] Lockhart's controversial lectures always proved popular, and covered a wide range of themes, such as (in 1862) 'Catholic and Protestant Missions to the Heathen', with 'statistics chiefly drawn from Protestant sources'.[55] His listeners would have witnessed the familiar sight of 'the table piled up with books which he had by his side'.[56] Indeed, he had gained the reputation of being a talented preacher. Shortly after coming to Kingsland, Newman included his name on a list of preachers for his Catholic University in Dublin and he went over for this purpose in February 1857.[57] *The Weekly Register* in 1858 reported Lockhart's lecture 'before a large audience of Protestants' in which he dealt with 'the revelations of "Maria Monk" and [Judge] Jeffreys'. The correspondent commented that

> seldom have we heard a subject handled with such eloquence, power and ability. The voice, gesture, and attitude bespoke the orator – fluent, clear, distinct, and audible in his delivery, even his lowest whisper was heard by all; the vigour and earnestness of his manner won over his hostile auditors.

The writer was impressed that 'here is this excellent Priest, formerly a member of Exeter College, Oxford, coming down and selecting by preference a pauper locality for his arena of toil ... "He deserves a Cathedral," said an Irish friend'.[58]

Distinguished visitors to the parish included Ambrose Phillipps[59] and Archbishop Polding of Sydney, a friend of Lockhart's whose chaplain was a relation of Miss Athy, one of the schoolmistresses and companions of Mrs Lockhart.[60] In February 1858, Lockhart admitted into Kingsland's Confraternity of the Blessed Sacrament Sarah Frances Russell, who was visiting London and had first met Lockhart during his preaching tour of Ireland. She was the sister of Lord Russell of Killowen, later to become the first Catholic Lord Chief Justice of England, and she herself entered the Sisters of Mercy.[61]

Converts were encouraged and received into the Church at Lockhart's hands. One of the most notable of these was William Wilberforce (the younger), eldest son of the abolitionist and brother of Samuel, the Anglican bishop of Oxford. Compared to the glittering careers of his siblings, William was considered something of a disappointment. Despite coming top of the poll for Kingston-on-Hull in 1837, the election was declared invalid the following year and he failed to contest Taunton and Bradford in 1841. For the next fifteen years he lived at St Germain-en-Laye, on the outskirts of Paris, where Lockhart was an occasional guest. The early 1850s had seen the conversion of his wife and two brothers, but William was reluctant to rush Romewards and he was not received into the Church until 1863. The immediate occasion for his conversion was a book by his brother, Robert, *An Enquiry into the Principles of Church Authority* (1854), which explained his own reasons for conversion and which was used many years later by Lockhart in a series of apologetic lectures. Wilberforce read the book three times before writing to his wife that he had 'discovered that the Protestant religion is a sham'. Lockhart accompanied him through the final stages of the process, 'as he had written and received many letters on controversial subjects from Dr Pusey and from his brother the Bishop of Oxford it was necessary to make good every step of the way'.[62] Lockhart received William Wilberforce at Epiphany 1863 and the conversion caused a great sensation in both England and St Germain.[63]

Another notable 'catch' was Edmund Bishop, the liturgical

scholar, described by David Knowles as 'one of the great English autodidacts',[64] who was received by Lockhart at Clapton on 16 August 1867 and went to the priest for spiritual direction in subsequent years. Edward Walford, the journalist and compiler of reference works, was also a spiritual client.

Beyond Kingsland

Lockhart was frequently away from Kingsland on account of poor health, which, as we have seen, had paralyzed him just after his conversion and during his preaching in Ireland. He once compared himself to 'an American clock which goes very well for a short time and then nothing can be made of it'.[65] His general complaint seems to have been of a nervous nature – 'severe headaches, want of memory, instability of nerves and a feeling of incapacity for anything involving responsibility'. He attributed this to juggling parish business with other duties, such as retreat-giving and work on behalf of the Institute.[66] On one occasion, Newman wrote to him, 'you do not allow yourself long enough rests enough to get well'.[67] At the end of November 1861 Lockhart took the famed hydropathic treatment at Malvern Wells. His physician, Dr Gully, told him to abstain from 'all that is laborious for mind or body for many months'; otherwise he would risk 'a general paralysis that would be incurable'.[68] A few weeks later he was acting as chaplain at Grace Dieu, following a relaxed regime of celebrating Mass, breathing country air and 'horse exercise, which is much recommended'.[69] In the New Year (1862) he stayed with 'my friend Mr Pugin' at Ramsgate[70] and went on to Paris, only being forced to return to Kingsland in March when Fr Lewthwaite was stricken with typhoid. By June of that year he declared the doctor had again forbidden him 'to preach or to have any parochial business on my mind'.[71]

Between September 1864 and July 1865, Lockhart was at Ratcliffe acting as Vice-President, a position which was supposed to provide him with a rest in the country air of Leicestershire. As always he was accompanied by his mother, who hoped to occupy the farm house near the College, and a tradition has been passed down that his classes with the boys lacked an element of discipline.

In 1873 and 1874 Lockhart, while remaining Rector of Kingsland, moved to Cardiff to look after the mission in succession to Fr Signini, who transferred to Kingsland. The Institute had accepted care of Cardiff in 1854, when the town was 'a rapidly developing sea-port of South Wales, the principal place of embarkation for the coal and iron ore of the mining districts'.[72] A splendid church, designed by Charles Hanson, was opened in September 1862. However, the mission had a large debt and Lockhart reported in January 1874 that 'the churches are well filled and we hope that Divine Providence will enable us to meet the interest of the debt which the Provincial has taken on himself. Perhaps in time it may be liquidated, at present we can think of nothing but bringing all our energies to bear to pay the interest'.[73]

Lockhart had ambivalent feelings towards the Cardiff mission and for many years recommended that the Institute leave the area. In 1872 he had written to Fr Rinolfi that 'we should spend no more at Cardiff but seek to withdraw and bring our forces to London'. This formed part of his long-standing argument, already referred to, for a regular community in London in which the Institute's resources would be concentrated and parochial duties minimized in favour of retreat-giving and education: 'if we do not make a central house in London, I believe that the spirit will die out of our Institute and then the body will soon be buried and forgotten'. Indeed, in September 1873 the bishop had picked up on the Institute's uncertainty and considered offering the Cardiff mission to the Benedictines or Oratorians.

In Cardiff, Lockhart became close to the third Marquis of Bute, a Catholic convert and wealthy local landowner. He had made the opening of St Peter's School possible in August 1872 and was also responsible for rebuilding Cardiff Castle as a gothic fantasy. The first post-Reformation Corpus Christi procession in Wales was held there in 1874, with the involvement of the Fathers of Charity. The Marquis later proved to be a great supporter of the restoration of St Etheldreda's, Ely Place.

The briefness of Lockhart's stay in Cardiff did not prevent him from involving himself in local politics during the 1874 General Election. It was usual for the Irish to vote for the Liberal Party, then under Gladstone, which favoured Irish Home Rule. Indeed, the Liberal MP for Cardiff was none other than James Crichton-

Stuart, the cousin of the Marquis of Bute. However, the Liberals opposed denominational schools being supported by the rates, thus putting Catholic schools in danger, and Lockhart encouraged his Irish parishioners to vote Tory. This was despite the fact that a third party had emerged onto the political scene, the Home Rule League, which would have appealed strongly to Irish Catholics. Lockhart was widely criticized for trying to manipulate the election in Cardiff, although Crichton-Stuart was safely returned to his seat.[74]

Elizabeth Lockhart and the Bayswater Franciscan Sisters

Lockhart's sister, Elizabeth, was meanwhile persevering in the Religious Life and, in 1857, had moved with her community of the Sisters of Charity of the Precious Blood from Greenwich to Bayswater.[75] Here they settled into three adjoining houses on Elgin Crescent and could enjoy the support of Manning, the Superior of the Oblates of St Charles at the nearby church of St Mary of the Angels. Manning closely supervised the community, acting as Superior and Confessor and providing £100 a year for its upkeep. The Sisters were suffering from a crisis of identity and it was Manning who was instrumental in their move to Bayswater, where they could assist the Oblates in charitable and educational work, and in their adoption of the Franciscan Rule in 1858. In order to be recognized canonically, new communities had to follow one of the older Rules, to which a Foundress could add her own Constitutions. Manning himself was a great devotee of St Francis. He had been impressed by a visit to the Franciscan Convent in Inverness and went on to establish several Franciscan communities in Westminster, including the Franciscan Sisters Minoress (1888).

Elizabeth and another Sister, Margaret Anne Burton (Sr Mary Francis), were duly dispatched for three months to the Convent of the Franciscan Sisters of the Immaculate Conception in Charlotte Street, Glasgow, a community with roots in France and in the tradition of St Angela of Foligno. The two convert ladies received the Franciscan habit on 26 October 1858 and returned with the promise of a Glasgow Sister who could assist in training the rest of the community in London.

This was not an easy time for Elizabeth Lockhart. Already in her late forties and having acted as Superior at Wantage and Greenwich, it took a great deal of humility to submit to the strict formation of a novitiate. Added to this were the tensions surrounding the change from the Rosminian to Franciscan vocation, which led four of the original community to leave Bayswater. This was a great blow since they included women of means, on whose incomes the community greatly relied. Moreover, the Sister sent from Scotland was younger and less refined than many of the London community and 'she made frequent remarks disparaging the arrangements at Bayswater and comparing things there unfavourably with the Glasgow house, thus creating dissatisfaction'.[76]

However on 26 October 1859, Elizabeth took her vows before Manning and was elected Prioress. The following month many of the original Greenwich community took the Franciscan habit, including Mary Reid, the veteran of Wantage (Sr Mary Magdalen), and another middle-aged convert, Mary Anne Kingston (Sr Mary Joseph). The youngest of those professed at the time, Mary Carter (Sr Mary Aloysius), lived until 1921.

On Elgin Crescent, one of the houses served as the convent, another as the orphanage and the third as the hostel for converts – a similar work of charity to Lockhart's St Joseph's Institute at Kingsland, although it was closed in 1859. The dining rooms of two of the houses were knocked through to form the chapel, where Cardinal Wiseman celebrated the first Mass. The Sisters were engaged in many good works in the area and taught in the school for poor girls at St Mary of the Angels where, within a year of arriving, they had a hundred pupils. By 1861 there were ten orphans living next to the convent. The Sisters eventually moved to larger buildings on the Portobello Road, where they ran a school, cared for lady-boarders and opened St Elizabeth's Home for the training of domestic servants. The buildings still exist and were for many years occupied by Dominican nuns.

In 1862, Sr Mary Francis replaced Elizabeth as Superior. The Foundress subsequently acted as Sub-Prioress and Vicaress and could now concentrate on the literary apostolate. She died on 21 July 1870, aged 59, after an illness of only four days. According to her biographer:

The illness with which she was seized admitted only passing moments of consciousness. Notwithstanding the torture of her state, her soul seemed to be with her God, inwardly praying all the time, though practically unable to articulate a word, save in rare instances when the prayers of the Church caught the ears of those around her. In these glimpses of light, her eyes, though partially dim, searched always and besought for prayers from her spiritual daughters, who prayed continually by her bedside. As soon as vocal prayers began, she calmed and her smitten face bore a look of smiling peace. The chaplain gave her the last Blessing and within a few minutes she passed away. Two days later Requiem Mass was sung by her brother, Rev. Father Lockhart, and she was laid to rest in the Convent cemetery.[77]

The Franciscan Sisters eventually settled in Braintree, Essex, where there is even a road called 'Elizabeth Lockhart Way'. In 1964 the community amalgamated with the Missionary Franciscan Sisters of the Immaculate Conception, which had been founded in 1873 by Elizabeth Hayes (Mother Mary Ignatius), the former associate of Elizabeth Lockhart at Wantage, Greenwich and Bayswater.

Around the time of her daughter's death, Mrs Lockhart's health began to fail and she finally died on 15 January 1872; 'she had the full use of her mind to the last, and died, not so much through any active disease, as through decay of nature'. Her Requiem was celebrated at Kingsland on 19 January and her body taken for burial at Ratcliffe College. Lockhart paid tribute to her as

> one of the gentlest, most unselfish, and wisest of mothers, to whose earliest training he owes, under God, whatever good there may be in himself; for, though she followed him into the Church, she was the means of placing him on the right road by her example of conscientious love of truth.[78]

Notes

1. Belti, *The Rosminian Question*, p. 31.
2. Ibid., pp. 32–4.
3. ASIC Box 7.4/24 (Lockhart to Provincial).
4. ASIC Box 7.4/24.
5. Lang, *Life & Letters of John Gibson Lockhart*, vol. ii, p. 396.
6. Pastoral Letter, 13 May 1856.
7. AAW W3/49/1 (Lockhart to Wiseman, 20 May 1856).

Kingsland

8. *Tablet,* 9 July 1904, p. 68.
9. After the death of his wife and children, Pope was accepted by the Birmingham Oratory, in whose school he had been teaching, and ordained in 1869. He accompanied Newman to Rome for the reception of the Cardinal's hat in 1879 and translated several works for publication, including Cardinal Capecelatro's classic life of St Philip Neri (1882), *The Imitation of Christ* and the *Prayers of St Gertrude and St Mechtilde* (both of which appeared posthumously in 1907). McLeod, who was the brother of the Countess of Caithness and, like Lockhart, a graduate of Exeter College, Oxford, later entered the Society of Jesus. He was ordained priest in 1861 and was for many years based at Manresa House, Roehampton.
10. Hirst, 'Necrology', p. 334.
11. ASIC AG 118/94 (Lockhart to Bertetti, Low Sunday 1863).
12. ASIC AG 118/97 (Lockhart to Bertetti, 30 April 1863).
13. Lockhart, *Popular Lectures on the Catholic Religion,* pp. 1–3.
14. ASIC AG 118/31–32 (Lockhart to Bertetti, 7 December 1861).
15. Hirst, 'Necrology: Father Lewthwaite', p. 288.
16. Ibid., p. 290.
17. ASIC AG 118 (Lockhart to Bertetti, 3 April 1862).
18. ASIC AG 118 (Lockhart to Bertetti, 7 October 1862).
19. ASIC AG 118/79 (Lockhart to Bertetti, 17 October 1862).
20. ASIC AG 118/209 (Lockhart to Bertetti, 5 August 1865).
21. ASIC AG 118/290 (Lockhart to Bertetti, 22 August 1867).
22. ASIC Kingsland Parish Notice Book (1 June 1862).
23. ASIC Kingsland Parish Notice Book (March 1864).
24. *Tablet,* 13 April 1867, p. 235.
25. ASIC Box 66.5.
26. ASIC AG 118/80 (Lockhart to Bertetti, 17 October 1862).
27. ASIC AG 118/117–18 (Lockhart to Bertetti, 26 August 1869).
28. *The Four Synods of Westminster,* p. 141.
29. Ibid., p. 187.
30. ASIC AG 118/11 (Lockhart to Bertetti, 4 July 1861).
31. ASIC AG 118/280 (Lockhart to Bertetti, 25 July 1867).
32. ASIC AG 118 (Lockhart to Bertetti, 27 November 1864).
33. AAW W3/49 (Lockhart to Wiseman, 5 August 1857).
34. Hirst, 'Father Lewthwaite', p. 287. Daniel Gilbert was a priest at St Mary Moorfields.
35. Fisher, *Our Lady and St Joseph, Kingsland,* p. 9.
36. *Weekly Register,* 10 September 1864, p. 164.
37. ASIC AG 118/17 (Lockhart to Bertetti, 27 July 1861).
38. *Catholic Directory 1863,* p. 250.
39. Hirst, 'Necrology', p. 338.
40. A church was finally opened in 1882. The current church was opened on 29 September 1962 and a daughter parish, St Jude, Clapton Park, established two years later. In 1972 the Retreat moved to Princess Risborough, Buckinghamshire, where it still provides accommodation for Catholics aged sixty and above. Much

of the information concerning St Scholastica's is taken from a typescript in the Westminster Diocesan Archives, AAW/DOW/DC/1/PAR/21, *A Short Historical Record compiled by the Warden, Major H. Gilmore, 1966*.
41. ASIC AG 118/118 (Lockhart to Bertetti; undated, 1863?).
42. ASIC AG 118/28 (Lockhart to Bertetti, November 1861).
43. ASIC AG 118/17-18 (Lockhart to Bertetti, 27 July 1861).
44. ASIC AG 118/21 (Lockhart to Bertetti, 30 July 1861).
45. ASIC AG 118/50a (Lockhart to Bertetti, 7 July 1862).
46. ASIC AG 118/135 (Lockhart to Bertetti, 7 May 1864).
47. ASIC AG 118/137 (Lockhart to Bertetti, 10 May 1864).
48. ASIC AG 118/130 (Lockhart to Bertetti, 11 March 1864).
49. ASIC AG 118/219 (Lockhart to Bertetti, 11 December 1865).
50. ASIC AG 118/308 (Lockhart to Bertetti; undated, 1867?).
51. ASIC AG 118/398 (Lockhart to Bertetti, 17 June 1872).
52. ASIC AG 118/368 (Lockhart to Bertetti, 4 July 1870).
53. ASIC Kingsland Notice Book (27 May 1864).
54. ASIC Kingsland File 26.
55. *The Times*, 3 May 1862, p. 10.
56. Hirst, 'Necrology', p. 331.
57. Ibid., p. 340; LD xvii, p. 534 (diary entry for 28 February 1857).
58. *Weekly Register*, 10 July 1858, p. 2.
59. ASIC AG 118/46 (Lockhart to Bertetti, 7 July 1862).
60. ASIC AG 118/253 (Lockhart to Bertetti, 25 July 1866).
61. Russell, *Three Sisters of Lord Russell of Killowen and their Convent Life*, p. 217.
62. ASIC AG 118//88 (Lockhart to Bertetti, 20 January 1863).
63. His obituary in *The Tablet* (7 June 1879) states this happened at Kingsland, though there is no reference to it in the parish registers.
64. Abercrombie, *Edmund Bishop*, p. xi.
65. ASIC Box 7.4/24.
66. ASIC AG 118/52 (Lockhart to Bertetti, 26 January 1862).
67. LD xxi, p. 142 (Newman to L., 3 July 1864).
68. ASIC AG 118/29 (Lockhart to Bertetti, 20 November 1861).
69. ASIC AG 118/31 (Lockhart to Bertetti, 7 December 1861).
70. This was, of course, Edward Pugin, the eldest son of Augustus (who had died in 1852).
71. ASIC AG 118/79 (Lockhart to Bertetti, 21 June 1862).
72. Lockhart, *Life of Rosmini*, vol. ii, p. 116.
73. ASIC 118/594 (Lockhart to Caccia, 9 January 1874).
74. *A History of St Peter's Parish, Roath, Cardiff*, pp. 16 and 18.
75. Their property at 70 Crooms Hill became the home of St Mary's Orphanage for boys, founded by Rev. William Gowan Todd at Chislehurst.
76. Breffny, *Unless the Seed Die*, p. 69.
77. SMA, *Mother Mary Elizabeth Lockhart*, p. 20. When the Sisters moved to Braintree, their Foundress' body was translated from Portobello Road to St Mary's Cemetery, Kensal Green.
78. *Tablet*, 27 January 1872, p. 117.

Chapter VII

Ely Place

Lockhart had long dreamed of moving to a better location where a central house of the Institute could be established. In 1871 Manning revived Wiseman's idea of combining the missions of Baldwin Gardens and (Great) Saffron Hill and Lockhart wrote to the Provincial in an upbeat mood: 'my opinion is that we could not select a more advantageous position'. At the time, Mrs Lockhart was dying and he hoped to use her legacy in setting up a new house: 'I think we have always agreed that Kingsland is not a place fitted for a foundation and now providence seems to open the way to a change, with the full sanction and to some extent by the initiative of the Archbishop.'[1]

The mission of St Bridget, Baldwin Gardens, had been opened in 1851, partly as a reaction to the proselytizing of the Irish in the area by the Evangelical Central School. According to an *Appeal* issued four years later,

> the congregation numbers between 6000 and 8000 of the poorest class of Irish and Italians who inhabit the densely crowded courts and alleys of Gray's-inn-lane, and Leather-lane, and its neighbourhood. Their Chapel is a warehouse or workshop fitted up to serve for the divine offices of Sunday, for Mass and the evening functions of week days – as a day school for boys, as a day school for girls, as a night school for boys, and as a night school for girls.[2]

The church of the Holy Family on Great Saffron Hill was opened by Wiseman on 29 June 1854 and was a more substantial structure built in the Gothic style, complete with a bell turret. By the 1870s the lease on Baldwin Gardens was nearly finished and, although the Saffron Hill property was freehold, doubts were raised about its suitability as a religious house, especially since there was no room for expansion due to the raising of the surrounding roads and the erection of the Holborn Viaduct.

In December 1873 the Institute's legal agent, Mr Harting, noticed that the medieval chapel of St Etheldreda in nearby Ely Place was to be auctioned. Built at the end of the thirteenth century, St Etheldreda's was the only surviving part of the old London palace of the bishops of Ely. John of Gaunt died there in 1399 and Shakespeare later put on the dying man's lips the famous 'this sceptr'd Isle' speech in *Richard II*. The palace continued to be owned by the bishops of Ely until the eighteenth century, although it was used by the Spanish Embassy in the 1620s and the Catholic Mass was once again celebrated in the chapel. After the so-called 'Doleful Evensong' in 1623, when a floor collapsed during Vespers at the French ambassador's house in Blackfriars, killing about a hundred Catholics, eighteen of the victims were buried in the crypt of the church.

In 1775 Ely Place was built on the site of the palace and the surviving chapel was let for use by the Church of England and then the Welsh Episcopalians. In 1874 Ely Place was sold by order of the Court of Chancery, in order to settle a lawsuit between the descendants of the original buyer. This came just at the right moment for the Rosminians and Lockhart later related in his small book, *S. Etheldreda's and Old London*, how the old chapel fell into Catholic hands once again:

> We heard of the proposed sale, and sent an agent to bid for the Chapel and other portions of the property. For the Chapel we paid £5,400, which was less than the value of the freehold ground on which it stands. The day after we had made the purchase, the clergyman of the Welsh congregation called on me to offer a considerable advance on the sum we had paid. It seems that the Welsh people had got the notion, that if the price ran up beyond the £5,000 they were prepared to pay, Sir Watkins William Wynn, the great Welsh magistrate, would authorize his agent at the sale to go on with the bidding. Their agent, when he had made his last bid, looked across the room to our agent [Mr Harting], whom he supposed to be the person authorized to act for the Welsh baronet. 'I suppose,' he said, 'it is all right in your hands?' 'Certainly,' was the reply of our agent, and making the next bid it was knocked down to him. It was only after the sale that they

learned that the property had passed into Catholic hands. 'Well, sir,' said the Welsh clergyman when I declined to sell, 'I am sorry we have lost the old place, but this I will say, if we were to lose it I am glad it has passed into your hands, for you will appreciate its beauty and, I have no doubt, restore it in a way we should never do.'[3]

On 22 June 1874, Fathers Lockhart and Signini and Brother Atkinson moved to Ely Place, together with their two maids who lodged in a separate building at the bottom of the garden, and the following day Lockhart said Mass in the quickly-fitted domestic oratory. It was the feast of St Etheldreda. A festive breakfast was served in the parlour afterwards, attended by a number of friends and benefactors. That evening, the Fathers returned to Kingsland for a large farewell Tea Party. The Archbishop was present and spoke affectionately of 'my dear old friend Father Lockhart', whom he had known 'intimately as one man can know another'. Manning claimed responsibility for recommending the appointment of the Fathers of Charity to the mission in 1854: 'feeling a great interest in this part of London, I looked about me to see whom I could recommend to the Cardinal ... and I fixed my eyes on ... Father Lockhart whom I have known for thirty years'. The Archbishop acknowledged the sadness at their departure for pastures new:

> The zeal and power of the Fathers of Charity have outgrown the Kingsland Mission. The power which is in them demands a larger and more difficult field than that afforded by the calm and tranquil congregation here. They must be placed in a central position for this great London, in a position where they may have more opportunity of bringing masses of sinners to salvation, and spreading the wholesome influence of their sacred ministries to a wider circle than they could do here in Kingsland. It is for this that I have felt it my duty to decide as I have done, though I should cause grief to you.[4]

Lockhart later recalled Manning's words to him regarding Saffron Hill: 'I wanted you to come here because I wished you to launch into the deep and let down your nets for a draft.'[5]

Not surprisingly, the Kingsland parishioners were distraught at the loss of their pastor and sent petitions to Cardinal Manning and the Father Provincial, with some 529 signatures. The Cardinal was told that 'we need hardly say that the very thought of losing these holy Fathers has filled our hearts with bitter grief for have they not guided and consoled us in all our troubles and who can tell how deeply we love them.' The parishioners suggested to the Provincial that 'our saintly superior Fr Lockhart might be Parish Priest of Kingsland as well as Holborn and Fr Lewthwaite remain with us still.'[6] However, the move went ahead and the outgoing Rector of Saffron Hill, Fr James Hussey, succeeded Lockhart at Kingsland. The Sisters of Providence stayed on to help at the Girls' and Infants' Schools until 1877.

The first task at St Etheldreda's was to prepare the crypt for public use, although there were complaints when the ancient floor of the crypt was lowered and modern stone pillars replaced the old wooden ones. 'St Bridget's-in-the-Crypt' was opened for worship in June 1876 and the Cardinal himself came to celebrate a Low Mass, in the presence of the Duke of Norfolk, the Marquis of Bute and the Dowager Marchioness of Londonderry. Lockhart was proud that 'some declare that they can say their prayers here better than anywhere they know'. The thick walls kept out 'all the roaring of the wheels in Holborn' and the temperature was constant 'so that it is, so I am told, the coolest place in summer and the warmest in winter in all London'.[7] The crypt was divided into two aisles by the columns, at the end of each of which was an altar, taken from Baldwin Gardens and Saffron Hill. A convert of Lockhart's, Frederick T. Hirgame, made his First Communion in the crypt in 1877 and remembered 'how the moisture dropped from the great beams of the roof on to our prayer-books.'[8]

Meanwhile, a Restoration Committee (including eight Catholic peers) was established so that funding could be provided for 'the restoration of the church to its sacred purpose for which it was built by the piety of our forefathers and to do this in a way as faithfully to preserve every part of the original work'. Lockhart calculated that £6,000 would be needed and hoped that the upper church would be ready by the summer of 1878.[9] Though work soon began on the oak roof, the opening was postponed until the following year.

The raising of funds was not helped by a controversy concerning the origins of the building. It was suggested that St Etheldreda's had actually been the hall of the bishops of Ely, only becoming a chapel at a much later date. Critics pointed to the unusual timber floor of the so-called church and the similar size of the windows at the east and west end. Writing in *The Tablet* in 1919, 'Senex' recalled that

> those who held that the building had never been a chapel but was the ancient banqueting hall of the palace, assigned another use to the crypt and especially to its recesses. One great argument that the building had been a chapel was removed when the sedilia in the upper church was destroyed to make a door into the priest's house.[10]

However, perhaps the strongest defense of St Etheldreda's came from the distinguished architect, Sir Gilbert Scott, who wrote a paper on the subject for the Middlesex Archaeological Society.[11]

There was much discussion about the nature of the upper church's restoration and debates between the antiquarians involved in the restoration. It was feared that the medieval structure would be too small for the combined congregations of Baldwin Gardens and Saffron Hill and some suggested the building of a new chancel, which would turn the east window into an arch, but this was condemned by the medievalist and artist H. W. Brewer. There were, moreover, ambitious plans for 'a presbytery on one side of the church and a convent on the other, suggestive of St Pancras station ... The church was to be entered through a porch in the northern building leading under a covered way through an open space to the north-western door'. In the end, however, 'the sole structural enlargements were the small annexe at the south-west, incorporating the scrap of Ely House that remained, topped by the wooden bell turret, and the small wooden three-sided cloister on the site of about a quarter of the old cloister garth'.[12]

Much excitement was caused on 19 April 1875 when part of the covered ceiling was removed 'in a shower of birdnests and cobwebs' to reveal the medieval roof, which was substantially intact.[13] Lockhart relished removing the Royal Arms, which dated from the reign of Charles I and had once hung over the Protestant Communion table. He placed this in the porch with the inscription, 'This emblem of the Royal Supremacy was removed from the Church of S. Etheldreda when it was restored to the Roman obedience'. Lockhart enjoyed recalling the words of Burke, an Irish labourer, who carried the Royal Arms into the porch – 'there, that's the finest job of work I ever did, and I won't forget it to my dying day, glory be to God'.[14] Bernard Whelan, the architect of the restoration and an alumnus of Ratcliffe, recounted how Lockhart insisted on inspecting the restored roof before 'the narrow platforms which stretched from tie-beam to tie-beam was about to be removed', despite having a terror of heights. 'Nerving himself, he climbed the ladder and stood upon the frail-feeling platform. I have not forgotten the pallor of his sensitive face'.[15]

Vincent Harting, who had been Lockhart's agent at the auction and who also acted as solicitor to the archdiocese, donated part of St Etheldreda's hand, a family heirloom recently deposited at the Dominican Convent of Stone in Staffordshire where his daughter was a Sister. Lockhart made the journey to Stone to receive the relic, which had been detached from the rest of the relic by Bishop Ullathorne. He boldly deduced,

> it would seem not unlikely that this relic has been restored to the chapel that was originally built for it, ... because as the body of S. Etheldreda was always preserved, until the dispersion of relics, in her cathedral at Ely, so it would seem likely that if a portion of her sacred body were removed from the original shrine, it would likely to be found in the chapel of the Bishop of Ely, in London.[16]

Lockhart himself gained great personal satisfaction in claiming descent from a kinsman of the Saxon patroness, though he told his cousin, the Princess di Cassano: 'you see, little Mary, the bother is, they were not saints from the vulgar classes, so it would be such an absurd dandyism to speak of the connection. I will just enjoy the blessed privilege for my own sake, and we won't talk about it to anybody.'[17]

The opening of the upper church was delayed and finally scheduled for 22 June 1879, when the ceremony of the reconciliation of a desecrated church was performed by Lockhart, after First Vespers for the feast of St Etheldreda had been recited in the crypt. A procession was formed and the relics of the patroness borne from the side altar in the crypt, as the choir sang the Litany of the Saints and the church sprinkled with holy water. After the prayers prescribed in the *Rituale* were said, the Blessed Sacrament was brought in with great solemnity and placed in the newly-blessed tabernacle.

The following morning, the Feast of St Etheldreda, the Rosminian Provincial, Fr Gazzola, celebrated the High Mass and the Cardinal 'preached from the Altar one of his striking sermons, in the course of which he expressed in words of touching pathos his love for England, and his hopes of her returning one day to the fold of Christ and of St Peter'. Lockhart's old University friend, Fr Ignatius Grant, SJ, preached at Solemn Vespers, noting that 'if these old walls could speak and could cry out, we should need but to interrogate them, and we should hear a history so interesting and so true, so alluring to the antiquary and so instructive to Catholics, that the intervention of human voice or human pen would be unnecessary.'

Slowly the windows were filled with coloured glass, thanks to sponsors such as the Duke of Norfolk, Edward Bellasis (the Lancaster Herald) and Edward de Lisle (son of Ambrose). Conscious of the historical connections, Lockhart planned a window in honour of the English Martyrs since St Etheldreda's was 'the only ancient public Catholic church in London where in those days they could have heard Mass'.[18] An early design, before the beatifications of 1886, even included Mary, Queen of Scots as one of the martyrs.[19] Lockhart hoped to restore Ely Place to its former glory, erecting an oak screen in the sanctuary in 1883, 'without in the least impeding the view of the high altar',[20] and, following a suggestion of Gilbert Scott, by placing statues of St Peter and St Paul on corbels between the windows. These were based on figures on the tomb of St Sibald at Nuremburg, a plaster cast of which was displayed at the South Kensington Museum, and it was hoped that a complete set of Apostles and Evangelists would one day stand along the wall.[21] Lockhart also desired 'a style of music in harmony with the church' and developed a choir made up of 'gentleman who have leisure for practice and love the Gregorian plain song and harmonized music of the school of Palestrina'.[22]

Ely Place spoke of the past; the presbytery even came with a resident ghost and Lockhart is said to have seen 'a lady with a lighted candle in her hand, going down the stairs'.[23] He was particularly excited by a stone bowl that had been found embedded in concrete under one of the oak pillars of the crypt and was moved upstairs beside the south door. He asked the opinion of Gilbert Scott, who thought it 'British or Roman, for it is older than the Saxon period'. Ever aware of the apologetic value of the fabric of Ely Place, Lockhart jumped to a dramatic (though unprovable) conclusion:

> [The bowl] must have belonged to an ancient British Church, and, as a sacred vessel no longer in use, it was buried according to the Catholic custom in such cases, in order that it might not be desecrated to common uses. Here then stood not improbably the earliest Christian Church of London on this very spot, which was then a wild and wooded hill; outside the walls of the Roman City, like the British Church of S. Martin, just outside the city walls of Canterbury. If this be so, it may have been here that the British Bishop of London, who afterwards attended the Council of Arles, received the news of the martyrdom of S. Alban at Verulam on the outbreak of the Persecution of Dioclesian A.D. 303. This font is evidently a holy-water vessel for it is much too small for a baptismal font of that early date, since these were always made large enough for baptism by immersion, as we see in all examples of ancient fonts in England. It is now restored to its ancient use, and, on the morning of the restoration of the Church to Catholic worship, I had the honour of blessing the water in it, after an interval of at least 600 years since last it had contained holy water.[24]

For Lockhart, that was the great secret of Ely Place: not only a centrally-located house for the Institute but a powerful symbol of Victorian Catholicism's continuity with 'the Old Religion'.

'Exiles of Erin'

Despite the impressive historical connections and the occasional visits from antiquarian and architectural associations, the area around Ely Place was not then a prosperous part of London. Indeed, the surrounding streets found their place in some of Dickens' grimmest descriptions of London, including 'Fagan's Den' and the 'Thieves Kitchen' in *Oliver Twist*, and the Anglican vicar of St Andrew's, Holborn, is reported to have only ventured into the Saffron Hill area accompanied by two police constables. Lockhart recalled that the area had once been fashionable and 'many an historical mansion now pulled down, many of which I remember, and some which are still in occupation of the working classes in the neighbourhood, are of historical interest, shewing, by their carved staircases and the dingy gilding on the ceilings, that here had once been the abode of wealth'.[25] Writing in 1903, the Catholic historian Johanna H. Harting noted:

> one peculiarity of the parish is the very large number of flower-girls who belong to the congregation, and who, on feast-days, bring their flowers to decorate the altars. The majority of the girls who sell flowers in front of the Royal Exchange, at the General Post Office, and at Tottenham Court Road, belong to the confraternities here, where there are Guilds for both men and women.[26]

The mission was full of the Irish poor and in his guide to St Ethleldreda's, which took the form of an imaginary dialogue between a visitor and the Rector, Lockhart paid tribute to the 'exiles of Erin' who had built up the old missions of Baldwin Gardens and Saffron Hill:

> Many of them were once tenant-farmers in Ireland, on the same farms that had been tilled by their ancestors for centuries, some of them the remnant of the old Irish aristocracy, who had kept the memory that the lands they tilled at rack-rent were once the property of their own families, of which they are lineal descendants. At last, driven from ruined homes by savage land-laws, old gentry and peasants in their thousands have been banished from Ireland to labour or to starve in the great cities of England and America.[27]

Indeed, Lockhart made a political point by combining the dedication of St Etheldreda with St Bridget, the original dedication of the chapel in Baldwin Gardens:

> The English S. Etheldreda and the Irish S. Bridget represent the English and Irish elements of England's Catholic population. In the parochial banner the same idea is repeated, where the English and Irish saints are seen clasping each other's hand, while S. Patrick gives a blessing on their union, indicating that the time is at hand when, class warfare being over, the people of the two islands will forgive and forget the wars and oppression of their rulers and of a military aristocracy, through which the two nations have been kept at variance for

centuries. There is a good time coming, and the good example of the steadfast faith of the Irish through centuries of persecution is helping to bring back the English people to the 'Faith of their Fathers'.[28]

Pastoral Duties in Holborn

Lockhart flung himself into pastoral work in Holborn, although he was increasingly in demand as a preacher and retreat director and from 1875 had to spend half the year in Rome as the Institute's Procurator General. A typical Sunday at Ely Place consisted of four Masses, including a Children's Mass with hymns in the crypt. The afternoon and evening were taken up with Catechism and Benediction (in the crypt) and Vespers, Sermon and Benediction (in the upper church). During the week there were meetings of various Confraternities, dedicated to St Joseph, the Holy Family and the Sacred Heart, which provided further opportunities for Rosary, Instruction and Benediction. The patronal feast was celebrated with great splendour each year, with a procession of the relic, and much publicity was given to the blessing of throats on St Blaise's day, which, despite becoming common around the country, seems to have been first practised in this country at Saffron Hill.

The Sisters of Providence opened a school for girls and in September 1876 a middle-class school for boys in the presbytery. The school for the poor at Baldwin Gardens continued. In July 1876 a letter by Fr Richardson appeared in *The Tablet*, complaining that many of the parish children had started attending a local Protestant establishment (Fox Court School) in order to obtain tickets for an excursion into the country. Fr Richardson pleaded for money so that a similar trip could be organized: 'our little ones, who are really the fringe of society, will be content with a very poor conveyance, provided only they can see the daisies and the buttercups, hear the birds sing and run after butterflies'.[29] The old mission church of the Holy Family, Saffron Hill, no longer needed once St Etheldreda's was ready, was eventually converted into a school building and by 1890 over 300 children attended the schools there. As at Kingsland, the Sisters of Providence taught the girls and infants, while lay teachers looked after the boys.

Lockhart continued his concern for the welfare of young men in the capital and provided a safe refuge for them in St Joseph's Club, which had formerly been established in Kingsland: 'young men who are willing to do something for God, by singing in the choir, serving in the sanctuary, or collecting for the support of the schools, will always be welcomed at the Presbytery and at St Joseph's Club'.[30] For a time he even invited students from London University (especially medical students) as lodgers although, as he had found at Kingsland, it had a negative effect on the religious atmosphere of the presbytery.

Sunday evening lectures were organized, covering topics such as 'Sketches from the History of Christendom' (1881), 'Roman Catholicism and Primitive Christianity' (1881) and 'Rationalism' or 'What do we know about God?' (1882), during which series the church was crowded and 'supplemental benches and forms had to be brought in'.[31] In 1885 he turned his attention to 'the foul literature that is flooding our streets'. He declared that 'in thirty years' experience of London he could not recall a time when the devil seemed to be so much abroad' and attacked the 'Disclosures' concerning 'the grossest forms of vice' which could be found in the popular press and which were 'giving young boys and girls a knowledge which they had not before and which will inevitably be harmful to them'.[32] Lockhart explained the Catholic teaching on purity and recommended confession as the most effective antidote to this 'moral plague'.

The League of the Cross

Lockhart came to love the Irish and this, together with his own Celtic roots, led him to tentatively support Home Rule, along with other English Catholics (including, at least eventually, Manning). On St Patrick's Day 1878, for example, Lockhart attended a 'grand national banquet' at the Westminster Palace Hotel, organized by the Irish Home Rule Party, whose founder, Isaac Butt, had been invited but was unable to attend.[33] Nine years later Archbishop Walsh of Dublin, while introducing a talk given by the Rosminian at Ringsend, Dublin, said that 'Father Lockhart was not an Irish priest, but he was a priest with an Irish heart and with Irish principles'. *The Tablet* reported that 'the large hall was crowded and the temperance band was present. A large number of people assembled outside, and tar barrels were burned'. In his address, Lockhart praised the contribution made by the Irish in London but criticized 'the unjust laws which drove them from their native valleys, and the economic laws from which their country suffered. They did right to combine and to use the means placed in their hands to obtain liberty to live in their own land; combine peaceably with the grand movement which was going on through the country' with the blessing of the Church.[34]

However, much as he admired the 'exiles of Erin', Lockhart thought that 'intemperance was the one thing which put a blemish and a stain upon the fair fame of Ireland'.[35] The issue of intoxicating drink became a key concern for Lockhart in his later life, as seen in a series of stories he provided for *The Lamp* in 1875, entitled 'Ruined by Drink', and his active work for the League of the Cross.

This was a common concern in nineteenth-century English Catholicism. The first specifically Catholic temperance society was founded in Chelsea by Fr Sisk in 1838, and the visit in 1843 of the Irish apostle of temperance, Fr Theobald Mathew, encouraged the rapid growth of the movement. During his three months in England, 200,000 are reported to have taken the 'Total Abstinence Pledge'.

Teetotalism was not only a preoccupation for Catholics and in 1853 the non-denominational United Kingdom Alliance was established to promote the reformation of people's habits. At the beginning of 1867 they sent a deputation to Archbishop Manning, who quickly became a great promoter of the cause and four years later became a Vice-President of the Alliance. The vice of drunkenness, the Archbishop argued, not only ruined the body but led to the falling away from the Faith. For St Patrick's Day 1867, he proclaimed a 'Truce of St Patrick', which 'appealed to the two strongest feelings in the Irish heart, Religion and Nationality'.[36] Shamrock was distributed at the altar, bearing the words of the 'Truce' round the stem:

> I promise, in honour of St Patrick, to abstain from intoxicating liquors (except one glass at meal time) from twelve o'clock at noon the 16th

of March, till twelve o'clock at noon the 18th of March, and I offer this act of mortification for the good of my soul, and to avert the anger of God, so justly deserved on account of the prevalence of the sin of drunkenness. O Mary, conceived without sin, pray for us who have recourse to thee.[37]

In 1873 he set up his own organization, the Total Abstinence League of the Cross, which has been called 'the crown of all Cardinal Manning's labours as a philanthropist'.[38] The organization had a military structure, unashamedly borrowed from the Salvation Army, with bright sashes and ranks of Major, Officer, Captain and 'Cardinal's Guard'. The League kept a number of festivals: the St Patrick's Day 'Truce', an annual Whit-Monday parade in central London, a meeting to celebrate Fr Mathew's birthday and a fête at the Crystal Palace. According to Manning's biographer, Purcell, 'the march past the Cardinal at the Crystal Palace, and the beating of drums, and the marshalling of the soldiers of the League of the Cross by the Cardinal's "Guards", excited enthusiasm and attracted public attention.' The crowds were swelled by the many sightseers who came to witness the spectacle. Although Manning requested that alcoholic beverages should not be sold, the managers of the Crystal Palace pointed out that their profits were the largest in the year that day, presumably because so many of the 'tourists' enjoyed drinking to the prosperity of the League.[39]

A young member of the League in the 1880s was William Francis Brown, later an auxiliary bishop in Southwark. He compared the Crystal Palace function to the

> triumphal progress of Catherine the Great to the Crimea, staged by Potemkin, with its improvised towns and palaces, all of which were demolished after the Empress had passed by, to be re-erected further on; because, in point of fact, only a small proportion of those in the procession were members of the League of the Cross. People anxious to please the Cardinal provided badges and regalia and caps for bandsmen for the day, in order that a brave show might be made for His Eminence. I used to wonder if he was really deceived.[40]

Despite such misgivings, these temperance festivals were one of the highlights of the Cardinal's year. Manning was clearly at his ease during these gatherings and comes across as a gifted orator able to jest with the crowd just as much as preach the gospel of teetotalism – an impression not readily given by his stern appearance in portraits. For example, during the celebrations for Fr Mathew's ninetieth birthday at Exeter Hall, which Lockhart attended, the Cardinal caused much laughter by his mention of the membership statistics presented to him: 'he did not say that their good Secretary broke his pledge and saw "double" (laughter) but the number was so great that he was afraid to believe them to be quite accurate'.[41]

Needless to say, Manning's opposition to drink was not appreciated by everyone, including many of his clergy. A joke made the rounds that the Cardinal encouraged Divorce by putting asunder the legitimate union between brandy and soda.[42] Manning later recollected that 'the fine gentleman heresy, the high life below stairs, and the free living of the middle class have kept educated and half educated laymen and priests from joining'.[43] In the early years of the League, Manning was only assisted by a handful of priests. However, by the final years of Manning's life many London parishes had a branch of the League.

Lockhart was asked by the Cardinal to take a central role in organizing the League. On St Patrick's Day 1875, for example, he chaired the large meeting held by the League at Exeter Hall. Manning was in Rome, preparing to receive the red hat, but a letter he had written to Lockhart five days earlier was read out:

> I would ask you to give to the meeting my blessing and tell them to persevere in the light privation of renouncing all intoxicating drinks, and in endeavouring to make as many as they can do likewise. Above all, tell them to bring up their children without so much as a taste of such drink; they will then grow up and help them in life and to pray for them after death.

Lockhart ended the meeting by reading Manning's telegram pronouncing the Pope's blessing (in Latin), which was 'followed by three cheers for Fr Lockhart himself'.[44]

On Whit Monday 1877 Lockhart attended the customary parade, which had previously been held in Hyde Park but on this occasion consisted of a march from the Thames Embankment via Oxford Street and Whitehall to the vacant site awaiting the construction of Westminster Cathedral. The League processed through the streets 'with bands of music and open carriages for the clergy'. At the Cathedral plot 'many thousands of people had collected, and sundry tents were erected' for refreshments of a non-alcoholic nature. Eventually 'an arm chair was procured, which Father Lockhart first mounted' to make a speech and introduce the Cardinal, who admitted to the crowd: 'Now I have laid a sort of trap for you. I have got you here on my ground, and if any man goes off this ground without making up his mind [to take the pledge] ... I shall be very sorry'.[45]

Lockhart was again present at the large demonstration on Tower Hill at the end of September 1877, at which *The Tablet* estimated a crowd of 10,000. He had trouble getting to his place due to the volume of people and was one of those who spoke while awaiting the arrival of Manning. He was 'expostulating with some noisy gamins who had taken possession of a vantage site on a huge mass of paving stones near the vans [which formed the speakers' platform], when the Cardinal was descried making his way to the spot' to huge cheers.[46]

In Manning's old age, Lockhart often acted as his delegate at meetings and, as the *Athenaeum* magazine noted, 'never was his fine military figure seen to greater advantage than on the public platform'.[47] Lockhart's obituary in *The Ratcliffian* noted that 'many thousands of "pledges" were given at his hands, and his wan, ascetic look, and the knowledge that for many years, as long indeed as the doctors would allow him, he himself was a strict teetotaler, gave force to his words, and kindled enthusiasm in his hearers'.[48] It went on to say:

> Perhaps at no time did Fr Lockhart appear so thoroughly happy, so truly the Parish Priest as when, on Sunday afternoons, preceded by the parish band and a banner of St Etheldreda, and surrounded by a goodly company of his chosen and faithful young men, he would repair to Robin Hood Court, to Bleeding Heart Yard, or to the slums and alleys of Grays Inn Road, and there, mounted on a tub or barrow, midst the cries of 'God bless your Riverence!' and 'Long life to the Father of London's Irish poor!' he would plead with them to give up drink and to live the lives of good Christians and Catholics.[49]

A friend of Lockhart's wrote of the sometimes uneasy relationship with the local police:

> Truly it was a glorious sight to see the Father in cassock and bareheaded, giving the pledge to young and old: men, women and little children, hundreds of whom bore the sad marks of habitual intemperance – nay, many of whom were actually the worse for drink while kneeling at his feet. It was on an occasion like this, in the summer of 1890, that I accompanied Fr Lockhart to an Irish Court in his parish: the afternoon was intensely hot, the narrow Court was densely-packed, while the doors and windows were swarming with those anxious to see and hear him who, in the estimation of all, was second only to the great and good Cardinal himself. Hardly had he spoken when an over zealous Police Sergeant ordered him to 'move on'. And in no ante-camera at the Vatican, at no Papal audience, did our Father look so truly grand and so noble as when, with head erect and step majestic, and in obedience to the rough command of that minion of the law, he descended to the pavement, and, after briefly apologizing for coming to preach temperance to Erin's exiled children, amid the mingled cries of 'shame' and 'God bless ye, Father,' from the women and children, and strong expressions of disapproval from the men, he was hustled out of the Court by the police. The conduct of the police now becoming aggressive, and the temper of our people being sorely tried, a regular street fight was imminent; but by the words of Fr Lockhart, what might have proved a serious matter, was averted and peace restored: not however until one man had been knocked down and roughly handled by the police. The result of all this was that many of next morning's London papers bore testimony to the esteem in which our Father was held by Catholics and Protestants alike, and severely called to account those officers who had obstructed a Catholic Priest in a Catholic district while looking after the welfare of his people. Next Sunday, again with band and banner, and preceded by the very policeman who had acted so unwarrantably but a week before, Fr Lockhart went to the same place, where the second officer in immediate command of the City (himself a Protestant) came in plain clothes; and after apologizing on behalf of his men, shook hands with Fr Lockhart, and bore testimony to the good work being done, adding that nothing would give him greater pleasure than to attend our temperance meeting that night, were he not engaged to speak on the same subject in Southwark.[50]

Notes

1. ASIC AG 118/384 (Lockhart to Bertetti, 21 October 1871).
2. *Catholic Directory 1855*, p. 40.
3. Lockhart, *S. Etheldreda's and Old London*, pp. 39–40.
4. Hirst, 'Necrology', p. 336.
5. Lockhart, 'Some Personal Reminiscences of Cardinal Manning', p. 379.
6. ASIC Kingsland File.
7. Lockhart, *S. Etheldreda's and Old London*, pp. 31–2.
8. *Tablet*, 22 February 1919, p. 218.
9. *Tablet*, 29 July 1876, p. 46.
10. *Tablet*, 23 January 1919, p. 3.
11. *Tablet*, 30 November 1878, p. 691. The paper was read to the Society after the architect's death by his son, George Gilbert Scott.
12. Sleigh, *Saint Etheldreda's and Ely Place*, pp. 73–4.
13. Ibid., 74.
14. Lockhart, *S. Etheldreda's and Old London*, pp. 33–4.
15. Whelan, 'Father Lockhart', p. 8.
16. Lockhart, *S. Etheldreda's and Old London*, p. 47.
17. Hirst, 'Necrology', p. 344.
18. *Tablet*, 1 January 1887, p. 22.
19. *Tablet*, 16 July 1881, p. 113.
20. *Tablet*, 10 March 1883, p. 392.
21. *Tablet*, 20 November 1880, pp. 660–1.
22. *Tablet*, 30 March 1878, p. 396.
23. *Shane Leslie's Ghost Book*, p. 57.
24. Lockhart, *S. Etheldreda's and Old London*, pp. 41–2.
25. Ibid., p. 29.
26. Harting, *Catholic London Missions*, pp. 130–1.
27. Lockhart, *S. Etheldreda's and Old London*, p. 30.
28. Ibid., p. 45.
29. *Tablet*, 15 July 1876, p. 79.
30. Lockhart, *S. Etheldreda's and Old London*, p. 65.
31. *Tablet*, 17 June 1882, p. 952.
32. *Tablet*, 5 September 1885, p. 391.
33. *The Times*, 19 March 1878, p. 11.
34. *Tablet*, 14 May 1887, p. 781.
35. *Tablet*, 26 May 1877, p. 659.
36. Purcell, *Cardinal Manning*, vol. ii, p. 595.
37. *Tablet*, 26 January 1867, p. 53.
38. Purcell, *Cardinal Manning*, vol. ii, p. 591.
39. Ibid., pp. 597–8.
40. Brown, *Through Windows of Memory*, p. 123.
41. Tablet, 16 October 1880, p. 499.
42. Purcell, *Cardinal Manning*, vol. ii, p. 593.
43. Ibid., p. 604.

44. *Tablet*, 20 March 1875, p. 372.
45. *Tablet*, 26 May 1877, pp. 659–60.
46. *Tablet*, 6 October 1877, p. 434.
47. Hirst, 'Necrology', p. 338.
48. Ibid., p. 338.
49. Ibid., p. 340.
50. Ibid., pp. 340–1.

1. Elizabeth Lockhart, foundress of three religious communities

2. Satirical print of Newman's foundation at Littlemore: *The Newman-Ooth College*

3. John Henry Newman: lithograph by J. A. Vintner, 1850, after the painting by Maria Giberne

4. Antonio Rosmini: portrait by Francesco Hayez, 1853

5. Luigi Gentili

6. Ratcliffe College, the east front (1843–4) and chapel (1848–9) by A.W.N. Pugin with the south gable as altered (1854) by C.F. Hansom, and his north wing addition (1857–8). Anon. watercolour by an amateur hand c. 1858

7. Church of Our Lady and St Joseph, Tottenham Road, Kingsland, opened by Fr Lockhart on the upper floor of an old paper-drying factory

8. Fr William Henry Lewthwaite

9. St Etheldreda's, Ely Place; the Chapel exterior in 1813 (some 60 years before its purchase by Fr Lockhart)

10. Henry Cardinal Manning

11. Pope Leo XIII

12. Frontispiece from *The Chasuble: its geniune form and size* (1891)

Chapter VIII

The Apostolate of the Press

Lockhart combined his pastoral initiatives with an active concern for publishing and the encouragement of writers. This was something of a family occupation – not only were there connections with Sir Walter Scott and John Gibson Lockhart, but both Lockhart's mother and sister showed a keen interest in writing. Despite her responsibilities in the convent, Mother Mary Elizabeth was able to translate books and produce articles for a number of journals, including *The Dublin Review*. According to Gillow, she displayed 'a rare gift of idiomatic translation',[1] preparing English editions of *The Life of St Teresa of the Order of Our Lady of Mount Carmel* (1865), *The Spirit of St Teresa* (1866) and *The Life of St Francis of Assisi from the Legenda Santa Francisci of Saint Bonaventure* (1868). She was also one of the translators of the *Fioretti* (1863), together with Lady Georgina Fullerton (herself a Franciscan Tertiary) and the Marchesa di Salvo. The two lives and *Fioretti* were edited by Archbishop Manning, who kept in touch with his spiritual daughter.

Shortly after her conversion, Mrs Lockhart translated two devotional works by Pagani (who had received her into the Church at Loughborough) and a short life of Rosmini (edited by her son). After unsuccessful attempts as a religious and teacher, she concentrated on the 'apostolate of the press', converting the premises at Wine Office Court into St Joseph's Press, which produced cheap Catholic literature and journals, including many of Lockhart's pamphlets, and raised money for the education of poor boys and other charitable works. It was said that 'many good and trained compositors and pressmen can trace their success to the day when she presented them with "indentures" and fair wages'.[2]

Fr Lockhart himself was involved in the running of popular Catholic journals and published many pamphlets, articles and books during his lifetime. Though he was encouraged by Manning, this literary work brought him into conflict with his immediate superiors, who feared it distracted from his priestly ministry and carried imprudent financial risks. Some of his initiatives were even begun without seeking the necessary permission, although he wrote contrite letters afterwards to justify his actions. Pagani thought the apostolate of the press was foreign to the Institute and 'not proper to our vocation, the salvation of souls'. Lockhart wrote:

> I am not such a fool as to compare my penny literature to Rosmini's great works, yet I do not forget that his time was devoted to literature by the desire of the Pope and that mine has been as pointedly directed to popular Catholic literature by my own Archbishop who wished me to leave as much parish work as I could to Fr Lewthwaite.[3]

Catholic Opinion (1867–73) and *The Lamp* (1871–90)

A number of sophisticated Catholic journals and weeklies had been started prior to the Restoration of the Hierarchy, including *The Dublin Review* (1836), *The Tablet* (1840) and *The Rambler* (1848). However, there was little in the way of cheap literature for the masses. An early attempt at producing a popular Catholic magazine was *The Lamp*, founded in 1846 by Thomas Earnshaw Bradley and priced one penny (as opposed to *The Tablet*'s sixpence). It described itself as 'A Weekly Catholic Journal of Literature, Science, the Fine Arts, &c., devoted to the Religious, Moral, Physical and Domestic Improvement of the Industrious Classes'. Much of its pages were filled with edifying stories, but it also provided news and summaries of important speeches. It was plagued by financial difficulties and its founding editor ended up in the debtors' prison at York Castle.

In 1867 another penny Catholic magazine was established by an Irish printer, Richard Archer of 15 Wine Office Court. It was entitled *Catholic Opinion: A Review of the Catholic Press at Home and Abroad* and, as the name suggests, it presented extracts from the national and international Catholic press. Mrs Lockhart bought a share in the magazine on 23 March 1867 and, after the sudden death of Archer just three days later, became the sole proprietor. Her son later wrote that 'many of the Notices of Books in *Catholic Opinion* were written by her hand; and a large quantity of MS, now printed in the Magazine, was carefully read and selected, and, when put in type, corrected by her'.[4]

The journal had been purchased 'partly to prevent it falling into Fenian hands' but it also solved a problem at Kingsland. The schoolmaster, Joseph Atkinson, did much of the editorial work and Lockhart declared that, since he was a parishioner,

> I have a perfect right and strict duty to advise him for the good of religion. Atkinson has laboured in the service of this Mission for twelve years with only a nominal salary and I was glad of an opportunity of putting him in a position in which he would have support for his declining years. If there is any profit beyond this on the paper I am sure he will devote it to works of charity through my hands.[5]

A series of articles in *Catholic Opinion* resulted in Lockhart's most popular book, *The Old Religion; or, How Shall We Find Primitive Christianity?* (1868). This originated in Lockhart's correspondence with the American Fr Isaac Hecker, a charismatic convert who founded the Paulist Fathers in 1858. He set up the Catholic Publication Society (now the Paulist Press) to distribute cheap literature and ran two popular magazines, *The Catholic World* and *The Young Catholic*. He was a man after Lockhart's heart. In the 'Preface' to *The Old Religion*, Lockhart noted that

> the idea of throwing Catholic doctrine into the form of conversations, and combining them together by a thread of narrative so as to form a tale, was first suggested to the author by the celebrated Father Hecker ... and the first chapters appeared in the *Catholic World*, a periodical published in New York, under Father Hecker's direction.

The experiment was continued in *Catholic Opinion*, which boosted sales and won much admiration. Bishop Brown of Newport and Menevia told Lockhart that the articles were 'entertaining, convincing, adapted to our actual times, and altogether the most valuable work of dogmatic instruction for general readers, which has issued from the press for many years'.[6] Due to popular demand, the series was brought together in one volume. One reviewer noted that 'many people shrink from the ordeal of a formal course of instruction who have no objection to receive it through the more attractive medium of lively conversations like the present, not unmixed with stirring incidents and witty repartee.'[7]

The conversations are largely set in America and a voyage 'from New York to Old Rome', cover a wide range of polemical topics and involve a number of characters, including Fr Dilke of New York, 'one of the most remarkable men of our Church in the States', who was modeled on Hecker himself:

> Himself a convert, and a man of large views and great sympathies, no one was better able to enter into the scruples and difficulties of religious Protestants on their first contact with Catholic doctrines and Catholic worship ... There was a stamp of originality about him; tall in stature, not exactly what we are used to call clerical in appearance, with a thoroughly American type of face, and with the national peaked beard instead of being closely shaven as is the custom with our clergy generally. I had met him before, without his clerical (religious) garb, on a journey on board a steamboat. At first, I remember, I had set him down as a Yankee skipper or trader of some sort; but when by chance we got into conversation, I found him a hard-headed man, shrewd, original, and earnest in his remarks; but when our conversation turned to religious topics, and got animated, I shall never forget how all that was common and national in his physique disappeared. And when he spoke of the mystery of God's love for man, his countenance seemed as it were transfigured, so that I felt that an artist would not wish for a better living model from which to paint a St Francis Xavier, making himself all things to all men amidst his shipmates on his voyage to the Indies.[8]

At the end of 1873, a year after Mrs Lockhart's death, *Catholic Opinion* was purchased by Bishop Vaughan of Salford and became a sort of supplement to *The Tablet*, which the Bishop also owned. Lockhart had in the meantime become preoccupied with *The Lamp*, which had been purchased by his mother in 1871. Although editorial responsibilities had been passed to her friend, Mrs Tayler, widow of Rev. Archdale Wilson Tayler of Stoke Newington and mother-in-law of Thomas Alder Pope, Fr

Lockhart acted as editorial adviser. The agreement with the proprietors of the journal had occurred so quickly that (not for the first time) he had not had time to seek permission from his superiors before acting. He explained in the first issue that 'I have allowed my name to be connected with *The Lamp* at the persuasion of friends, who think it sufficiently well known to be some guarantee that nothing shall appear in its pages which is against orthodoxy, charity or good taste'. Moreover, 'my colleagues and myself are willing to work without fee or reward of any kind: but it is our hope, sooner or later, to find remunerative employment for many able pens, which now rest idle, or else contribute to swell the tide of that ocean of non-Catholic literature, with a few marked exceptions, sets dead against us'. He hoped that the publication would 'blend amusement with instruction' and believed in the power of fiction as a 'form of teaching by parable', inspired by the recent successes of Wiseman's *Fabiola* and Newman's *Callista*.[9] However, he failed to win the active support of Newman, who assumed that if the publication included articles on the religious affairs of the moment, 'it is impossible, considering your position in London, that those Articles should not be in general accordance with the views of *The Tablet* and *Dublin Review*, and *id genus omne*; and such views have no attraction for me'.[10]

For Lockhart, *The Lamp* realized a long-held dream: 'we are deluged with non-Catholic literature, most attractive in appearance to our youth, when we have not one really attractive periodical in England and Ireland'.[11] The first number, for example, was illustrated by fine engravings and included an article on the 'Home of the Exiled Stuarts', an edifying account of the Franco-Prussian War (translated by Lady Herbert) and a tale by the magazine's former proprietor, Fanny Margaret Taylor, 'Eveleen's Victory or Ireland in the Days of Cromwell'.[12] Lockhart himself provided 'The Sacristan's Legacy', the first of a series of stories supposedly found among the papers of his former sacristan, who was given the *nom de plume* 'Edward Challice'.

The Lamp was printed by St Joseph's Press and was welcomed by the *Dublin Review*, which noted that 'the lack of an illustrated Catholic serial to compete with the numerous Protestant publications evincing both spirituality and talent in their lavish engravings, has long been felt'.[13] Lockhart's barrister friend, James Coen, later became editor, offering his work gratuitously, and was helped by his brother, Joseph, and sister, Nora, together with other volunteers. The magazine was eventually sold in 1890 to Charles Gilbert Ellis.

Controversial Works

Lockhart combined his concern for the production of popular Catholic literature with more learned and polemical contributions. At the time of his death, *The Tablet* noted an apparent contradiction in the priest's character: 'he had no enemy in this world, and he could not bear the thought of any estrangement in the world to come ... With all his love of peace, he was fated to be in the wars of controversy from first to last.'[14]

Lockhart's published works covered many subjects, including apologetics, autobiography, philosophy and hagiography. His first work was the life of St Gilbert of Sempringham for Newman's series of *Lives of the English Saints*. The young man was working on this when he was received into the Church and, as already noted, his tour of sites connected with the saint provided him with an excuse to visit Gentili at Loughborough. The manuscript was used and completed by Dalgairns and published in 1844.

Another early effort, in 1856, was a translation of Baron de Bussières' account of *The Conversion of Marie-Alphonse Ratisbonne*, a French Jew who became a Catholic after receiving a vision of Our Lady at the church of Sant'Andrea delle Fratte in Rome in January 1842. He went on to become a priest and devoted his life to apostolic work with the Jews, founding (with his brother) the Congregation of the Religious of Our Lady of Sion. Lockhart used his account of this celebrated conversion to show that miracles were not restricted to the Scriptures, being found even in the nineteenth century, and to demonstrate the importance of devotion to Mary and the saints. He also indirectly paid tribute to the grace of his own conversion: 'this narrative is of conversion, of Mary's tender pity towards those who know her not ... We know, by manifold experience – we have heard with our ears, and our fathers have declared it to us – the reality, the range, and the patience of that compassion'. Paraphrasing Newman, he prayed 'for those who, from amidst their gathering gloom, are casting wistful, timid looks towards the one unwavering light, that God's grace may still lead them on'.[15] Lockhart later returned to the subject of the Communion of Saints in a pamphlet of 1868.

It would be tedious to examine each of his works in detail, many of which were part of the large contemporary literature of apologetics and controversy aimed against the perceived threat of Protestantism. Many of his public lectures at Kingsland were published in the late 1850s, including *A Christmas Greeting to all Christians* (1856), *Popular Lectures on the Catholic Religion* (1858) and *Popular Lectures on Who is the Anti-Christ of Prophecy?* (1858). His 1864 *Reasons for Rationalists, and Thoughts for Thoughtful People* was designed as 'a General Address to the principles of Colenso, Renan, and other Rationalising writers of the day'.[16]

To give a feel for Lockhart's writings, let us examine three important themes: Corporate Reunion, Temporal Sovereignty, and Liturgy.

1) Lockhart and Corporate Reunion

Perhaps Lockhart's most controversial writings concerned the sensitive issue of Corporate Reunion, which sparked off many polemical exchanges during the second half of the nineteenth century. Although ecumenism belonged properly to a later chapter of Church history, there were several nineteenth-century initiatives that tried to promote unity, largely the product of enthusiasts and visionaries who soon found themselves at odds with the ecclesiastical authorities. As early as 1838, the convert Fr George Spencer, who later became a well-known Passionist, founded the 'Association of Universal Prayer for the Conversion of England' and preached on 'the Great Importance of a Reunion Between the Catholics and the Protestants of England and the Method of Effecting It', arousing the suspicions of the Vicars Apostolic (with the exception of Walsh) and the 'old Catholics'. He was helped in this scheme by Ambrose Phillipps, who went on to establish his own Association and publish a pamphlet on the subject in 1857, entitled *On the Future Unity of Christendom*, stressing the need for 'the three great denominations of

Christians' (Catholic, Greek and Anglican) to meet together.

Lockhart, a friend of Phillipps and a frequent visitor to his Leicestershire home of Grace Dieu, attended the inaugural meeting of the Association on 8 September 1857 at the London chambers of Frederick George Lee, an Anglican theologian and medievalist. Lockhart was one of the few Catholics present, though a number of founder members later converted, including Henry Oxenham and Henry Collins (then curate at St George's in the East and later to become a Cistercian). It was proposed 'that a Society, to be called the Association for the Promotion of the Unity of Christendom [APUC], be now formed for united prayer that visible unity may be restored to Christendom'. The Provost of St Ninian's, Perth, Edward Bowles Knottesford-Fortescue, was named as 'Master' and Lee as 'Secretary', and the purpose of the new organization defined as uniting 'in a bond of intercessory prayer members both of the clergy and laity of the Roman Catholic, Greek and Anglican Communions', who 'lament the divisions among Christians [but] look forward for their healing mainly to a Corporate Re-Union of those three great bodies which claim for themselves the inheritance of the priesthood and the name of Catholic'.[17]

Lockhart had his reservations about the Association but wrote to Phillipps that 'it seems to me that if people agree together in the main they may work together'. He added:

> Arguing from the progress that has been made during these fourteen years since I left the Establishment, I do not see that anyone has a right to blame those like yourself for the most sanguine expectations of what another ten years may produce. I confess I cannot but think that the Catholicising party cannot go much farther than they have gone without bringing on a collision with the State, with the high establishment party, and the evangelicals, as will oblige them to join the Catholic Church as individuals, feeling that their work has been stopped, or else form a kind of Free Church party for a while.[18]

He noticed that since being involved in the APUC, he 'had more Anglicans applying for instruction and actually received into the Church than during the two years previously', many of them readers of the *Union Newspaper*, which had been founded by Lee.[19]

By 1862 the Association boasted 8,000 members, roughly an

eighth of which was Catholic. Bishops Clifford of Clifton and Moriarty of Kerry expressed their support though did not formally join. However, Manning (then Provost of Westminster) and others were suspicious of the APUC and angered by some of the contributions in the *Union Review* (as Lee's journal was now called). These pushed forward the 'branch theory,' as had Phillipps' earlier pamphlet, and seemed to discourage individual conversions while corporate reunion was being discussed. Many of the writers, also, were disgruntled converts and their opinions could offend Catholic sensibilities, particularly a series of articles by Edmund Salisbury ffoulkes, 'Experiences of a "Vert"'.

Wiseman decided to place the matter of the APUC before Rome and Ullathorne was given the task of drafting a letter. He noted that 'the Anglican sect is tacitly assumed to be part of the catholic church' and that *The Union Review* created 'a refuge for imprudent catholics who can let their imaginations run to offensive lengths, where episcopal authority cannot reach them'.[20]

Catholic involvement in the Association was eventually banned by the Holy See on 16 September 1864, with the rescript *Ad Omnes Episcopos Angliae*. Not only did the Association encourage indifferentism and scandal, the document declared, but it wrongly assumed that 'the three Christian Communions, the Roman Catholic, the schismatic Greek, and the Anglican, though separated and divided one from another, yet with an equal right claim the title of Catholic'. Prayers for the return of 'heretics and schismatics' to the Church were to be commended, but it stressed 'that the faithful in Christ, and that ecclesiastics, should pray for Christian unity under the direction of heretics, and, worse still, according to an intention stained and infected by heresy in a high degree, can in no way be tolerated'.

Lockhart quickly withdrew his membership but revealed to Lee in 1887 that 'I have never changed my views as to the soundness of the original basis of the APUC. What we meant was misunderstood by those among us in authority, to their decision I was, however, bound to bow'.[21] He encouraged Phillipps to resign, drafting for him a statement to be sent to the *Union Review* 'in which you say that you "withdraw your name *under* protest as an act of submission to authority even though you hold that authority has been deceived by a false relation of facts".'[22]

Phillipps wrote to Wiseman a few days later, hoping that, despite the condemnation, he would let Rome know 'the real truth, that if they do not sympathize with it and encourage the *Romeward* longings of the Anglicans, it will be disastrous to the Catholic Church, and the movement will turn to the Greeks, and then settle down into *a fearful combination against the claims of the Papacy*'.[23] In another letter, he confessed

> I certainly never held or for a moment dreamt of holding any one of the Principles or propositions condemned by Cardinal Patrizi – and as a fact I know that no one who drew up the Programme of the APUC, including the Rev. Father Lockhart who proposed the very clause most objected to by Bishop Ullathorne, ever for an instant held such monstrous propositions, which have been so maliciously imputed to them by those who misrepresented the case to the Holy See.

Phillipps feared that the condemnation 'cannot fail to produce in the minds of Englishmen an unpleasant impression against Rome' at a moment when 'a powerful section of English churchmen and English politicians were looking to Rome with longing eyes'.[24]

Lockhart's views on the reunion of Churches continued to be 'liberal' in their generosity and placed him against the 'Ultramontane' party and its great organ, the *Dublin Review* under the editorship of W. G. Ward. This could clearly be seen in Lockhart's review of Pusey's *Eirenikon, the Possibilities and Difficulties of Reunion* (1866), originally published in the *Weekly Register* of 18 November and 2 December 1865. Pusey's work, the first of three such eirenicons, was the latest salvo in a debate with Manning over the Church of England. Pusey had stated that

> while I know that a very earnest body of Roman Catholics rejoice in all the workings of God the Holy Ghost in the Church of England (whatever they think of her), and are saddened in what weakens her who is, in God's hands, the great bulwark against infidelity in the land, others seemed to be in an ecstasy of triumph at the victory of Satan.[25]

Manning replied in *Workings of the Holy Spirit in the Church of England, a Letter to the Rev. E. B.Pusey*, in which he conceded that 'no Catholic ever denies the workings of the Spirit of God or the operations of grace' in the Church of England but denied that it was a bulwark against infidelity; indeed it 'must be recognised as the mother of all the intellectual and spiritual aberrations which now cover the face of England'. Pusey responded with *The Church of England, a Portion of Christ's One Holy Catholic Church and a Means of Restoring Visible Unity. An Eirenicon in a Letter to the Author of 'The Christian Year'.* It vigorously rejected Manning's charge that 'the Church of England is the cause of the unbelief in England' and surveyed the doctrines held in common: for example, there was a common rejection of the ancient heresies, a common recognition of the sacramental system and the 'real, objective presence of Christ's blessed body and blood in the Holy Eucharist', a common respect shown to the Church, which was one, holy, catholic and apostolic and was entrusted with a Divine authority. Pusey even suggested that Anglicans did not deny that the Church had a visible head, that they were 'not more independent of Rome than Africa was at the time of St Augustine'.

Pusey's intentions were admirable but the 'eirenical' nature of his work was compromised by the criticisms he made of current Roman usage, especially with regard to the invocation of the Blessed Virgin and the saints. He quoted the more 'extreme' writers of the day, including Faber and Ward, referred to 'forged Decretals' being at the heart of many topics of controversy and recounted how he had heard of the dogmatic definition of the Immaculate Conception (1854) 'in silent sorrow' since it was an obstacle to reunion and 'an insoluble difference between the modern Roman and the ancient Church'.[26]

Lockhart noted Pusey's errors and misunderstandings of Catholic doctrine, but broadly welcomed his 'peace offering' since it sought unity rather than division and was 'the most unequivocal advance in that direction made since the Reformation'.[27] The Rosminian was under no illusions about the imminence of any such reunion and he looked to the distant future: 'if Anglicans were liberated from State control, the Catholic element being set free would fly as it were of its own nature to the Centre of Unity'.[28] However, corporate reunion was surely to be preferred to perpetuated schism and it 'cannot be impossible, since it has been realised by the Church at the Council of Florence, as well as in various other transactions with separate bodies'.[29] Lockhart was careful to state that his views did not go beyond Wiseman's *Letter to Lord Shrewsbury* (1841), which had spoken encouragingly of reunion. He also addressed himself to the members of the (recently condemned) APUC, 'inviting them to join with us in petition, that all the Baptized may be brought within the Fold of Visible Unity under the Successor of Peter'.[30]

In the first part of his review, Lockhart implied that Newman had 'originally enunciated' the statement about the Church of England being 'the great Bulwark against infidelity in this land'. On 19 November Newman wrote to the *Weekly Register* denying this, stating that 'it does not express my real judgment concerning the Church of England'. What he had actually written in his recent *Apologia* was that 'doubtless the National Church has hitherto been a serviceable breakwater against doctrinal errors more fundamental than its own'.[31] However, Lockhart had drawn his former mentor into the debate and had forced a comparison between Manning's hostility towards the English Church and Newman's general sympathy.

Newman wrote to Pusey that he was 'much surprised and much rejoiced' by Lockhart's piece; only recently the journal 'would not insert a review of a book *because* it was *not* according to Ward, who *is* according to Manning, who *is* according to the Pope. But this review, though not against the mind of the Pope, is certainly contrary against [*sic*] Ward and Manning'.[32] Meanwhile, Newman congratulated Lockhart on the review but feared that 'there will be some attack on it'.[33]

Given the delicate nature of the subject, Lockhart had shown a draft to Manning, who had 'suggested some alterations but assented to its going in as expressing a conciliatory spirit'. However, after its publication the Archbishop complained that 'I had not made the Alterations as fully as he could have wished – that it had been attacked to him from several quarters and he had defended me – and he bids me write another article bringing out the incompatibility of the Anglican branch theory with any Catholic basis of reunion'.[34] This led Newman to write to Pusey:

> I abominate the fierce tyranny which would hinder an expression of opinion such as his [Lockhart], and calls to account everyone who

ventures to keep clear of ultra-isms. You may be sure that Manning is under the lash as well as others. There are men who would remonstrate with him, and complain of him at Rome if he did not go all lengths, – and in his position he can't afford to get into hot water, even tho' he were sure to get out of it.[35]

In the meantime, Lockhart wrote an article clarifying his position, as requested, published on 2 December as 'Dr Pusey's Eirenicon and the Difficulties of Reunion'.

The *Eirenicon* led to the writing of many articles and pamphlets. One of Lockhart's converts, Henry Nutcombe Oxenham, published *Dr Pusey's Eirenikon Considered in Relation to Catholic Unity: a Letter to Revd Fr Lockhart of the Institute of Charity* (1866). In his 'Preliminary Remarks', he addressed Lockhart:

> You have never sneered at the Catholic aspirations, or ignored the conscientious difficulties, or slighted the doctrinal approximations, or laughed at the ritual developments, or mistrusted the sincerity, or discredited the zeal, or repelled the friendly advances of those without our pale, but who in heart, even when they know it not, are often very near us.[36]

Newman himself reluctantly stepped into the fray and published *A Letter Addressed to the Rev. E. B. Pusey, D.D., on Occasion of His Eirenicon* (1866). He noted that Pusey had discharged his olive branch as if from a catapult and tried to present a true eirenicon by focusing on the Church's Marian beliefs and devotions. He told James Hope-Scott that writing about Pusey's work was 'the most inoffensive way of alluding to Faber and Ward' and rejecting their exaggerations:

> ... how can you say that, either as to the doctrine about the B.M.V. or the Holy See, English Catholics are extreme? Who have been, in the passing generation, our chief writers? Cardinal Wiseman, Dr Lingard, Dr Rock, Mr Tierney, Dr Husenbeth, which of them is extreme on either doctrine?[37]

At issue were deeper divisions within the Catholic community. Lockhart had earlier written to Newman that 'Wardian Christianity is in the ascendant with us here' and feared that 'we shall have precious souls dropping off from us sooner or later'. Those who dissented from the 'Wardian' view 'must remain in deep silence, or speak out and be branded as "unsound Catholics".' In the same letter, Lockhart stated his opposition to the definition of papal infallibility and thought that Catholics in England, France and Germany should clearly declare their opposition to 'these new views', which he considered an obstacle to reunion.[38] In his reply, Newman mentioned the dilemma that they faced: 'if we do not speak out, we let an exaggerated doctrine be mistaken for Catholic truth to the injury both of Catholics and Protestants,' but 'if we do speak, then we create a great scandal'.[39] As Dessain notes, 'when an Anglican, Newman's mission had been to restore Revealed Religion in its integrity: now his duty lay in moderating excess.'[40]

Lockhart returned to the issues raised in the debate throughout the late 1860s. In 1866 he wrote *The Communion of Saints; or, the Catholic Doctrine concerning our Relation to the Blessed Virgin, the Angels, and the Saints*, which the *Dublin Review* praised for 'the union of orthodoxy and moderation which F. Lockhart exhibits, in dealing with the alleged excesses of Catholic language concerning our Blessed Lady, on which Dr Pusey has laid so much stress.'[41] Lockhart thought the fault lay with English Protestant readers:

> Italian Catholics, speaking to pious Italian Catholics, would be understood by them according to the whole tradition of Catholic faith in which they had been taught from their mother's knee; but the same words translated into English, and read by English Protestants whose early training had not been tinctured by the same accurate theology and living tradition, would most likely be misunderstood.[42]

In an 1868 pamphlet *Secession or Schism*, Lockhart reviewed a posthumously printed sermon by John Mason Neale that promoted the 'Branch Theory' and laid down that 'those who leave the Anglican Church have been led by Satan, under the guise of an angel of light, into a great sin'. Lockhart was careful to 'utterly deny that Anglicans form any part of the visible Church' and to attack Neale's 'futile attempt to charge certain of our doctrines as modern'. Lockhart posed the question, 'would S. Bernard, if he returned to earth, feel himself most at home at an

Anglican Evensong, from the Book of Common Prayer, or joining in the old *Salve Regina* at Catholic Vespers, and in the Litany of the Blessed Virgin at Benediction?' However, he concluded,

> for my own part, I must say that I have no inclination to hold controversy with Anglicans; on the contrary, I have watched the movement for five-and-twenty years with the deepest interest and sympathy, I am sure the impulse of that movement is from God, and have not a doubt whither it is tending and what will be its result, so sure am I of this, that not knowing that I can help them on, I have always preferred to leave Anglicans to the guidance of the grace of God, acting on those Catholic premises which have become fixed principles in their minds, rather than to put in my own oar to make or mar the work.[43]

At the time of the Vatican Council it was suggested that reunion should be included among the subjects discussed by the Fathers. Victor de Buck, a Jesuit who had written a favourable review of the *Eirenicon* in 1866, told Pusey that he had suggested to Cardinal Billio, Secretary to the Inquisition, that a small committee should be appointed in Rome, under the Cardinal, to discuss reunion and open negotiations: 'all converts, except, perhaps, Lockhart and Newman, ought, he thought, to be rigidly excluded from this committee'.[44]

Nothing came of the plan and the Council that opened in 1869 put an end, in Pusey's mind, to any useful discussions regarding corporate reunion. Lockhart continued to pray and hope for unity. In 1881 he confessed, 'I have always retained a great sympathy with my former co-religionists, and have never felt that I could treat the Ritualistic movement with less than the respect due to the religious conviction of earnest men.'[45] Though writing as an apologist rather than a theologian, Lockhart made a modest contribution to these attempts to promote reunion in the 1860s, despite the volatile ecclesial environment, which prefigured the ecumenical movement of the twentieth century and more recent developments, including *Anglicanorum coetibus* (2009).

2) The Roman Question – *Non Possumus* (1868)

Non Possumus or the Temporal Sovereignty of the Pope and the Roman Question (1868) originated as two sermons preached at Kingsland during the Garibaldian invasion, when Manning directed parishes to have 'special devotions and sermons explaining the rights of the Pope and his spiritual and temporal capacity'.[46] Lockhart argued that the spiritual and temporal powers of the Pope could not be morally separated; 'both one and the other were together in the intention of God, were manifested gradually, and grew up together under the action of natural and supernatural causes'.[47] Lockhart stated that 'if the Romans have any zeal for a United Italy, it is for a federal union of the Italian State, with the Pope at their head.'[48] This, indeed, is what Rosmini and Manzoni had originally suggested. Romans were not Italians and had their own nationality:

> much as the tradesmen of Oxford and Cambridge live by the Universities, so do the lay inhabitants of Rome live by the ecclesiastical population, and by the constant influx of visitors, lay and clerical, from all parts of the world ... With the free consent of the Romans, Rome can never become a secular city, and sink from the Capital of Christendom into the Capital of Italy.[49]

Young Catholic men all over the world were joining the Pontifical Zouaves to defend the Vicar of Christ, and special collections, like the Fund of SS Peter and Michael, were being made for the cause. *Non possumus* reflected the spirit of the 1860s by ending on a militant note: the small Papal Army was 'but the vanguard of that host which could, if necessary, be arrayed by the Catholic World'. Lockhart hoped that '"the sons of the Crusaders" will guard the Holy City, and beat back and crush the hosts of the "Disciples of Voltaire".'[50] These hopes were ultimately to be disappointed but Lockhart remained a defender of the Pope's temporal sovereignty. In one of his last works, on the *Roman Chasuble*, he related a convert friend once telling him with great enthusiasm: 'I love to see the dogs running about free in St Peter's, in and out between the legs of the Swiss Guards. It seems as if they too felt at home in their Father's house.' In a footnote, the author added that 'since the Italian occupation the dogs no longer frequent the churches. It would seem that they, too, have joined the party of the Quirinal.'[51]

Non Possumus would have been more pleasing to Manning than Lockhart's recent reflections on corporate reunion. The Archbishop himself argued 'that the temporal power of the Pope is ordained of God', that it had 'been the root, and the sustaining principle of Christian Europe' and that, consequently, 'the dissolution of the temporal power of the Pope would bring with it the dissolution of Christian Europe'.[52]

Newman, on the other hand, was one of the few leading English Catholics to distance himself from demands for the preservation of the temporal sovereignty. He professed himself to be 'lukewarm' on the issue and was even rumoured to have contributed to a fund in support of Garibaldi. He predicted that 'Italy requires a thorough castigation and clearing out. And, when matters are finally settled, he [the Pope] will be stronger and firmer than he has been for a long while.' Above all, he thought that 'temporal dependence was not inconsistent with spiritual independence *in se*'.[53]

Unsurprisingly, Lockhart's singing to the Archbishop's tune disturbed the critic of *The Union Review*, the mouthpiece of the APUC, who would have been only too aware of the recent controversy. The pamphlet was 'a mere milk-and-water reproduction of the same extravagant theory Dr Manning has familiarised us with *usque ad nauseam* in everything he has spoken or written – pastorals, pamphlets, speeches, sermons – for the last half-dozen years or more'. At least the author possessed 'too much both of moderation and of Christian courtesy to indulge in the rabid denunciations and insolent dogmatism' so typical of the Ultramontane party. The critic concluded: 'we are sorry to see Saul for the first time among the Ultramontane prophets, and the best wish we can form for him is a speedy return to better and more congenial company'.[54]

3) Rood Screens and Chasubles

Lockhart turned his attentions to liturgy at the beginning and end of his career as a controversialist. As a young priest he was probably partly responsible for a passionate exchange of views in

The Rambler and elsewhere on the subject of rood screens. A letter from 'A Country Priest' to *The Rambler*, published on 15 July 1848, has been attributed to the young Rosminian, then working at Shepshed. Indeed in April 1851 Newman wrote concerning 'the controversy about Skreens' to Bishop Ullathorne and stated, 'I believe it took its rise in a letter of F. Lockhart to the *Rambler*, written without any intention at all of making mischief.'[55]

The letter in question asked about the 'theological objections' to rood-screens, with reference to the recent opening of St George's, Southwark, and the criticisms that had been made of the new screen. Whether or not it was the writer's intention, the letter sparked off the famous 'rood screen controversy' and eventually resulted in Pugin's *Treatise on Chancel Screens and Rood Lofts: their Antiquity, Use and Symbolic Signification* (1851). The debate involved, firstly, a liturgical principle. 'Anti-screenites' held that the faithful should have an uninterrupted view of the sanctuary, particularly important moments such as the elevation of the Host or exposition of the Blessed Sacrament during the *Quarant' Ore*. Pugin and his fellow 'screenites', on the other hand, saw 'the idea of room worship, and the all-seeing principle' as 'a perfect novelty' and argued that a rood screen maintained a sense of mystery and sacredness.[56] Indeed, according to Michael Trappes-Lomax, 'this idea of the sacrosanct quality of rood screens had developed in Pugin's mind in the course of his studies of ancient examples. They do not appear in his earliest churches'.[57] Also at issue was 'whether Renaissance Italian or Mediaeval English ideas were to prevail in Catholicism in England'.[58]

Whether or not Lockhart was responsible for this passionate exchange of views, it is interesting that many years later he erected a chancel screen at Ely Place, as was fitting in a medieval building.

The Chasuble, written during Lockhart's last year, attacked the pointed gothic style of vestments so beloved of Pugin and examined what he believed to be the correct shape – such *minutiae* were of great concern to Victorian Catholics. This pamphlet was originally inspired by an old chasuble Lockhart had seen in November 1852, when he was preaching a mission in Galway with Fr Rinolfi. It was 'of ample and genuine Roman form', like the ones seen in well-known portraits of St Charles Borromeo and St Philip

Neri. Lockhart had made sure he took patterns of the Galway chasuble, which proved useful many years later when he commissioned vestments to be made for Ely Place. Passing through Bruges in 1891, a visit made in connection with the proposed Rosminian House of Aspirants at Warenghem, Lockhart undertook research in the public library and produced a small work on the chasuble and its correct shape.

Lockhart was concerned to avoid two extremes. First there were the vestments 'improperly called *Gothic*' and 'cut into a pointed form behind and in front'. He wrote that 'it has always seemed to me, though I have an abounded admiration of everything else that Pugin did, that this form of vestment was not a true return to that of the ancient medieval chasuble.'[59] They represented 'only a poor, superficial imitation' of medieval vestments, which were circular; 'of all sizes and shapes, according to the fancy of the priest, or of some pious benefactress', the 'gothic' chasuble prevented 'the restoration of the really majestic and authoritative chasuble of the *Roman Pontifical*'.[60] Lockhart also questioned whether they were tolerated or actually permitted by the authorities.

Lockhart was equally critical of

> the abortion of the chasuble that pervades France at the present day. Fiddle-shaped in front, not coming down to the knees, stiff with buckram, or paper pasted on the poverty-stricken half-cotton-half-silk material of Lyons manufacture. They are as stiff as tea-boards and crack if they are bent.[61]

He criticized the way in which convenience and private judgment determined the shape of the vestment rather than the guidelines and traditions of the Church: 'having once begun to clip the vestments; in a hot country like Italy, the lighter the vestment the better for the convenience of celebrant'.[62]

For Lockhart, a true Roman chasuble came down to near the heels and was wide and square behind. Vestments that were pointed were 'as great a departure from ancient traditionary forms as the vestment reaching hardly to the knees, behind and in front, cut into a shape of a fiddle'. Lockhart hoped that the restoration of the traditional design would gain the sanction of Rome, though he would be disappointed. The wider debate about the correct design of vestments continued into the following century and was taken up by proponents of the Liturgical Movement. A 1925 rescript issued by the Congregation of Rites actually forbade the use of fuller vestments in the Roman Rite, although a decree in 1957 left the matter to the prudence of the local bishop and chasubles of ample form (though not always of the design or artistic quality envisaged by Lockhart) soon entered common usage.

'A Symposium of the Nether Gods'

As at Kingsland, Lockhart provided lodgings for young men at Ely Place to preserve them from the corruptions of the great capital and strengthen their Faith. They were encouraged to help him both in the parish – serving at the altar or singing in the choir – as well as in various publishing projects. Perhaps the most notable of his young protégés was Wilfrid Meynell, who came from a northeastern Quaker family and was received into the Church at the age of eighteen at the Dominican church in Newcastle. When he came to London he quickly found a home at Ely Place. According to his daughter, Viola Meynell, the young man

> assisted in the work of the parish, and caught a life-long habit of being unable to pass a beggar without making a momentary friend of him. He shared the Fathers' habits of self-denial, and never abandoned them. He had a unique opportunity for an entry into Catholic journalism, and in the pages of *The Lamp*, edited by Father Lockhart, appeared his serial 'Lost and Found, or the Story of a Girl's Life' (which all too inevitably proved to be the story of her death) with its now nostalgic illustrations of whiskered middle-aged-looking young men, and fichued and full-skirted young women swooning.[63]

One day in 1876, he read in the *Pall Mall Gazette* a review of *Preludes*, a book of poems written by Alice Thompson, a convert whose sister would become the celebrated war artist, Lady Elizabeth Butler. Meynell formed a strong desire to meet the young poetess and told Lockhart, who knew the Thompson family. The priest arranged for Meynell to be invited to an afternoon gathering at their house. It proved a great success and, on New Year's Day 1877, Wilfrid and Alice announced their engagement. This took even Lockhart by surprise but he wrote to Alice the same day: 'You have determined to link your lot with one who is chivalrous in honour, tender in pity and love and who will be faithful to the end and true as steel in weal and woe. For him you have been willing to forgo a more brilliant but not, as I believe, a happier lot'.[64]

Wilfrid's lack of means was a serious problem in the eyes of his prospective father-in-law. In an attempt to help, Lockhart offered him editorship of *The Lamp* but this would hardly add to his income. In the end, Mr Thompson relented, thanks in part to the Rosminian's intercession – in a letter of 5 February, Alice mentioned a 'sweet little note' from Lockhart that touched her father and reduced her mother to tears.[65] The couple was married in the Servite church on Fulham Road on 16 April. The ceremony was conducted by the bishop of Northampton, Dr Bagshawe, and Alice wore the golden rosary of Mary, Queen of Scots, a precious family heirloom.

The Meynells went on to make a valuable contribution to Catholic publishing. Wilfrid edited *The Pen* (1880–1), *The Weekly Register* (1881–98, at Manning's insistence) and *Merry England* (1883–95), which first published the poems of Francis Thompson. Viola Meynell later reflected that her father had learnt from Lockhart 'that complete brotherliness with the uncouth, the ragged, and the unpresentable, which when Francis Thompson crossed his path made him always uncritical of his outward condition'. Alice continued to write poetry and, following the death of Tennyson, was even considered for the position of Poet Laureate.

Another member of the priest's literary circle was Edmund Bishop, whom Lockhart had received into the Church at Clapton in 1867. Bishop would become an important scholar in his own right and collaborated with several prominent clerical writers; in later years he researched for Stanton's *Menology* of British saints and Gasquet's works on monastic history. Lockhart provided him with some early experience in the late 1860s when Bishop researched many of the arguments used in the priest's series on apologetics in *Catholic Opinion* (later published as *The Old Religion*) and wrote an article for the journal on 'Chalcedon and the Creed'.

The poet Lionel Pigot Johnson, cousin of Lord Alfred Douglas and (for a time) friend of Oscar Wilde, was received into the Church by Lockhart at Ely Place on 22 June 1891 and lived nearby in Gray's Inn Square. Lockhart did not live to see his published works, such as *The Dark Angel* (and, indeed, *Pax Christi*, dedicated to the memory of the Rosminian), or his tragic decline into alcoholism. Wilde said of him: 'every morning at 11 o'clock you can see him come out very drunk from the Café Royal and hail the first passing perambulator.'[66] Another colourful literary character known to Lockhart was Henry Nutcombe Oxenham, a former Anglican minister who had been received into the Church by Manning in 1857 and begun studies for the priesthood at St Edmund's, Ware. He eventually left, though he continued to wear ecclesiastical dress for the rest of his life since he had received Minor Orders and also apparently believed in the validity of his Anglican Orders. He hoped for the Reunion of Christendom, being active in the APUC, and refused to accept Papal Infallibility at the First Vatican Council. However, despite remaining on the margins of the Church and maintaining a close friendship with Döllinger, Lockhart remained faithful to him as a friend and attended him on his deathbed in March 1888. The priest read to the dying man the *Dream of Gerontius* and they soon reminisced about their mentor, both concluding that 'there was no one like Newman'.[67]

Towards the end of his life, Lockhart was in contact with Wilfrid Scawen Blunt, the poet and breeder of Arabian horses, who had grown up at Petworth House and whose mother was a Catholic convert and a friend of Manning and the Lockhart family. Blunt met with Lockhart during stays in Rome and Dublin and the Rosminian was an occasional guest at Crabbet Park. The younger man lived a hedonistic lifestyle but went through periods of repentance in which he returned to the Catholic Faith – and during these moments he sometimes went to Lockhart. In April 1888, for example, Blunt had met the priest at Epsom and went on to stay at Ely Place, intent on living a better life. 'My meeting Father Lockhart at Epsom was a Providence, as I have confessed my sins', he wrote. 'I suppose there never was a worse record than mine has been in certain ways'.[68] Lockhart not only acted as an occasional confessor but was sympathetic to Blunt's outspoken views regarding Home Rule.

In 1892 the bohemian figure of Frederick Rolfe, self-styled as

Baron Corvo, made a brief entrance into life at Ely Place. He had been recently expelled from the Scots College, Rome, and had since been supported by various long-suffering benefactors, including the Duchess Sforza-Cesarini, at whose palace in Genzano he had spent a happy summer. Now the writer found himself in London, homeless and penniless. It seems that he had asked for lodgings at St Joseph's Convent, Chelsea, but was turned away and, unwilling to try a 'common Lodging-house', made the long walk to Ely Place. He explained his situation to Lockhart after morning Mass and was given lodgings at the Priest's House. In an attempt to help the penniless writer, Lockhart wrote a letter to Meynell asking him to help the failed seminarian. Unfortunately the communication was left unopened and Rolfe was turned away eight times, although there was a correspondence between the two men the following year, in which Rolfe referred to 'Fr Lockhart (on whom be blessing)'.[69]

Lockhart encouraged female writers as well. He is described as a 'dear and intimate friend' of Mary Howitt, a convert from Quakerism and author of the famous poem *The Spider and the Fly*. He attended her as she lay dying during a visit to Rome in 1888.[70] Younger female writers also received his patronage, including Theodora Louisa Lane Clarke, whose literary debut was commissioned by Lockhart for *The Lamp* following her conversion. Her marriage to Captain Bartholomew ('Bartle') Teeling, a former Papal Zouave decorated by Pius IX, was the first to be solemnized at Ely Place.

After Lockhart's death in 1892, some of his 'disciples' paid tribute to his cherished memory. Bernard Whelan stated in rather exaggerated tones:

> In him the genius of friendship combined the authority of paternity with the equality of fraternity ... Generosity, hospitality, sympathy were his clothing, more real and more obvious than his sombre cassock. His humour and his laughing smile transformed that pathetic front kitchen in the basement [of Ely Place], which was his dining room, into a symposium of the nether gods.[71]

Here the Rosminian was following in the footsteps of Newman, who also had a great genius for friendship. He did not impose upon others a set of rules or propositions but worked through personal contact, 'heart speaking unto heart'. Wilfrid Meynell eulogized that 'perhaps one of the secrets of his [Lockhart's] life was this. So delightful himself, he brought out only what was delightful in others. Therefore were all men delightful, at least to him. And as for him, he was delightful always to all men.' He also displayed mildness in temperament; his 'instincts were all towards freedom – in Religion, in politics and in the details of daily life'.[72]

Notes

1. Gillow, *Bibliographical Dictionary of English Catholics*, vol. iii, p. 298.
2. Hirst, 'Necrology', p. 339.
3. ASIC AG 118/694 (Lockhart to Pagani, 8 March 1874?).
4. *Tablet*, 27 January 1872, pp. 116–17.
5. ASIC AG 118/608 (Lockhart to Ceroni, 26 March 1868).
6. Lockhart, *The Old Religion*, Preface (unnumbered).
7. *Irish Ecclesiastical Record*, February 1884, p. 135.
8. Lockhart, *The Old Religion*, p. 188.
9. *The Lamp*, 1 July 1871, p. 4.
10. Newman, LD XXV, pp. 346–7 (Newman to Lockhart, 19 June 1871).
11. ASIC 118/379 (Lockhart to Provincial, 14 June 1871).
12. The popular author of *Tyborne and Who Went Hither*, who had just founded the Poor Servants of the Mother of God as Mother Mary Magdalen.
13. *Dublin Review*, vol.17 (1871), p. 521.
14. *Tablet*, 21 May 1892, p. 804.
15. Lockhart, *The Conversion of Marie-Alphonse Ratisbonne*, p. 17.
16. *Tablet*, 16 July 1864, p. 458.
17. Chapman, 'Fantasy of Reunion', p. 60.
18. Purcell, *Life and Letters of Ambrose Phillipps de Lisle*, vol. i, p. 396.
19. Ibid., p. 398.
20. Pawley, *Rome and Canterbury*, pp.174–5.
21. F. G. Lee, *Reginald Pole* (1888), p. 287 fn.
22. Purcell, *Life and Letters of Ambrose Phillipps de Lisle*, vol. i, p. 399.
23. AAW V1/25 (Phillips to Wiseman, 26 December 1864).
24. AAW V1/25 (Phillips to Wiseman, 3 January 1864 – probably dated in error and should be 1865).
25. Liddon, *Life of Pusey*, iv, p. 95.
26. Pusey, *Eirenicon*, p. 121.
27. Lockhart, *Possibilities and Difficulties of Reunion*, p. 31.
28. Ibid., p. 50.
29. Ibid., p. 5.
30. Ibid., p. 29.
31. Newman, LD XXII, p. 105 (letter of Newman, 19 November 1865).

The Apostolate of the Press

32. Ibid., p.106 (Newman to Pusey, 19 November 1865).
33. Ibid., p.107 (Newman to Lockhart, 21 November 1865).
34. Ibid., p. 107 fn (Lockhart to Newman, 22 November 1865).
35. Ibid., p. 109 (Newman to Pusey, 23 November 1865).
36. Oxenham, *Dr Pusey's Eirenikon Considered in Relation to Catholic Unity*, p. 4.
37. Newman, LD XXII, p.112 (Newman to Hope-Scott, 26 November 1865).
38. Ibid., p. 84 (Lockhart to Newman, 24 October 1865).
39. Ibid., p. 85 (Newman to Lockhart, 26 October 1865).
40. Dessain, *John Henry Newman*, p. 132.
41. *Dublin Review*, January 1869, p. 222.
42. Lockhart, *Communion of Saints*, p. 6.
43. Lockhart, *Secession or Schism*, p. 21.
44. Liddon, *Life of Pusey*, iv, p. 178.
45. *Tablet*, 30 July 1881, p. 180.
46. ASIC AG 118/306 (Lockhart to Bertetti, 20 December 1867).
47. Lockhart, *Non possumus*, p. 15.
48. Ibid., p. 29.
49. Ibid., pp. 30–1.
50. Lockhart, *Non possumus*, p. 53.
51. Lockhart, *The Chasuble*, p. 6.
52. Manning, *Temporal Power of the Pope*, p. 2.
53. MacDougall, *The Acton-Newman Relations*, pp. 64–5.
54. *The Union Review* (1868), pp. 284–5.
55. See Margaret Belcher, *A. W. N. Pugin: An annotated critical bibliography*, pp. 250–1, which provides some notes on the subject. An editorial note in Newman LD XIV, 258n, identifies the 'country priest' as 'presumably' Lockhart. Sadly, this remains unproven and possibly unprovable.
56. Trappes-Lomax, *Pugin*, p. 230.
57. Ibid., p. 222.
58. Ibid., p. 226.
59. Lockhart, *The Chasuble*, p. 4.
60. Ibid., p. 5.
61. Ibid., p. 17.
62. Ibid., p. 19.
63. Meynell, *Francis Thompson and Wilfrid Meynell*, p. 5.
64. Ibid., p. 6.
65. Ibid., p. 8.
66. Ellmann, *Oscar Wilde*, p. 391.
67. Tristram, *Newman and his Friends*, p. 33.
68. Longford, *A Pilgrimage of Passion*, p. 264.
69. Benkowitz, 'Frederick Rolfe, Baron Corvo, writes to Wilfrid Meynell', p. 16.
70. Howitt, *Mary Howitt*, vol. 2, p. 358.
71. Whelan, 'Father Lockhart', p. 6.
72. Meynell, 'Further Reminiscences of Father Lockhart', pp. 162–3.

Chapter IX

The Rosminian Question

On 27 August 1875, shortly after the move to Ely Place, Lockhart was named Procurator General of the Institute of Charity, while continuing as Rector in London. This important new role necessitated his spending half the year in Rome, where he liaised with the Holy See on behalf of the Institute and lived on the Via Alessandrina, beside the Forum.[1] He worked closely with two Generals: the saintly Giuseppe Gioacchino Cappa, who governed the Institute for three and a half years before succumbing to heart problems, and, from 1877, Luigi Lanzoni.

The period saw some growth for the Institute. Foundations were made, for example, at Schillingsfürst in Germany (1877) and Clonmel in Ireland (1884), and a new English novitiate was opened at Wadhurst in Sussex (1882), much to Lockhart's delight. However, these achievements were overshadowed by the so-called 'Rosminian Question', which caused much ink to be spilt and old tensions with the Jesuits to be re-ignited.

The decree *Dimittantur* of 1854 had vindicated Rosmini's writings but its effects were limited since it was never made fully public. Pius IX had no wish to unduly humiliate the Society of Jesus, certain members of which had been the chief supporters of the condemnation. As a result Rosmini and the Institute continued to be followed by a dark cloud. Suggestions were frequently made in the press that the verdict on Rosmini was unresolved and that further examinations of his writings were needed. In the main, matters calmed down until 1876, when an anti-Rosminian campaign began in the pages of the *Osservatore Romano* and the Milanese *Osservatore Cattolico*. This tried to restrict the meaning of the 1854 decree and once again question Rosmini's orthodoxy.

In 1879 Leo XIII published his Encyclical *Aeterni Patris*, making St Thomas Aquinas the standard for philosophical teaching throughout the Catholic world. A demonstration was arranged in Rome for 7 March 1880 to present addresses to the Pope thanking him for the letter and Lockhart was chosen to represent the English Province of the Institute. Such representation was important because there were claims that Rosmini's teaching was opposed to that of the 'Angelic Doctor'. One 'party' claimed that *Aeterni Patris* had implicitly condemned Rosmini and petitioned the Pope to go one step further and make it explicit, so that 'his adherents may either be led to abandon his system, or else stand confessed as no longer owning the name of Catholic'.[2]

Lockhart used his visit to Rome to seek a private audience with the Holy Father. He was able to use his connections, especially now that his old mentor, Newman, had recently been elevated to the Sacred College. The new cardinal promised to write a letter of introduction for Lockhart:

> I have said to the Pope that you are an old friend of mine, one of a set of men who are *optimi nominis*, that you want an audience of his Holiness and deserve it ... I have ever had a great reverence for Father Rosmini and should rejoice to find that your anxiety was at an end but I am ashamed to say that I never read any of his works.[3]

Years earlier, in October 1846, Newman had nearly met with Rosmini during a visit to Milan, though the latter sent a message saying 'that he did not call since he did not speak Latin, nor Newman Italian'. Newman confessed then, 'I cannot get at the bottom of his philosophy. I wish to believe it is all right, yet one has one's suspicions.'[4]

Lockhart gained the desired papal audience and described it in his *Life* of Rosmini, rather confusingly referring to himself in both the first and third person:

> The Pope received him most graciously. After he had made the usual acts of reverence, the Holy Father bade him rise, and with great kindness of manner thus addressed him: 'Father Lockhart, I am informed by Cardinal Newman that you Rosminians are much grieved, fearing that it is my intention to condemn the works of your Founder Rosmini. This is not true; up to this moment such a thought

has not entered my mind. In my Encyclical *Aeterni Patris*, in which there is not a word that I had not well weighed, there is nothing that has any application to Rosmini. It is true that I have commended the works of St Thomas as the foundation of Philosophical teaching, but I have never intended to exclude the study of other writers. Let Rosmini and other authors be read, in order to throw light upon questions, but let St Thomas be taken as the text-book.'

I replied, 'Holy Father, I am greatly consoled by your Holiness's words, but Cardinal Newman has not quite expressed our meaning. We are not afraid that your Holiness will ever condemn Rosmini; but we cannot accept the censures of Journalism as if this was the voice of the Holy See. We believe that in following Rosmini we are following St Thomas, but if ever the Holy See should instruct us that we are in the wrong, we are prepared to obey. We are Rosminians by conviction, but first of all we are obedient children of the Holy See.'

To this the Pope replied, 'Bravo; and are all your Italian Fathers of the same mind as you English Rosminians?' I assured the Holy Father that this was the case. He was evidently well pleased with the few words I said to him. I then asked leave to present a little work I had written some years before, *On the Temporal Sovereignty of the Popes and the Roman Question*, saying, 'Holy Father, you will see from this work, which has the *imprimatur* of Cardinal Manning, and which was published with the sanction of my Religious Superior, that we Rosminians are not the *Liberali* they report us to be, in the Italian Journals.' At this the Pope laughed, saying, 'No, no, I know you are not *Liberali*, but excellent Religious.'

He then began to ask me many questions as to religious affairs in England and the work there done by our Institute. The audience must have lasted nearly half an hour. I was then preparing to make my exit in the usual way, by walking backwards to the door and making the three customary genuflections. But the Pope rose from his seat, and with most unusual condescension conducted me to the door, which was opened from without. The Holy Father then stood conversing with me at the entrance of the Apostolic Chamber in sight of the crowd of officials and persons waiting in the *Anti-camera*. He inquired very affectionately after the health of Cardinal Newman, sending him his blessing as I knelt to take leave.[5]

In June 1880 the Congregation of the Index issued a declaration confirming that *Dimittantur*, which had been continually devalued by critics of Rosmini, 'signifies only this – that the work which is "dismissed" has not been prohibited'.[6]

The year 1882 marked a new phase in the controversy, reaching a climax in the publication of *Rosminianism, a synthesis of ontologism and pantheism* by the Jesuit Fr Giovanni Maria Cornoldi. The title neatly summed up the book's argument. It was immediately criticized by supporters of Rosmini but, as Belti points out, 'from this time on, the accusation had been made, and everyone knows how, once things (whether true or false) have been put into people's minds, they remain there through inertia'. Moreover 'the men who maintained these accusations were from other points of view well worthy of respect; it was therefore easier to believe what they said'.[7]

Lockhart stated that 'the violence and calumnies of the Jesuits have caused a reaction throughout Italy'.[8] He told Meynell that Cornoldi's '*rechauffé* of the old objections is really an insult to the Holy See, which commanded silence. Something will have to be done soon to restrain the licence to calumniate exercised by a portion of the Italian Catholic press'.[9] The Institute was 'doing our best to bring good influences to bear on the Pope' but Lockhart compared the struggle to that of David and Goliath and feared 'the blunder of Galileo' would be repeated if Rosmini was condemned.

> There is no doubt we have been shamefully treated by Leo XIII. The permission tacitly accorded to the *Civiltà* to break the precept of silence and the permission to Cornaldi to publish his book in Rome are enough to make us lose all hope in the good will of the Pope – but, for all that, I look not to Gioacchino Pecci but to the Vicar of Christ, who in this capacity must act as Pope and not as a private doctor.[10]

The Rosminians continued to find themselves under suspicion. In November 1882 Lockhart complained to Manning:

> the persistent calumnies of the *Civiltà* &c have this effect: that no one who comes under the influence of any priest in England who is at all in the current of the stream of Roman talk, has a chance of being allowed to come to the Rosminian Order. I have quite lately had instances of this in the case of the London Oratorians and Oblates of St Charles. A priest recently staying in Innsbruck found a number of well-educated German priests who had never heard of Rosmini except as a heretic or atheist like Kant, Hegel &c.[11]

Moreover, 'some of our convert priests, who have been to Rome come back, if not *Gesuiti, Gesuitante* in the sense that the *Compagnia* is a sort of barometer of orthodoxy and that which they condemn will, later on, be condemned by the Church ... So, what is read in the *Civiltà* is taken like the words of prophecy'.[12]

In 1883, Lockhart was asked by the Cardinal Vicar of Rome to be one of the English preachers at the Epiphanytide devotions at Sant'Andrea della Valle, a custom inaugurated by St Vincent Pallotti in 1836. Lockhart himself saw the invitation as highly significant and used it to further his defense of Rosmini at a critical moment. He noted,

> my name was published on the doors of all the Churches of Rome and in the Journals of the Vatican, amongst the appointments of the Cardinal Vicar to preach the English sermons in Rome ... The moral of this was understood in Rome to be that, notwithstanding all the accusations of *heterodoxy* against the Rosminians, the representative of the Order in Rome was selected, with the full sanction of the Pope, to be one of the public instructors in *Christian Doctrine*.[13]

Moreover in 1883 and 1884 he was chosen as one of the Lenten preachers at Sant'Andrea delle Fratte and the Santissima Trinità on the Via Condotti respectively. This led him to be introduced to the Pope once again, along with the other preachers; in 1884 the Holy Father was proudly reported by Lockhart as commenting '*Ah P. Lockhart le predica agli Inglesi, bene, bene.*'[14]

In a leader in *The Tablet*, Cornoldi was quoted as reporting a private audience with the Pope, who was interested to hear of improvements in the philosophical curriculum at colleges like Stonyhurst but stressed that the professors 'should strictly adhere to the teaching of St Thomas, and entirely reject the doctrines of more recent schools and especially those of Rosmini, which are now in some favour in this country'.[15] Lockhart wrote to the paper, stating that 'the Rosminians claim only that their School of Philosophy is free to be studied' and that 'remarks of the Pope, made in private audience, should be repeated with great caution'.[16] He remained convinced, through his personal connections with the Holy See, that the pope would not do anything dramatic. Lockhart had been assured by the Secretary of the Index that 'the Rosminian affair is not before the Holy See and it would never be revived during the reign of Leo XIII'. If there was to be a new examination, the Institute would be the first to know about it.[17]

However, on 14 December 1887 Leo XIII signed the *Post obitum* condemning forty propositions of Rosmini. It was not promulgated until 7 March 1888 and Lanzoni only received news of the decree on 25 March. The previous day Lockhart wrote to the *Tablet* saying that he had not heard confirmation of the decree but stressed that 'we accept beforehand whatever comes to us with the authority of the Holy See'.[18]

The forty condemned propositions were drawn from works published posthumously and left unfinished, such as the *Theosophy* and the *Commentary on the Introduction to the Gospel according to John*. The General issued a declaration pronouncing surprise at the condemnation but stressing that, 'though our obedience in these days is put to a severe proof, ... authority must be obeyed, and may the will of God be done! ... We are not philosophers, but religious, and the Holy Father himself, in his letter to the Bishops of Upper Italy [on 25 January 1888], distinctly separated the cause of the Rosminian school from that of the Institute of Charity'.[19]

Lockhart had been well aware of the strength of anti-Rosminian sentiment but never doubted that Leo would stand by his predecessor's previous decree. In 1882 he had written to Manning that 'personally [the Pope] is disinclined to Rosmini's philosophy, but has decided that he will never be induced to condemn it by authority, but will leave it to find its own level in the Catholic Schools – this is all we could desire'.[20] At the end of 1886 he compared the situation of the Institute to

> an armour-clad vessel that has passed and re-passed the Dardanelles under the heaviest fire that the Turks could bring to bear upon her, without damage to her armour-plating. This does not prove that the vessel is invincible, but it need cause no wonder if the crew feel confident that no projectile that can be forged is likely to do the good ship any serious damage.[21]

The Institute was not indeed invincible. Lockhart now stressed that *Post obitum* did not condemn all of Rosmini's writings nor did it prohibit their study or publication.[22] He revealed his inmost thoughts in a letter to a mature student at the Venerable English College, George Ambrose Burton, an *alumnus* of Ratcliffe and future bishop of Clifton (1902-31):

> We are bound to respect the Act of the Congregation, but only as an act of obedience to legitimate authority, not bound to interior assent, as the authority is not infallible. We must accept the propositions in the sense in which they are condemned, as containing matter, as they stand, which to ordinary minds uninstructed in the grammar of the system would convey a wrong meaning and not be by them distinguished from dangerous ontologism ... Speaking for myself, I can accept the act of the Holy See, without in any way doubting of the soundness of Rosmini's philosophy as a whole ... Of course, this is a heavy and most unexpected blow, but I hope our prompt submission, after the example of our saintly founder, will disprove to all honest minds the charge of disloyalty to the Holy See so industriously circulated.[23]

Burton himself was a keen supporter of Rosminian philosophy and out of sympathy with many of his professors at the Roman College. On hearing of *Post obitum*, he recorded in his diary: 'I feel this as a heavy blow ... What a triumph to those damned Jesuits! ... What do I believe in now? In God, in his Christ, in Christ's Church, in Christ's vicar and in nought else – *omnis homo mendax*'.[24]

Shortly afterwards Lockhart preached a retreat to the clergy of Westminster and wrote to the Provincial that his texts had been 'distinctively Rosminian, but expressed in the words of St Augustine and St Thomas &c and I hear that the younger and best educated priests were particularly pleased with the theological undercurrent of the sermons'. Cardinal Manning said that 'he had listened to every sentence and that there was not a proposition I laid down which he was not willing to defend as a thesis'.[25] The archbishop had indeed showed himself as a true friend to the Rosminian cause and, following the condemnation, wrote to the pope in support of the Institute. The cardinal was assured that *Post obitum* 'does not in any way affect the meritorious Institute of Charity' and that Pope Leo 'esteems and honours the Institute of Charity as he has always esteemed and honoured it'.[26] Other English bishops were less generous in their views. Ullathorne, in whose diocese the Rosminians had a strong presence, thought that the condemnations did not go far enough, leaving out the 'worst' proposition 'which aperts that creation is division in God' or the passage in the *Antropologia* 'in which the generation of man is described as the deposit of matter touched by the divine light thus giving no substance to the soul'. The bishop had long been critical of his writings and admitted that 'whilst Rosmini was yet living, I warned his leading disciples in England, both by letter and voice, of these fundamental errors, and some of my letters were sent to Rosmini'.[27]

Overseas the attacks on Rosmini continued. In 1889 the Jesuit Fr Liberatore published his *On Universals, an Exposition of Thomistic Doctrine*, in which he boasted of his long-standing struggle with Rosminianism and how he now thanked God that 'in my old age I am obliged again to break a lance against it'.[28] Lockhart was resolute in abstaining from all controversy,

> in obedience to the commands of our General and out of respect to the Decrees of the Holy Office. The continual attacks of Professor Liberatore and others in journals and reviews would seem calculated to destroy our good name among those who do not know us; the justification of our orthodoxy we leave, however, to those who for fifty years have known us in England, Ireland and Scotland; especially the bishops and priests who have called us again and again to give retreats to their clergy and missions to their people.[29]

He remained upbeat. Shortly before Christmas 1888, Burton recorded in his Roman diary:

> Walked for some minutes on Pincio with Fathers Lockhart and Hirst [President of Ratcliffe] and took them to see Rosmini's bust (the extremity of the nose of which has been put on anew). I remarked that the chipping the nose off a statue did not imply any signal dishonour to the personage represented since the busts of so many great men on Pincio had been so treated; on which Fr Lockhart remarked smiling, 'Then you don't think it's been any designing Jesuit?' or some such words. I couldn't help laughing as he said before parting, 'some people would seem to have imagined that we were going to swell up and die, as the good Maltese expected Paul to do when stung by the viper.' Both were in capital spirits.[30]

Behind the scenes in the Roman Curia, Lockhart did his best to defend the Founder's good name. Suspicions abounded that the Institute was allied to the '*liberalissimi*' of the north and supported radical journals such as the *Nuovo Rosmini*. At the beginning of March 1890, Lockhart told Burton about a recent rearguard action he had fought in the face of attempts at getting more propositions condemned and even placing the entire Rosminian corpus on the Index:

> When it became apparent that proceedings were again impending, he had an interview with Cardinal Monaco [Secretary to the Congregation of the Inquisition] and wrote him a letter in which he spoke of the submission of the Institute to the decree, against which they had never written, complained of the tone of the journals towards them, and stated that though they were ready to bow to any decision of the Holy See, they did not intend to take the law from the *Civiltà Cattolica*. He sent the Cardinal a letter of submission which had appeared in the *Tablet*. The Cardinal went off to the Pope and placed before him Fr Lockhart's letter to the *Tablet* as well as his other representations. The Pope's reply was: '*Sare che il Padre Lockhart sia franco e leale*: – let the General only endorse what Fr Lockhart here says and disavow publicly any connection with the *Nuovo Rosmini* and 'twill do!' Shortly after the General's disclaimer appeared in the *Unità Cattolica* of Turin; and then [Mgr] Critone[31] to Fr Lockhart's surprise called upon him in a carriage from the Vatican and told him that he was charged to inform him that the General's letter was in everyway satisfactory to His Holiness and the Congregation, and that the Congregation had decided to stop all further proceedings.[32]

Lockhart, who was about to return to Ely Place, was immensely relieved and commented: 'we were to have been hanged on a gibbet as high as that prepared by Aman for Mordechai ... But it's all smashed!! There'll be no more trouble. I never left Rome with a greater sense of relief.'[33]

Post obitum was, of course, a huge blow to the Rosminians and left them in a state of shock. The Institute contracted, experiencing a drop in vocations and fewer new missions, and for many years exercised caution in promoting the works of their Father Founder, suspending publication of *Bollettino Rosminiano* and the review *Il Rosmini*.

At the time of the decree, Lockhart referred to Rosmini's maxim that 'the seed cannot bring forth much fruit until it die' and predicted an eventual resurrection of Rosminianism.[34] Lockhart did not live to see this but in *Fides et Ratio* (1998), John Paul II commended Rosmini as one who had courageously promoted the 'fruitful relationship between philosophy and the Word of God', though he expressed some reservations.[35] As Prefect of the Congregation for the Doctrine of the Faith, Cardinal Ratzinger signed the *Note on the Force of the Doctrinal Decrees Concerning the Thought and Work of Fr Antonio Rosmini Serbati* in 2001. This admitted that, although the Holy See was correct to condemn the forty propositions in 1887, these did not truly represent Rosmini's thought; 'the meaning of the propositions, as understood and condemned by the Decree, does not belong to the authentic position of Rosmini, but to conclusions that may possibly have been drawn from the reading of his works'.

Post obitum was to be explained partly by the resurgence of Thomism, which 'created the premises for a negative judgement of a philosophical and speculative position, like that of Rosmini, because it differed in its language and conceptual framework from the philosophical and theological elaboration of St Thomas Aquinas'. Moreover,

> the condemned propositions were mostly extracted from posthumous works of the author. These works were published without a critical apparatus capable of defining the precise meaning of the expressions and concepts used. This favoured a heterodox interpretation of Rosminian thought, as did the objective difficulty of interpreting Rosmini's categories, especially, when they were read in a neo-Thomistic perspective.

The document also admitted that 'one finds in Rosmini's system concepts and expressions that are at times ambiguous and equivocal. They require a careful interpretation and they can only be clarified in the light of the overall context of the author's work'.[36]

Only six years after the rehabilitation, the former Cardinal Prefect – now Pope Benedict XVI – approved the beatification of Rosmini, which took place in Novara on 18 November 2007. In his sermon, Cardinal Martins said that 'Rosmini's voice is a modern echo of that of the great Fathers of the Church, with whom he can easily be set side by side for the acuteness and vastness of his speculative interests, well harmonized with the Gospel ardour of the shepherds of souls'. There were some cries of protest, especially by those who sensed an attack on Thomism, but Rosmini was effectively rehabilitated and entered the mainstream of Catholicism. Lockhart would have been well pleased.

Translating the Works of Rosmini

As an admirer and disciple of Rosmini, Lockhart was never shy in speaking of his writings and his philosophical system. As well as defending the Founder's name in Rome, Lockhart was a key player in translating his more important works and effectively introducing Rosmini to the English-speaking world.

In 1856, as he was establishing the Kingsland mission, Lockhart edited an English edition of Vincenzo de Vit's *Cenni Biografici di Antonio Rosmini*, published the previous year in Milan. Entitled *An Outline of the Life of the Very Reverend Antonio Rosmini, Founder of the Institute of Charity, Translated from the Italian by Sisters of the Convent of Our Lady at Greenwich*, it contained a brief preface on the Rosminian system drafted by Fr Gastaldi. The chapter on Rosmini's virtues was looked over by Cardinal Wiseman himself.[37]

At Christmas 1864 Lockhart reported to Bertetti that he was resting at Ratcliffe and busy reading the works of the Founder. He had translated most of the *Sistema Filosofico* and confessed: 'I have such an attraction for the works of Rosmini and though my understanding of them is no doubt very imperfect I feel sure that they do me more good intellectually and I think morally than any other writings.'[38]

It was an on-going project and, given the polemics in Rome, undertaken amid a degree of secrecy. Lockhart wrote to his fellow Rosminian, Fr William Ward, in an undated letter from the early 1880s, that during his stays in Rome he had 'kept out of the way of the Pope, as much as possible':

> I did not want the Pope to ask me any Questions about the Translations or he might express a wish that we would leave them

alone. He cannot do it publicly but he might say something privately that would be embarrassing ... Depend on it, we cannot be too quiet about our doings in England and elsewhere. It may console our friends in Italy to hear of our doings but it furnishes matter to those blackguards for the constructing [of] their lies.[39]

Despite this, it was a work of great importance for the Institute and in 1883 Lockhart told Ward that 'the General wishes us to use the balance of the income of the Ely Place property ... in publishing Father Founder's works in England and the *Life* in French'.[40]

Manning had initially been reluctant for translations to appear in England but in 1879 told Lockhart 'he should not object to our publishing in England and in English any work of Rosmini which we could get permission to publish in Italian and in Rome. He added that he should advise us to do this and considered the time propitious'.[41] With the help of Fr Signini, who had known Rosmini intimately, several translations of the Founder's works were begun, including the *Sistema Filosofico* (1882), *Nuovo Saggio* (1883), which Lockhart regarded as 'the key to the whole of that vast system – universal and yet one – which has been developed in a great variety of writings by the same author',[42] and *Psicologia* (1885). For the best part of a century the Lockhart-Signini translations remained the only major philosophical works of Rosmini available in English, with the exception of H. Liddon's edition of the *Five Wounds of the Church* and Thomas Davidson's *Rosmini's Philosophical System*, both of which appeared in 1882.

Lockhart declared that at last 'Rosmini twenty-five years after his death will begin to speak in the English tongue'.[43] He thought that 'great numbers of persons Catholic and Protestant, some in imminent danger of Rationalism, are most anxious to read Rosmini, but do not know Italian'. He saw Rosmini as 'the best antidote to Rationalism' and recalled the words of Pius VIII to the Founder that 'the world must be brought to faith by reason'.[44] Moreover, 'the General [Lanzoni] sees that the future of Rosminian philosophy is through the English-speaking races both sides of the Atlantic, and greatly outside the Church; like the false philosophy of Locke which entered the Catholic Schools through having become popular outside'.[45]

Lockhart also edited a two-volume *Life* of Rosmini, published in 1886. The first volume was written by Gabriel Stuart Macwalter, covering the life of the Founder and first published separately, and Lockhart produced a companion volume including a useful description of the activities of the Institute in England, studies of Rosmini as a 'holy man' and philosopher, and a summary of the 'Rosminian Question' up until 1886. Lockhart included 'Anecdotes and Reminiscences by Father Signini', who had been the great man's *amanuensis*, and Bishop Ferré's defense of Rosmini, *Saint Thomas of Aquin and Ideology*. Lockhart also incorporated his previously published translation of *A Short Sketch of Modern Philosophy, and of his own System*.

The two-volume *Life* was well received in many quarters, *The Tablet* commenting that all clergy should read it as well as 'all educated Catholic laymen who are interested in the great problem, How the Church is to overcome the powers of evil, found in modern society ... It is not that he [Rosmini] has solved all our problems, but that he has studied many of them, with all the force and penetration of an extraordinary intellect'. In Rosmini, the anonymous review continued, could be found the 'rare combination of intellect and sanctity devoted to the study of the problems presented by modern society'.[46]

The *Life*, of course, constituted an apologia for Rosmini in the light of current controversies and what Lockhart referred to as 'journalistic assassination'. Had the work been published after *Post obitum* then it is unlikely that these sections would have been so extensive. The condemnation of the forty propositions led to difficulties when foreign translations of the *Life* were prepared. Lockhart complained that the Italian translator 'has taken great liberties with the original: has refused admission to our act of submission to the Holy See in respect of a recent decree of the Holy Office concerning certain propositions of Rosmini and he has added a postscript most disrespectful of the Holy See, implicitly impugning its authority'. Lockhart was so disgusted that he telegraphed a statement via his lawyer friend, James Coen: 'I prohibit the publication, otherwise legal proceedings will be taken.'[47]

As already mentioned, Lockhart stressed that *Post obitum* did not condemn Rosmini's teachings *per se* nor did it prohibit their study, translation or publication. Up until his death Lockhart continued to promote the works of the Founder. However, the condemnation severely restricted the fruitfulness of his labours. Any interest in 'Rosminianism' that had existed in English-speaking countries was soon replaced by suspicion, as Rosmini became included in the list of *errores* taught in seminary philosophy. The editions of Lockhart and Signini were quickly forgotten by all but a tiny minority. This situation remained until the second half of the twentieth century, when Rosmini House, Durham, was founded to promote the translation of Rosmini's works. Although his translations were often too florid for modern taste and occasionally inaccurate, Lockhart helped build the foundations of this revival of interest in Rosmini.

Notes

1. The complex consisted of 24 rooms on three floors, a small chapel and cortile. The Institute left this site in 1907, when a new Generalate was opened at San Carlo al Corso. The buildings on the Via Alessandrina (including the church) were demolished by Mussolini and the street only survives today as a path leading towards the Colosseum.
2. Lockhart, *Life of Rosmini*, vol. ii, p. 336.
3. ASIC AG 156/21–22 (Newman to Lockhart, 12 April 1880).
4. Newman, LD XI, p. 263 (Newman to Dalgairns, 18 October 1846).
5. Lockhart, *Life of Rosmini*, vol. ii, pp. 337–8.
6. Belti, *The Rosminian Question*, p. 62.
7. Ibid., p. 65.
8. ASIC AG 118/628 (Lockhart to Costa, 17 November 1882).
9. Meynell, 'Further Reminiscences of Father Lockhart', p. 163.
10. ASIC Box 66.5 (Lockhart to Cavalli, 18 February 1882).
11. AAW Capel Papers, Lockhart to Manning (20 November 1882).
12. AAW Capel Papers, Lockhart to Manning (27 November 1882).
13. Lockhart, *Life of Rosmini*, vol. ii, p. 340.
14. ASIC AG 118/787 (Lockhart to Lanzoni, 26 February 1884).
15. *Tablet*, 2 April 1887, p. 523.
16. *Tablet*, 9 April 1887, p. 579.
17. Mariani, *Rosminian Generals and Bishops*, p. 55.
18. *Tablet*, 24 March 1888, p. 484.
19. *Tablet*, 7 April 1888, p. 558.
20. AAW Capel Papers, Lockhart to Manning (27 November 1882).
21. Lockhart, *Life of Rosmini*, vol. ii, p. 341.
22. *Tablet*, 2 February 1889, p. 178.
23. VEC, Liber 824 (Ambrose Burton's Roman Diary), 14 April 1888.
24. Ibid., 17 March 1888.

25. ASIC 118/758–761 (Lockhart to Provincial, 7 July 1888).
26. Mariani, *Rosminian Generals and Bishops*, p. 57.
27. AAW Manning Box 11/134 (Ullathorne to Manning, Easter Sunday 1888).
28. *Tablet*, 19 October 1889, p. 610.
29. *Tablet*, 2 November 1889, p. 702.
30. VEC, Liber 824, 17 December 1888.
31. Mgr Serafino Cretoni, *Assessore* of the Inquisition.
32. VEC, Liber 824, 3 March 1890.
33. Ibid., 2 March 1890. Lockhart is referring to an episode in the Old Testament Book of Esther.
34. Ibid., 14 April 1888.
35. John Paul II, *Fides et Ratio*, 74.
36. *Note on the Force of the Doctrinal Decrees Concerning the Thought and Work of Fr. Antonio Rosmini Serbati*, 1 July 2001.
37. AAW W3/49/1 (Lockhart to Wiseman, 20 May 1856).
38. ASIC AG 118/157 (Lockhart to Bertetti, 24 December 1864).
39. ASIC Box 7.4 (Lockhart to Ward, 13 November, no year).
40. ASIC Box 7.4 (Lockhart to Ward, 2 May 1883).
41. ASIC AG 118/455 (Lockhart to Lanzoni, 7 June 1879).
42. Ferré, *St Thomas of Aquin and Ideology* (1875), vi (translator's preface).
43. ASIC AG 118/626 (Lockhart to Costa, Christmas 1881).
44. ASIC AG 118/623 (Lockhart to Ceroni, 2 January 1879).
45. ASIC 118/630 (Lockhart to Costa).
46. *Tablet*, 2 April 1887, p. 529.
47. *Tablet*, 21 April 1888, p. 650.

Chapter X

'That we may persevere to the end'

The Affair of Mgr Capel

Lockhart's regular presence in Rome meant that he was sometimes asked by Manning to represent him in diocesan affairs, as is shown by the case of Mgr Thomas John Capel. He had won fame preaching at society weddings and funerals and claimed as many as 3,000 converts, including the Marquis of Bute and the Duchess of Norfolk. It was little surprise that his cartoon appeared in the *Vanity Fair* magazine in September 1872 with the caption 'Apostle to the Genteel'. In 1873 he founded the Catholic Public School at Kensington and the following year became Rector of Manning's Catholic University, also in Kensington. Capel may have been gifted in many areas but, under his leadership, the University suffered from financial problems and was soon faced with bankruptcy. At the request of the bishops, Capel resigned in 1878 and the College was closed. Accusations were also made, with compelling evidence to back them up, concerning Capel's private life, including drunkenness and charges of immorality with a string of women. His priestly faculties were suspended by Manning in 1879, but Capel appealed to Rome, where he had many supporters and hoped he would be acquitted.

Lockhart's frequent letters to the Cardinal on the subject reveal the familiarity the two men enjoyed. Lockhart is honest in his opinions: he fears that Mgr Stonor 'talks too much'[1] and told a convalescent Manning, 'I do hope you will not, as usual, do too much. This long weakness after illness proves that your stamina is not what it was'.[2] Lockhart believed the allegations against Capel and saw the Monsignor as 'a lesson and a warning. How many priests I have known, my own contemporaries, who have made shipwreck, and why not I, but for the unmerited mercies of God?'[3] Nevertheless he was disgusted by the scandal caused:

> His having leave to say Mass and, as it is supposed, to reserve the B[lessed] Sacrament, while he is known to be leading a life of horrible incontinence, is spoken of as reflecting discredit on the ecclesiastical authorities in England and in Rome. People are saying there are worse things in the Communion of the See of Peter than the marriage of the clergy in the Protestant Church, and that if the things known to exist and caused by the authorities (like Achilli's case and that ... of Capel) are going on in the nineteenth century what must have been the decadence of morals at the time when Protestantism began, and which gave it its first start as a Protest against clerical corruption? I wish the Holy See would take a strong line and degrade incontinent priests and let them marry and sink into the ranks of the laity.[4]

In his missives, Lockhart reported conversations with various Roman dignitaries and sent press cuttings illustrating the latest actions of Capel, who hoped to escape to Florence as a preacher and confessor. Lockhart interpreted the whole affair from the perspective of the Roman ecclesiastical politics in which he was so immersed. He told Manning, 'you have plenty of people in Rome that, to say the least, would delight in giving you a humiliation – and we need not say the Jesuits would work at it *con-amore*, that is to say, the mischievous, unprincipled clique that have fought us and undermined us this forty years'.[5] Indeed, after being accused of writing a strongly-worded article on Capel in the *Weekly Register*, Lockhart reflected: 'I have no doubt that S.J. [i.e. the Jesuits] has its finger in this affair of mine and that an attempt is being made to utilize this accusation ... in order to do me a bad turn in my official position'. As a result, Lockhart asked for Manning's support and protection.[6]

No letters survive after February 1883. Manning refused to grant faculties to Capel should he return to Westminster and, following the Roman appeal, it was arranged for the Monsignor to conveniently 'disappear' into comfortable retirement in Sacramento, California.

'Thank God I shall never be a bishop'

In one of his letters to the Cardinal, Lockhart commented, "...God I shall never be a bishop. These things would kill me .. the original edition of the *Dictionary of National Biography*, Tho. Seccombe wrote that Lockhart's 'diffidence and lack of initiat which rendered him so greatly dependant on others, first (Newman, then on Rosmini, prevented him from obtaining hig. preferment in his church'.[8] The previous pages have hopefully shown that Lockhart's life was marked by many initiatives, especially in the world of publishing and in the parishes of Kingsland and Ely Place. He was, however, easily influenced by charismatic personalities such as Newman, Manning, Rosmini, Phillipps and, not least of all, his own mother. In a sermon preached after Lockhart's death, Fr Jarvis commented that

> it has truly been said that Father Lockhart was not fitted by nature to be a great leader of men, although he was gifted with great talents ... [I]f Father Lockhart influenced others by word and example, he did it unconsciously. He had a shrinking from responsibility, and he was most distrustful of his own judgment, so that he was accustomed to lean in most things on the judgment of others. Thus, by nature, he was led to attach himself to others.[9]

Given Lockhart's ability as a writer and preacher and his connections in high society, it is not surprising that his name was regularly mentioned with regard to a mitre. As early as 1858 Archbishop Polding of Sydney was proposing Lockhart as bishop of Bathurst, judging him to be 'precisely the man we want for Australia, ... full of energy, disinterested, equal to all exigencies' and, crucially, acceptable to the Irish.[10] Furthermore, a letter of 1884 reveals that his name had been considered for Sydney a decade earlier, in succession to Polding. Lockhart was 'known to Propaganda', although they had not been properly informed about his '*Vescovibilità*' and had, he thought, made a sane decision by appointing a Downside monk, Roger Vaughan.[11] Also in 1874, Lockhart's name was mentioned as a possible candidate for Nottingham in succession to Bishop Roskell, whose health was declining. 'If I were not aware that the Holy Ghost knows me thoroughly and would never make a Bishop of me,' wrote hart, 'I should be a little uneasy about the reports which come to me on all sides.'[12]

In 1878, as plans for the restoration of the Scottish Hierarchy were being made, a report appeared announcing Lockhart's imminent appointment as bishop of a possible See at Rutherglen, which seemed appropriate given the Lockhart family's links to Lanarkshire. He wrote to Caccia:

> Many thanks for your kind letter of congratulations! I hope they are premature ... I do not believe a word of it ... However, I wrote yesterday to our Cardinal in Rome [Howard] to say that if there was any truth in the project of making me a Bishop, it would never be done with my free-will except under the force of my vow of obedience and begging him to use his influence against it.

Lockhart thought it merely 'a trick of the Jesuits to get me out of London, where I occupy too large a place on the *Stage* by reason of the Temperance movement'.[13] Moreover, in the eyes of the Society, 'St Etheldreda's is too grand a position for the Order of Charity'. *The Lamp* also 'contributes to give me influence amongst the Middle Class' and the Jesuits 'know I am an active collaborator in the translation of Rosmini'. The proposed diocese would be 'an out of the way district, peopled by a low class of Irish, where the duties of a Bishop would be to do the work of our priests in Cardiff or rather of the wretched missions in the mountains of Wales'.[14]

In 1884, rumours connected Lockhart's name to the Archdiocese of St Andrews. He tried to persuade Manning to intervene, but the Cardinal wrote: 'I shall not send the letter to Scotland nor in any way cross what may be God's will. If He chooses you it will be, if not it will not be, and if it be, He will give you all needful from health to Canon Law.'[15] At Septuagesima Lockhart wrote triumphantly that Cardinal Howard had told him 'the *terna* for the Archbishopric of St Andrews has arrived, without my name. *Deo gratias!*'[16]

In the last year of Lockhart's life, rumours abounded that he would be appointed as Coadjutor in Westminster with right of succession. Leo XIII secretly sent Archbishop Rotelli, the nuncio in Paris, to London for three days to make enquiries and observe Lockhart. According to a *Memorandum* in the Rosminian archive, 'Mgr Rotelli came up to [Lockhart] one morning when he was unvesting after Mass in the crypt of St Etheldreda's and when he was not at first recognized made himself known and going upstairs with him into the Library had a long chat with him, telling him the purpose for which he had come to London unknown, accompanied by one servant'. He was staying in a hotel near Holborn and Lockhart found it extraordinary to think of such a high prelate visiting London incognito and using a public omnibus. Lockhart's name was favoured, it appeared, by the 'Irish party in Rome [and] the Irish and American Episcopacy'. It might seem surprising that a prominent Rosminian should be considered for such high office just a few years after *Post obitum*, but Pope Leo apparently told Rotelli that 'Rosmini has been treated with too great severity; we must find some way of making compensation to the Institute of Charity.'[17]

After Manning's death, Lockhart's name was still being mentioned in connection to Westminster and in a letter to Lanzoni in February 1892 he enclosed a cutting from the liberal *Lloyd's Weekly Messenger*, reporting that 'according to a correspondent, there is a consensus of opinion in favour of the Very Rev. Dr [sic] Lockhart of St Etheldreda's, Ely Place, the favourite of the clergy and the people'. Lockhart explained this away by referring to the paper's pro-Irish sympathies.[18]

Last Years

By the 1880s, Lockhart, though only a sexagenarian, was fast ageing and declining in health. The future Cardinal Archbishop of Boston, William O'Connell, remembered seeing him during a visit to London: 'a venerable figure with stooped form and long white hair, and a face that bespoke a high order of intelligence'.[19] In 1883 Lockhart had been told by his Roman doctor that the wall of his heart was so attenuated that a chill or sudden exertion could prove fatal. This led him to jest that he might die at any time after climbing one of the many long flights of stairs in the Eternal City. George Burton recorded visiting the Via Alessandrina as a seminarian in January 1887 and finding Lockhart 'confined to bed, but sat up reading the *Spectator*'.[20] During the winter of 1891–2 he suffered a serious attack of gout in Rome, which greatly worried his friends.

Despite such setbacks, Lockhart's last decade saw much activity and a surprising energy. He continued to spend half the year in Rome, preside over Ely Place and give numerous missions and retreats around the country. During these years he preached in Glasgow, Liverpool, Manchester, Sheffield and Derby, and directed retreats for various religious communities and seminaries, including the clergy of Galway, St Thomas' Seminary in Hammersmith, several Dublin convents and the Men's Association of the Sacred Heart at Irishtown. He preached at great occasions, such as the opening of the splendid new church of St James, Spanish Place in September 1890. In Rome he likewise gave retreats to the students of the English and Irish Colleges and preached a series of sermons on Revelation at San Silvestro in Capite during Epiphanytide 1890. In 1888 he wrote, 'I look upon it as another of the miracles of Father Founder that, at my time of life, I have a vigour I never knew when I was a younger man, and that I succeed in preaching, so far as I can judge, better than when I was younger'. He attributed this partly to the discipline of studying and translating Rosmini's works.[21]

As he entered the 1890s, Lockhart had to deal with the deaths of several close friends and mentors. After Easter 1890, for instance, Lockhart made the last of his annual visits to see Newman at the Birmingham Oratory:

> He sent for me to come to him, before he rose in the morning, saying that after dressing he might feel too much exhausted to receive me. I found him weak, weak indeed, in body, but as bright and clear in mind as ever. I told him news from Rome which I knew would interest him. He listened with all his old intensity of thought: fully appreciated the facts and the situation of matters ecclesiastical and political. I knelt down: took his hand, and kissed it. I felt sure I should not see him again. I thanked him for all the good he had done me, since, under God, he had been, as I hoped, the instrument of my salvation. I asked his blessing, which he gave me with great earnestness, simplicity, and tenderness. Three months later I stood by his bier.[22]

After the great man's death, Lockhart gave a public address on the late Cardinal at Ely Place and published a retrospect in which he proudly referred to himself as one of Newman's 'oldest living disciples'.

'That we may persevere to the end'

On 14 January 1892 Cardinal Manning died and Lockha̦
to Fr Grant from Rome that

> these deaths all around me remind me of the *Conciergerie* in
> where those destined for the guillotine were confined and calle
> one by one for execution. *Et vos estote parati* is always in my ears
> meditation always takes that shape. May our blessed Mother help
> all to say more often and earnestly: 'Pray for us now', that we may
> made ready, 'and in the hour of our death', that we may persevere
> the end.[23]

The Rosminian was conspicuous in attending the Solemn Requiem Masses held for the Cardinal at the English College and San Silvestro in Capite.

On Easter Sunday 1892, Fr Lewthwaite died. He had retired from Ely Place to the Yorkshire air to act as chaplain to the Institute's Reformatory at Market Weighton and was nursed in his final illness by Brother Anthony Wehrle, formerly a parishioner at Kingsland. Lockhart was invited to preach at Requiem Masses for Lewthwaite at Kingsland and Hoxton and these would be two of his last public appearances.

At the beginning of May 1892, the new Archbishop of Westminster, Herbert Vaughan, was enthroned at the Pro-Cathedral in Kensington. Lockhart was one of the nineteen clerical signatories to the official *Address of Welcome*, assuring Vaughan of 'our readiness to be loving and obedient to you; and by co-operating in your good works, to lighten the heavy burden which his Holiness, the Vicar of Our Lord, has laid upon you'.[24]

On 14 May, a Saturday, Lockhart had functioned as normal, hearing confessions in the crypt until ten at night, eating supper with his brother clergy and engaging them in genial conversation. A few days earlier he had noted that he had never felt better in his life and arranged to sing High Mass on Sunday morning and preach in the evening. The following morning he made his usual visit to the Blessed Sacrament but, about half past eight, came into the room of Fr Jarvis to ask him to sing the High Mass in his place. Lockhart said that he felt very unwell, fearing an attack of gout, and asked also for his confessor, Fr Bone, who was at that moment celebrating Mass. When Fr Bone entered Lockhart's about ten minutes later, he found the priest lying on his ple camp bed in what appeared to be a deep sleep. However, further examination, it became evident that the 72-year-old ad died suddenly and alone; as his obituarist pointed out, 'soli-.arily had ended a life devoted to others'.[25] The cause of death was later established as heart failure, resulting in syncope, and complicated by gout in the stomach. The 'grand old priest' was then vested in cotta and biretta, and a rosary placed in his hands. A journalist who paid his respects in the 'death chamber' noted that 'a beautiful smile lit up the worn countenance'.[26]

The announcement of his death to the congregation at St Etheldreda's resulted in 'pathetic' scenes of much emotion and glowing tributes were printed both in the Catholic and secular press. *The Tablet* declared that 'perhaps no man, except the Cardinal himself [Manning], had so strong a hold on varying classes and masses of men; and these are now united in a common sorrow over a common and irreparable loss'.[27] *The Catholic Times* quoted the words of one who knew the Rosminian well:

> The Catholic body in London has lost in him one of its most eminent figures, and the society to which he belonged one its best and dearest members. He was once described to me as 'the soul of kindness' and such he ever was to all who were brought into contact with him. He was a finished scholar and in his manner and bearing bore the stamp of the perfect gentleman.[28]

On 19 May, the Office of the Dead and Requiem were sung at Ely Place in the presence of the new Archbishop and many of the clergy. Lockhart's body was then carried to the hearse by members of the League of the Cross and taken to St Pancras station, where 'a large crowd collected, estimated at 6,000 in number, and in spite of the pelting rain which fell, showed their regard and esteem for the deceased by following the funeral train'. At Ratcliffe the body was solemnly received at the college lodge by the President, Fr Hirst, and 'all the religious community and all the boys, vested in cassocks and surplices'. Vespers of the Dead was chanted and the following day Fr Richardson (from Newport) celebrated the Requiem.

William Lockhart was buried in the college cemetery, beside his mother and the Athys and close also to Fr Lewthwaite. As one correspondent to *The Tablet* put it, 'as in life they loved one another, so in death they are not separated'.[29]

A window depicting St William was later placed in the Ratcliffe chapel in memory of Lockhart[30] and he also came to be represented by a lily on the College crest. Furthermore, up until 1972 one of the school's 'houses' was named after him. At his beloved Ely Place, Lockhart was shown in various stained-glass windows, though these were sadly destroyed during the Second World War. A window portraying the prophecy of Malachi with regard to the Eucharist depicted Lockhart as celebrant at Mass, while a series of medallions in the great west window depicted scenes from the Rosminian's life, culminating in the wigged and gowned Lord Chancellor presenting him with the title deeds of the church. A design was drawn up for an altar tomb, with an effigy of Lockhart vested for Mass, but this was never completed. However, a brass plaque was erected in his honour, which can now be found by the stairs leading to the upper church:

In Memoriam
William Lockhart, B.A. Oxon
Priest of the Order of Charity, founded by Rosmini.
Rector of this Mission, a man of great kindliness of judgment,
and loyalty of truth. Friend and disciple of Manning and Newman,
he preceded both in the great act of their lives.
By his instrumentality this ancient chapel of the Bishops of Ely,
wherein later, in times of persecution, as a Catholic embassy chapel,
the Holy Mass found for a time an inviolable sanctuary,
was, in (A.D.) 1876, restored to the old
religion of an undivided Christendom.
Born 22 August 1819; died May 1892.
ON WHOSE SOUL SWEET JESUS HAVE MERCY.

Notes

1. AAW Capel Papers, Lockhart to Manning (6 November 1882).
2. AAW Capel Papers, Lockhart to Manning (3 February 1883).
3. AAW Capel Papers, Lockhart to Manning (Septuagesima 1883).
4. AAW Capel Papers, Lockhart to Manning (4 October 1882).
5. AAW Capel Papers, Lockhart to Manning (6 November 1882).

5. AW Capel Papers, Lockhart to Manning (8 February 1893).
6. AW Capel Papers, Lockhart to Manning (4 October 1882).
7. Stephen and Lee (eds), *Dictionary of National Biography*, vol. xii, p. 52.
8. Hirst, 'Necrology', p. 343.
9. Birt, *Benedictine Pioneers in Australia*, vol. 2, p. 258.
10. ASIC AG 118/775–776 (Lockhart to Caccia, 7 February 1884).
11. ASIC Box 49.2 (Lockhart to Gazzola 20 April 1874?).
12. ASIC AG 118/597 (Lockhart to Lanzoni, 6 February 1878).
13. ASIC AG 118/435 (Lockhart to Lanzoni, 5 February 1878).
14. ASIC AG 118/777 (Manning to Lockhart, 5 February 1884).
15. ASIC AG 118/793 (Lockhart to Manning, Septuagesima 1884).
16. ASIC Box 66.5, Memorandum (undated).
17. ASIC AG 156/841–845 (Lockhart to Lanzoni, 21 February 1892).
18. O'Connell, *Recollections of Seventy Years*, p. 85.
19. VEC, Liber 824, 13 January 1887.
20. ASIC 118/761 (Lockhart to Provincial, 7 July 1888).
21. Lockhart, *Cardinal Newman*, pp. 56–7.
22. *Tablet*, 9 July 1892, p. 67.
23. *Tablet*, 12 May 1892, p. 764.
24. *Tablet*, 12 May 1892, p. 804.
25. Hirst, 'Necrology', p. 341.
26. *Tablet*, 12 May 1892, p. 804.
27. *Catholic Times*, 20 May 1892.
28. *Tablet*, 28 May 1892, p. 870.
29. This was removed in the 1960s when the new school chapel was built and placed in the Rosminian school near Lushoto, Tanzania, now the Junior Seminary for the diocese of Tanga.

Appendix

Cardinal Newman: A Retrospect of Fifty Years, by one of his oldest living disciples[1]

Affectionate veneration for my old Master in the Science of Truth has made me wish to say something in honour of his memory; but I am now conscious that I have undertaken more than I can perform, except most imperfectly.

It is, I think, rather more than fifty years since I first had the privilege of knowing John Henry Newman. It was not long after I went to Oxford. I saw him first on a certain day which I vividly remember. I was walking down High Street – it was between All Souls' and Queen's College. He was crossing, I think, to Oriel. My companion seized my arm, whispering to me, 'Look, look there, that is Newman!' I looked, and there I saw him passing along in his characteristic way, walking fast, without any dignity of gait, but earnest, like one who had a purpose; yet so humble and self-forgetting in every portion of his external appearance, that you would not have thought him, at first sight, a man remarkable for anything. It was only when you came to know him that you recognised or began to recognise what he was.

In speaking of my own reminiscences of Cardinal Newman and of his work, I shall necessarily have to speak of myself, but of myself merely as a type of the ordinary young Oxford man who came under Newman's wonderful influence. For there was about him a spiritual power, an influence, or rather an effluence of soul, the force of moral greatness, which produced on some a feeling of awe in his presence. There was a tradition in my time at Oxford, that once on market day when the upper end of High Street, near Carfax Church, was much crowded with roughs, and the 'Town' and 'Gown' element were apt to come into collision, Newman was walking past All Saints' Church in the line of march of a furiously drunken butcher, who came up the street foul-mouthed and blasphemous. When they were near together, Newman stood in his path; my informant, who was a 'muscular Christian', the stroke of his college boat, expecting violence, came close up to the butcher, and was just making ready to fell him, when he saw the man stop short; Newman was speaking to him. Very quietly he said, 'My friend, if you thought of the meaning of your words you would not say them.' The savage was tamed on the spot; he touched his hat, turned round and went back.

When Whately was Principal of S. Alban Hall, Newman was his Vice-Principal. He was afterwards Tutor, and I think Dean, at Oriel; this brought him into contact with the undergraduates. Oriel especially was a 'fashionable' college; there were always a good number of noblemen, baronets, gentlemen commoners, distinguished by their velvet, or 'tufted' gold tasseled cap, and silk gown. They were mostly fast young men, 'hunting in pink' was perhaps the smallest of their irregularities against university discipline. There was apt to be too much wine drunk at supper parties, and in consequence 'rows in quad' were frequent. Newman could do more by a few words than anyone living. 'What did he say to you?' was asked of one who had been called up by Newman for some more or less serious matter. 'I don't know,' said the other, 'but he looked at me.' Newman could read character; one felt in his presence that he read you through and through.

In that wonderful passage in his *Discourses to Mixed Congregations*, preached at Birmingham, he speaks, with certain adaptations about, what he had first learned of 'polished ungodliness' in young Oxford men of rank, 'tufts', as they were called, and of its bad imitations in the sometimes vulgar but superficially polished 'tuft hunter', who was sent to Oxford, principally, that he might get 'into good society and form useful connections'. To the latter the following passage applies:

> You my brethren have not been born splendidly; you have no high connections; you have not learned the manner or caught the tone of good society ... yet you ape the sins of Dives while you are strangers to his refinement ... you think it the sign of a gentleman to set yourself above religion ... to look at Catholic or Methodist with impartial contempt ... to walk up and down the street with your

heads on high, and to stare at whatever meets you, and to say and do worse things, of which these outward extravagances are but the symbol! The Creator made you it seems, O my children, for this office and work, to be a bad imitation of polished ungodliness.

And now one more word about Newman's personal appearance and his ways. Who that has had experience of it can forget the impression made on him by the majesty of Newman's countenance, when one came really to know him and to study it – his meekness, his intensity, his humility, the purity of 'a virgin heart in work and will'[2] that was expressed in his eyes, his loving kindness, his winning smile, the wonderful sweetness and pathos, and delicate unstudied harmony of his voice!

Then he had, also, according to times and persons, a wonderful caressing way, which had in it nothing of softness, but which was felt to be a communication of strength from a strong soul, a thing that must be felt to be understood. Then there was at times in him a great vein of humour, and at times a certain playful way which he had of saying things which were full of meaning, and called to mind some passages in St Paul's writings, suggesting, too, that perhaps there was in him, as in this, so also in other things, a certain likeness to the Great Apostle who made 'himself all to all that he might gain all to God'.

He impressed me in these ways more perhaps than any but one other man has impressed me – the great master of thought under whom I passed when I left Newman; another of the greatest minds of the age – Antonio Rosmini, the Founder of the Order to which I have the honour to belong.

When Newman read the Holy Scriptures from the lectern of St Mary's or at Littlemore, we felt more than ever that his words were the words of a Seer, who saw God, and the things of God. Many men are impressive readers, but we can see they *mean* to be impressive. They do not reach the soul; they play upon the sense and imagination: they are good actors, certainly; they may or may not be more. They do not forget themselves; you do not forget them. Newman's reading of the Nicene Creed was a sublime meditation, or rather contemplation. I remember his reading the passage in the Book of Wisdom about the making of idols, and the sublime scorn with which he read of the 'carving of the block of wood and the painting it with vermilion', impressed me with the blank stupidity of the attempt to put the idea of God, under any material form, and Newman's sermons were like his reading, the words of one who spoke with the utter conviction and intense earnestness – the quiet unstudied rhetoric – of one who saw truth and spoke what he saw.

These sermons were preached at St Mary's, the University Church, at the afternoon parish service, when the University Sermon was over. It was always crowded by undergraduates, Bachelors and Masters of Arts, the very flower of 'Young Oxford'. The effect of his teaching on us young men was to turn our souls, as it were, inside out; in measure and degree it was like what he says in the *Dream of Gerontius* of the soul after death presented before God,

> Who draws the soul from out its case
> And burns away its stains.

God the Creator was the first theme he taught us, and it contained the premises of all that followed. We never could be again the same as before, whether we 'obeyed the heavenly vision' or neglected it. We had gained some notion that there were false forms of Christianity to be avoided. Socinianism was one; Roman Catholicism was another; and this had been impressed upon us very strongly. But the Church of England, which we supposed was much the same in doctrine with the other Protestant Churches, we did not doubt was the old and true religion.

The next truth which we learned from the tenor of all his teaching was, that God who is so near us, that 'in Him we live and move and are', who is the ultimate hidden force and First Cause beneath the phenomena of the visible universe, and of our own spiritual consciousness and conscience, our Moral Governor, might be expected beforehand to have given a religion to man by supernatural revelation. He had done so. We accepted the Christianity of the Church of England as the original Revelation.

Being now convinced of the duties we owed to God and to Revelation, we set to work to practise the duties it taught – to repent of our sins and amend our lives, to pray very earnestly,

Appendix

and to frequent the Communion celebrated every Sunday morning early in the chancel of St Mary's. An important matter to us was the teaching of Dr Pusey on *Baptism* and on *Post-Baptismal Sin*. From hearing these doctrines, most of us came to hold that, as a fact, we had been made 'temples of God in baptism'.

What was our present condition, if by sin perhaps from early youth or even from childhood, we had driven out the Spirit of God and had become a dwelling place of evil spirits? I do not know what to say about others; for myself no words can express the dark terror of my soul. But the Anglican doctrine, clear as it is about baptism, could tell us no remedy for sin committed after baptism.

It was for me most providential that I happened at this critical moment to come across a Roman Catholic book, Milner's *End of Controversy*. I read it eagerly, for I was in sore distress. I saw at once, first, that I had been misled and mistaken as to the tenets of the Roman Catholics – that they believed in One God and in Jesus Christ as their only Redeemer and source of Grace; I saw that they taught that, in Baptism, we are made Temples of God, that sin deserves everlasting punishment, but that if we sin God has provided 'a second plank after shipwreck',[3] equivalent, if repentance is deep, to a second Baptism – the Holy Sacrament of Penance – Confession and Absolution. This was the first time I had ever heard of this Sacrament. It was Milner who sent me to the Anglican Prayer-book for the same doctrine of Confession and Priestly Absolution, and then I saw it clearly laid down in the *Ordination Service of Priests* and in the *Office for the Visitation of the Sick*. I afterwards read the same doctrine in the works of Jeremy Taylor, and of other Anglican Divines.

I was immensely relieved, and began to practise confession, but never without misgiving, since the first attempt I made with a very High Church cathedral dignitary, who was so scared by my asking him to hear my confession that he said he really could not do it until he had consulted the Archdeacon! It was clear therefore that he had never met with anyone proposing to go to confession until that moment. What then was to be thought of a Church which had neglected for 300 years an essential Sacrament in which it professed in words to believe – what confidence could one have that in other weighty matters it had not neglected its trust?

This led me to see for the first time the meaning of the words in the Creed 'I believe in One, Holy, Catholic, and Apostolic Church'. I saw that the Roman Catholic Church was by far the largest portion of the Church of the Creed. I saw too that England was, up to the time of Henry VIII, a visible part of that Church. I supposed it was so still, or ought to be.

Doubts had begun to arise in my mind whether I ought not to become a Roman Catholic at once, for I could not see how the Church of England could still be a part of that Church from which it had separated. Still the example of Newman, and of so many, more learned and better far than myself, made me wish to be able honestly to dispel my doubts.

But that now happened in the Church of England which awoke us all from our dream that it formed any part of Catholic Christendom. It was on this wise: The Established Church, by force of a new Act of Parliament, found itself committed by the consent of its Bishops to enter into communion with the German Lutherans and Calvinists, in the establishment of a Bishop of Jerusalem, consecrated by the Archbishop of Canterbury, through a mandate of the Sovereign. This Bishop was to preside over a mixed community of Lutherans, Calvinists, and members of the Church of England, and to enter into communion, if they found the way open – if those heretics were willing – with Nestorians, Eutychians and other Oriental Christians.

In short, the act to which the State Church was absolutely committed, was, to faithful men in the Church of England, a revelation of the false step taken in the 16th Century, when the English Sovereign, with the full consent of the Bishops, made himself Head of the Church, through his law courts, 'in all causes Ecclesiastical as well as Civil, supreme'.

But Newman and others in good faith tried to content us, and prevent our leaving the Church of England; for he did not believe as yet that it was in schism, and though he was convinced that all Christendom ought to be united with the Bishop of Rome, he did not as yet see that out of that visible unity, the visible Church has no existence.

At this critical moment he published the famous *Tract 90*, the object of which was to show that the Thirty-nine Articles of the Church of England were not irreconcilable with the Decrees of

Appendix

the Council of Trent, the last General Council of the Church; that the Articles were intended to include Roman Catholics if they would give up a certain technical dependence on the Bishop of Rome. *Tract 90* produced an immense sensation throughout the country. This was quite unexpected by Newman. Edition on edition teemed from the press, and he was actually enabled with the proceeds to purchase a large and valuable library. It is that which was first at Littlemore, and is now at Edgbaston. The heads of the University, however, and the Bishops now raised an universal protest against *Tract 90*, and against all attempts to minimise the differences between the Church of England and the Catholic Church. Newman felt that his Eirenicon had failed. On us young men *Tract 90* had the effect of strengthening greatly our growing convictions that Rome was right and the Church of England wrong.

Now, having taken my degree, I began for the first time very seriously to turn my mind to becoming a clergyman in the Church of England – or perhaps a Catholic priest. Hearing that Newman intended establishing a kind of monastery at Littlemore, near Oxford, I volunteered to join him, and was accepted. We had now arrived at the year 1842, when we took up residence with Newman at Littlemore. Father Dalgairns and myself were the first inmates. It was a kind of monastic life of retirement, prayer and study. We had a sincere desire to remain in the Church of England, if we could be satisfied that in doing so we were members of the world-wide visible communion of Christianity which was of apostolic origin.

We spent our time at Littlemore in study, prayer and fasting. We rose at midnight to recite the Breviary Office, consoling ourselves with the thought that we were united in prayer with united Christendom, and were using the very words used by the Saints of all ages. We fasted according to the practice recommended in Holy Scripture, and practised in the most austere religious orders of Eastern and Western Christendom. We never broke our fast, except on Sundays and the Great Festivals, before twelve o'clock, and not until five o'clock in the Advent and Lenten seasons.

We regularly practised confession, and went to Communion, I think, daily, at the Village Church. At dinner we met together, and after some spiritual reading at table, we enjoyed conversation with Newman. He spoke freely on all subjects that came up, but I think controversial topics were tacitly avoided. He was most scrupulous not to suggest doubts as to the position of the Church of England to those who had them not.

I remember him once saying that eternal punishment was to him of all Christian doctrines the most overwhelming; that not reason alone, but faith only, in God having revealed it by an infallible authority, could accept it.

Again, he once said that there were no doctrines of the Christian revelation which presented anything like the intellectual difficulties that might be made to obscure the doctrine of God the Creator. Pantheism solved nothing; it only said, 'We know nothing but what we see, and we can draw from it, only that what is, is'. Newman would never let us treat him as a superior, but placed himself on a perfect level with the youngest of us. I remember that he insisted on our never calling him Mr Newman, according to the custom of Oxford when addressing Fellows and Tutors of Colleges. He would have had us call him simply Newman. I do not think we ever ventured on this, though we dropped the Mr and addressed him without any name.

It was his wish to give us some direct object of study (partly to keep us quiet) in his splendid library, in which were all the finest editions of the Greek and Latin Fathers, and School-men, all the best works on scripture and theology, general literature, prose and poetry, and a complete set of Bollandist *Acta Sanctorum*, so far as they had been printed. He had a project of bringing out *Lives of the English Saints*, and a translation of Fleury's *Ecclesiastical History*. I was set to work on the history of the Arian period, with a view to undertaking the translation of a volume.

Newman was an excellent violin player, and he would sometimes bring his violin into the library after dinner and entertain us with exquisite sonatas of Beethoven. It is said that a well-known Protestant controversialist – Canon Hugh McNeill of Liverpool – a great speaker on anti-Popery platforms, once advised himself to challenge Newman to a public disputation. The great man's answer was like himself. He wrote saying that

> Canon McNeill's well-known talent as a finished orator, would make such a public controversy an unfair trial of strength between them,

because he himself was no orator. He had had in fact no practice in public speaking. His friends however told him that he was no mean performer on the violin, and if he agreed to meet Canon McNeill, he would only make one condition, that the Canon should open the meeting, and say all he had to say, after which he (Mr Newman) would conclude with a tune on the violin. The public would then be able to judge which was the best man.

I have said that Newman never alluded to Anglican difficulties, or unless pressed, in private, by direct questions. Once I had been to confession to him; and in other ways he knew I was in great distress about the position of the Church of England ever since I read Milner's *End of Controversy*. After I rose from my knees I said to him, 'But are you sure that you can give me absolution?' He did not speak for a few moments, then he said in a tone of deep distress, 'Why will you ask me, ask Pusey.' This was the first indication I had received that he himself was seriously shaken as to his own position in the Anglican Church.

He soon perceived that I was more unsettled than ever. One day he came to my room and said, very kindly but abruptly, as if it was something unpleasant that he must say: 'Now I must tell you that you must leave us at once, or else you must promise to remain with us for three years.' I answered, 'In my present state of mind I could not promise that.' He said, 'Will you go and see Ward and have a talk with him?' I assented, and the next day I went by appointment into Oxford to see Ward at Balliol. I remember he took me for a walk. I think we talked for three hours, walking round and round the Parks, beyond Wadham College. In the end, I found myself without an answer, thoroughly puzzled, but unconvinced. Ward had just published a huge volume, *The Ideal Church*, in which he made a great point of the relations between *Conscience* and *Intellect*. His line with me was, that I must know that however convinced in my intellect that I ought to leave the English Church, I must not trust it unless my conscience was up to the same measure as my intellect; and that, knowing myself, could I say that I had cultivated my conscience, by obedience to all that I knew was the Will of God, so as to justify me in being confident in the judgment of intellect?

I went back to Newman in a state of perplexed conscience; but not seeing what else to do, and hesitating in my judgment about the duty of submission to Rome, since I saw that such a learned, wise, and saintly man as Newman did not see it to be his duty, I gave him a promise to remain for the stipulated three years at Littlemore. Years after I found that Newman had not expected me to give the promise.

I kept my promise for about a year, but I was dreadfully unhappy. I thoroughly believed in sin and in Baptism, and that there was no revealed way for the washing away of post-baptismal sin except the Sacrament of Penance, Confession, and Absolution; now I doubted seriously about Anglican orders, but still more about Anglican jurisdiction, for I could see no Church on earth but the Visible Church, in which the successor of St Peter is the Visible Head and Source of Jurisdiction, with the power of binding and of loosing given by Our Lord to His Visible Church under the Visible Head appointed by Him.

At last I could bear the strain no longer, and with great grief I left my dear Master, and was received into the Catholic Church in August, 1843. Newman and my friends at Littlemore and Oxford were greatly pained by my secession. Newman considered himself so compromised by it, that he immediately resigned his parish of St Mary's, and preached his last sermon – his last sermon in the Anglican Church – at Littlemore. It is entitled 'The Parting of Friends'.

Two years later, in 1845, Newman and the rest of his companions at Littlemore, and many others, made their submission to the Catholic Church. One of the first things he did after this was to pay me a most kind and loving visit at Ratcliffe College, near Leicester, where I was studying. He and many other learned disciples left the Church of England, (and many others have followed them) because, through profound study, and earnest seeking after God, during long years of patient waiting, so as to test each step thoroughly, they had come to be utterly convinced that the English Church had forfeited all claim to teach, from the moment it separated from the Visible Church, whose centre is at Rome, its circumference the round world itself. They saw that they had to leave the Church of England as by Law Established under Henry VIII; rather than join which Sir Thomas More, Cardinal Fisher, and hundreds of others, priests and laymen in England, Ireland, and Scotland laid down their lives.

Appendix 169

Our work among English Church people was sundered. Few of the friends we had left cared any longer to associate with us. We had become, I will not say, 'the scorn of men', for most men believed we were sincere, however mistaken; but we were 'the outcasts of our people'. And still more was this the case when the storm arose throughout all England against the Catholics, on the occasion of the restoration of the English Hierarchy, and what was called the *Papal Aggression* Act of Parliament. But a reaction came: the New Act against Catholics was ignominiously expunged from the Statute Book, as the result of this revulsion of public opinion. After a time, too, we found our old friends, long estranged, venturing to come near us again.

But no event, and no person, has had so much to do with producing this revulsion of public feeling as Cardinal Newman. Nothing is needed to prove this beyond the daily papers and reviews of this month, which show that his death has been treated by the public opinion of England as the loss of one of the greatest, most venerated of England's sons. Yet he was a Catholic, a convert, a Cardinal of Rome, and the writer who has done more to expose the errors of Protestantism than any writer for three centuries.

But during the greater part of the past fifty years the work even of Newman, and still more of the most of us, as priests in the Catholic Church, has been chiefly among the masses of the Irish Catholics resident in England, and the faithful remnant of the old English Catholics.

Yet, as we have ministered to Catholic congregations, many of all classes, and of all Protestant denominations, and many from the ranks of Socinians, and of Rationalists of every degree, have come to us, by all manner of different roads, and lines of thought, and, convinced by the same ultimate reasons that convinced us, have become Catholics.

But in the Church of England itself, the work of Newman is not over. He has done much to save it from the deteriorating spirit of a *State religion*, tending fast to Socinianism and Rationalism, and raised in it a desire widely felt to prove itself a part of the Catholic Church. English Churchmen, generally, have a pervading consciousness that they are in the presence of the majestic Visible Unity of the Catholic Church. That was not the case fifty years ago.

Meantime great numbers of the ministers of the Church of England, with the prestige of their position, teach publicly nearly every one of those Catholic doctrines which our forefathers abandoned 300 years ago. They delight to call themselves Catholics, and to think that they are one in doctrine with the ancient Church, from the days of St Augustine up to the days of Henry VIII. Perhaps there is but one doctrine they have not yet reached – the key-stone of the arch – the See of Peter – the centre and the test of Catholic Unity.

Let us hope that in the Church of England, men are as earnest, now, in seeking after dogmatic truth, and 'the Church of the Living God, the pillar and ground of the truth', as those who were the first leaders in the *Catholicizing* Movement of fifty years since. Well, it took Newman and Manning many years to reach this point, after they had, already, come to believe most Catholic doctrines. Yet, men of thought and earnestness cannot put themselves into our position of fifty years ago. The case of the *Jerusalem Bishopric*, and the *Gorham case*, were a *revelation* that the Church of England has its public teaching authority solely from the State. Its clergy may teach almost every Catholic doctrine, because all doctrines have been reduced to such opinions on *religion* as public opinion, and the House of Commons, which roughly, but clearly enough represents public opinion, will tolerate; and it will tolerate nearly everything, short of open atheism and downright Popery.

William Lockhart, B.A. (Oxon)

Notes

1. Originally published by Burns & Oates, London, 1891, and reprinted from an article in *The Paternoster Review*.
2. Taken from Tennyson's poem 'Sir Galahad' (1842).
3. A phrase used by the Church Fathers, cf. Tertullian, *De Poenitentia*.

BIBLIOGRAPHY

Works of William Lockhart
As Author
St Gilbert of Sempringham (1844; completed by J. B. Dalgairns).
A Few Thoughts for Thoughtful Protestants (1853).
Reasons for Rationalists (1853; republished with the above in 1864 as *Reasons for Rationalists, and Thoughts for Thoughtful People, a General Address to the principles of Colenso, Renan, and other Rationalising writers of the day*).
A Christmas Greeting to all Christians (1856).
Popular Lectures on the Catholic Religion (1858).
Popular Lectures on Who is the Anti-Christ of Prophecy? (1858).
Possibilities and Difficulties of Reunion. A Review of Dr Pusey's Eirenikon (1866; reprinted in *Cardinal Newman*, 1891).
'Non Possumus', or the Temporal Sovereignty of the Pope and the Roman Question (1867).
The Communion of Saints: or the Catholic Doctrine concerning our Relation to the Blessed Virgin, the Angels, and the Saints (1868).
The Old Religion, or How shall we find Primitive Christianity? A Journey from New York to Old Rome (1868).
Secession or Schism. A Review of the late Dr Neale's Sermon on Secession; with an Appendix on the 'Altar Bread Controversy' (1868).
S. Etheldreda's and Old London (1889).
Cardinal Newman: Reminiscences of Fifty Years Since (1891).
The Chasuble: its genuine form and size (1891).

As Editor
An Outline of the Life of A. Rosmini (1856).
Life of Antonio Rosmini Serbati (2 vols, 1886; Italian edition, 1888).

As Translator
Bussières, Baron Théodore de, *The Conversion of Marie-Alphonse Ratisbonne* (1855).
Ferré, Pietro Maria (Bishop of Casale), *St Thomas of Aquin and Ideology: A Discourse Read to the Academia Romana, 18th August 1870* (1875).
Rosmini, Antonio, *A Short Sketch of Modern Philosophy, and of his own System* (1882, with an introduction by Lockhart).
Rosmini, Antonio, *The Origin of Ideas* (3 vols, 1883).
Rosmini, Antonio, *Psychology* (3 vols, 1884–8).

Articles by Lockhart referred to in the Text
'Some Personal Reminiscences of Cardinal Manning when Archdeacon of Chichester', *The Dublin Review*, 1892.
'On the Road to Rome: A Psychological Fragment', *The Month*, November 1893.

General Bibliography
Abercrombie, Nigel James, *The Life and Work of Edmund Bishop* (London: Longmans, 1959).
Anon., *A History of St Peter's Parish, Roath, Cardiff* (Archdiocese of Cardiff, 2001).
Anon., *Butler of Wantage. His Inheritance and His Legacy* (Westminster: Dacre Press, 1948).
Anon., *Life of Mother Mary Agnes Amherst* (Exeter: The Catholic Records Press, 1927).
Badeni, June, *The Slender Tree: A Life of Alice Meynell* (Padstow: Tabb House, 1981).
Belcher, Margaret, *A. W. N. Pugin: An annotated critical bibliography* (London and New York: Mansell Publishing Limited, 1987).
Bellasis, Edward, *Memorials of Mr Serjeant Bellasis 1800–73* (London: Burns, Oates and Washbourne, 1923).
Belti, Remo Bessero, *The 'Rosminian Question'*, translated by John Morris, IC (Loughborough: Quorn Litho, 1992).

Bibliography

Benkovitz, Miriam J., 'Frederick Rolfe, Baron Corvo, Writes to Wilfrid Meynell', *Columbia Library Columns*, vol. 34, no. 1, November 1984.

Birt, Henry Norbert, *Benedictine Pioneers in Australia*, 2 vols (London: Herbert & Daniel, 1911).

Blehl, Vincent Ferrer, *Pilgrim Journey: John Henry Newman 1801–1845* (London: Burns & Oates, 2001).

Breffny, Brian de, *Unless the Seed Die. The Life of Elizabeth Hayes (Mother M. Ignatius, OSF)* (Rome: Don Bosco Press, 1981).

Brown, William Francis, *Through Windows of Memory* (London: Sands & Co., 1946).

Browne, Edward George Kirwan, *The New Spring and the New Harvest: A Resume of the Annals of the Tractarian Movement to 1882* (London: H. V. Clements & Co., 1882).

Chadwick, Owen *The Victorian Church*, 2 vols (Oxford: Clarendon, 1966 & 1970).

Chapman, Mark D., 'The Fantasy of Reunion: The Rise and Fall of the Association for the Promotion of the Unity of Christendom', *Journal of Ecclesiastical History*, vol. 58, no. 1, January 2007.

Coleridge, Ernest Hartley, *Life and Correspondence of John Duke Lord Coleridge, Lord Chief Justice of England*, 2 vols (London: William Heinemann, 1904).

Ellmann, Richard, *Oscar Wilde* (London: Penguin, 1988).

Fisher, Bernard, *Our Lady and St Joseph, Kingsland, N1, 1854–1964* (London: Antwerp Printing Works Ltd, 1964).

Gilley, Sheridan, *Newman and his Age* (London: Darton, Longman and Todd, 1990).

Gillow, Joseph, *A literary and biographical history, or bibliographical dictionary, of the English Catholics from the breach with Rome, in 1534, to the present time*, 5 vols (London: Burns & Oates, 1885–1902).

Gwynn, Denis, *Father Luigi Gentili and His Mission (1801–1848)* (Dublin: Clonmore and Reynolds Ltd, 1951).

Harting, Johanna H., *Catholic London Missions* (London: Sands & Co., 1903).

Hill, Rosemary, *God's Architect: Pugin and the Building of Romantic Britain* (London: Allen Lane, 2007).

Hirst, Joseph *Brief Memoir of Father Hutton, First President of*

Ratcliffe College, with the Course of Studies followed in the same College (Market Weighton Press, 1886).

Hirst, Joseph, 'Necrology: Father Lockhart', *The Ratcliffian*, Autumn 1892.

Hirst, Joseph, *Biography of Father Lockhart Printed with Additions from the Autumn Number of 'The Ratcliffian'* (Ratcliffe College, 1893).

Hirst, Joseph, *Father William Lockhart of the Order of Charity* (abridged) (London: Catholic Truth Society, 1912).

Howitt, Margaret, (ed.), *Mary Howitt, An Autobiography*, 2 vols (London: William Isbister Ltd, 1889).

Ker, Ian, *John Henry Newman: A Biography* (Oxford: Clarendon, 1988).

Kinealy, Christine & Mac Atasney, Gerard, *The Hidden Famine: Hunger, Poverty and Sectarianism in Belfast* (London: Pluto Press, 2000).

Lang, Andrew, *Life and Letters of John Gibson Lockhart*, 2 vols (London: J.C.Nimmo, 1897).

Leetham, Claude, *Ratcliffe College* (Ratcliffe: The Ratcliffian Association, 1950).

Leetham, Claude, *Luigi Gentili. A Sower for the Second Spring* (London: Burns & Oates, 1965).

Leetham, Claude, *Rosmini, Priest, Philosopher and Patriot* (London: Longmans, Green and Co., 1957).

Leslie, Shane, *Shane Leslie's Ghost Book* (London: Hollis & Carter, 1956).

Letters and Diaries of John Henry Newman (LD), vols 1–10, ed. Ian Ker, Thomas Gornall, Gerard Tracey, Francis J. McGrath (Oxford: Clarendon, 1978–2006); vols 11–31, ed. Charles Stephen Dessain, Edward E. Kelly, Thomas Gornall (Oxford: Clarendon, 1961–72).

Liddon, Henry Parry, *Life of Edward Bouverie Pusey*, 4 vols (London: Longmans, Green and Co., 1893).

Longford, Elizabeth, *A Pilgrimage of Passion: The Life of Wilfrid Scawen Blunt* (London: Weidenfeld and Nicolson, 1979).

MacDougall, Hugh A., *The Acton-Newman Relations* (New York: Fordham University Press, 1962).

McClelland, Vincent Alan, *Cardinal Manning: His Public Life and Influence 1865–1892* (London: Clarendon, 1962).

McEvoy, Sr M. Agatha, MFIC (writing as 'S.M.A.'), *A Brief Account of the Life of Mother Mary Elizabeth Lockhart, O.S.F. and the Foundation of the Franciscan Sisters of the Third Order Regular of the Immaculate Conception* (London: A. Quick & Co., 1959).

Manning, Henry Edward, *The Temporal Power of the Vicar of Jesus Christ* (London: Burns & Oates, 1880).

Mariani, Domenico, *The Rosminian Generals and Bishops* (Wonersh: Rosminian Institute of Charity, 2004).

Meynell, Viola, *Francis Thompson and Wilfrid Meynell* (London: Hollis & Carter, 1952).

Meynell, Wilfrid, 'Further Reminiscences of Father Lockhart', *Merry England*, July 1892.

Middleton, Robert Dudley, *Newman at Oxford. His Religious Development* (Oxford: Clarendon, 1950).

Morando, Giuseppe, *Guglielmo Enrico Lockhart* (Firenze: Uffizio della Rassegna Nazionale, 1892).

Mozley, Dorothea, *Newman Family Letters* (London: SPCK, 1962).

Norton, Anne F., *A History of the Community of St Mary the Virgin, Wantage: Foundation and Early Development* (unpublished MA Thesis, Oxford, 1974).

O'Connell, William, *Recollections of Seventy Years* (Boston and New York: Houghton Mifflin, 1934).

O'Donnell, Roderick *The Pugins and the Catholic Midlands* (Leominster: Gracewing, 2002).

Oxenham, Henry Nutcombe, *Dr Pusey's Eirenikon Considered in Relation to Catholic Unity: a Letter to Revd Fr Lockhart of the Institute of Charity* (London: Longmans, Green & Co., 1866).

Pattison, Mark. *Memoirs* (London: Macmillan & Co., 1885).

Pawley, Bernard and Margaret, *Rome and Canterbury through Four Centuries* (London and Oxford: Mowbray, 1981).

Pawley, Margaret, *Faith and Family. The Life and Circle of Ambrose Phillipps de Lisle* (Norwich: The Canterbury Press, 1993).

Purcell, Edmund Sheridan, *Life and Letters of Ambrose Phillipps de Lisle*, 2 vols (London: Macmillan & Co., 1900).

Purcell, Edmund Sheridan, *Life of Cardinal Manning Archbishop of Westminster*, 2 vols (London: Macmillan & Co., 1895).

Rinolfi, Angelus, *Missions in Ireland: especially with reference to the proselytizing movement; showing the marvellous devotedness of the Irish to the Faith of their Fathers* (Dublin: James Duffy, 1855).

Rosmini, Antonio, *Counsels to Religious Superiors*, edited by Claude Leetham (London: Burns & Oates, 1961).
Russell, Matthew, *The Three Sisters of Lord Russell of Killowen and their Convent Life* (London: Longmans & Co., 1912).
Sleigh, Leonard, *Saint Etheldreda's and Ely Place* (London: Paternoster Publications, 1952).
S.M.A., see McEvoy, Sr M. Agatha.
Stephen, Sir Leslie and Lee, Sir Sidney, (eds), *Dictionary of National Biography from Earliest Times to 1917* (Oxford: Clarendon, 1917).
Thureau-Dangin, Paul, *The English Catholic Revival in the Nineteenth Century* (London: Simpkin, Marshall, Hamilton, Kent, 1914).
Trappes-Lomax, Michael, *Pugin A Mediaeval Victorian* (London: Sheed and Ward, 1932).
Tristram, Henry, *Newman and his Friends* (London: John Lane The Bodley Head Ltd, 1933).
Turner, Frank M., *John Henry Newman. The Challenge to Evangelical Religion* (New Haven and London: Yale University Press, 2002).
Ward, William, *William George Ward and the Oxford Movement* (London: Macmillan and Co., 1890).
Whelan, Bernard, 'Father Lockhart', *Merry England*, June 1892.

INDEX

Akeroyd, Joseph 47, 70
Amherst, Mother Mary Agnes 62
Anderdon, Fr William Henry 13, 19
Arundell, Lady Mary 34, 46
Association for the Promotion of the Unity of Christendom (APUC) 116–8, 125
Athy, Miss 72, 83
Atkinson, Joseph 73, 79, 93, 111
Augustinians 76, 78

Baines, Bishop Peter 30–2
Baldwin Gardens 66, 91, 94–5, 99
Barberi, Blessed Dominic 29, 45
Bathurst, Catherine Anne 63
Bayswater Franciscan Sisters of the Immaculate Conception *see* Franciscan Sisters of the Immaculate Conception
Belfast 52–3
Bellasis, Edward 1–2, 97
Belton 45, 49
Benedict XIV 60
Benedict XVI (Joseph Ratzinger) xii, 143–4
Bertetti, Fr Pierluigi 50, 56, 59–60, 75, 79–80, 144
Bishop, Edmund 83–4, 129
Bloxam, John Rouse 18, 34
Blunt, Wilfrid Scawen 130
Bowles, Frederick 1, 26, 48
Boyle, Co Roscommon 54
Brown, Bishop Thomas Joseph 111–12

Brown, Bishop William Francis 103
Burton, George Ambrose 140–2, 153
Bute, Third Marquis of 85, 94
Butler, William John 41–4

Cambridge Camden (or Ecclesiological) Society 70
Capel, Mgr Thomas John 149–50
Cappa, Fr Giuseppe Gioacchino 134
Cardiff 85–6
Catholic Opinion 73, 110–12, 129
Chichester 18, 39
Clapton 76–8, 80–1
Clarke, Theodora Louisa Lane 131
Coen, James 114
Coffin, Bishop Robert Aston 40
Coleridge, John Duke 35
Confraternity of the Blessed Sacrament, Kingsland 83
Cornoldi, Fr Giovanni Maria 137–8
Corvo, Baron *see* Rolfe, Frederick
Costa, Fr Joseph 72, 81
Coventry 46
Crichton-Stuart, James 85–6

Dalgairns, Fr John Dobre 14, 26, 34, 48, 165
de Buck, Victor 123
de Lisle, Ambrose Phillipps *see* Phillipps, Ambrose

de Lisle, Edward 97
de Mendoza y Rios, Anna
  see Mendoza y Rios, Anna de
Dimittantur 60, 134, 136
Dominican Congregation of the Holy Rosary 63
Dominican Convent, Stone 96
Douglas, Edward 19
Dublin (Catholic University) 82

Ely Place
  see St Etheldreda's
Etheridge, Fr 59
Exeter College, Oxford 13–24, 82

Faber, Fr Frederick William 16, 68, 81
Ferré, Bishop Pietro Maria 146
Franciscan Sisters of the Immaculate Conception xi, 63, 86, 88
Froude, Richard Hurrell 15–16
Furlong, Fr Moses 32, 46, 48, 55

Gagliardi, Joseph 70, 80
Galway 53, 126–7
Gazzola, Fr 97
Gentili, Fr Luigi 29–34, 54
  early life and ministry 29–32
  and Lockhart's conversion 32–4
  and Ratcliffe 47
  and Shepshed 49
Gilbert of Sempringham, St 27, 33, 114
Gladstone, William Ewart 41
Glasgow 86–7
Grace Dieu 31–2, 45, 84, 116
Grant, Ignatius 97
Grant, Johnstone Horace 18–19, 21–2, 35
Greenwich 61–3, 86, 144
Gregory XVI, Pope 57–8

Griffiths, Bishop Thomas 15

Hanson, Charles 85
Harrison, Elizabeth 76–8
Harting, Vincent 92, 96
Hartwell 7–8
Hathern 45
Hayes, Elizabeth 63, 88
Headford, Co Galway 53
Hecker, Fr Isaac 111–12
Hibbert, Washington 50
Hope-Scott, James Robert 19, 66
Howard, Cardinal Edward 152
Howitt, Mary 131
Hoxton 73, 75–6, 155
Hussey, James 94
Hutton, Peter 32, 47–9

Ireland 51–5
Irish at Ely Place 99–100
Irish Church Missionary Society 53
Italian Church, Clerkenwell 79–80

Jacob, Martha
  see Lockhart, Martha
Jacob, William 6, 10, 38, 42
Jesuits xi, 57–60, 81
Johnson, Lionel Pigot 129–30
Jumpers 51–3

Keble, John 13–15, 40
Kelly, Thomas 66–7
Kingsland (Our Lady and St Joseph) ix, 66–79, 82–4
  schools ix, 72–5
Knox, Mgr Ronald x

Lamp, The 102, 112–14, 128–9, 131, 152
Lanzoni, Fr Luigi 134, 145

Index

Lee, Frederick George 116–18
Leo XIII, Pope 135–41
Lewthwaite, William Henry 70–3, 75–6, 78, 84, 94, 155
Liberatore, Fr 141
Lipowski, Henry 70
Littlemore ix, 1–2, 23–9, 36
Liverpool (St Joseph's) 51
Lockhart, Charlotte 19, 66
Lockhart, John Gibson 56, 66–7, 109
Lockhart, Rev Alexander 4–7, 9
Lockhart, Elizabeth
  and Bayswater 86
  childhood 7
  conversion 43–4
  death 87–8
  Foundress of (Anglican) Communities xi, 41–4, 61
  and Franciscan rule 86–7
  literary output 109
  and Lockhart 33
  and Manning 40–4
  and Rosminian vocation 61
  and Tractarianism 14, 40
Lockhart, Martha
  ancestry 6
  conversion 39
  death 88, 91
  health 63
  at Kingsland 69, 72
  literary works 62, 109
  and Lockhart 33, 38, 80–1
  and Manning 38–40
  marriage 6
  and Ratcliffe 84
  and Rosminian vocation 61
  schools 72–3
Lockhart, Fr William
  ancestry, birth and early years 4–6, 7–8
  and Mgr Capel 149–50
  at Cardiff 85
  conversion 20–1, 28, 34–7, 38–9, 168
  death, funeral and memorials 155–7
  and Gentili 32–4
  and Ely Place 93–106
  health 55, 153
  and Ireland 51–5, 98–107
  and Kingsland ix, 66–73, 93
  and League of the Cross 101–6
  and Leo XIII 135
  literary concerns 109–32
  literary works
    The Chasuble 124, 126–8
    A Christmas Greeting to all Christians 115
    Communion of Saints 115, 122
    Conversion of Marie-Alphonse Ratisbonne 114
    Life of Rosmini 60–1, 145–7
    Life of St Gilbert of Sempringham 27, 33, 114
    Non Possumus 124–5
    An Outline of the Life of Rosmini 62, 144
    Popular Lectures on the Catholic Religion 115
    Reasons for Rationalists 115
    Review of Pusey's Eirenikon 118–22
    Secession or Schism 122–3
    A Short Sketch of Modern Philosophy 146
    Thoughts for Thoughtful People 115
    Who is the Anti-Christ of Prophecy? 115
  and Littlemore 24, 26–9, 165
  liturgy 74–5, 125–8
  and Manning ix, 15, 19–20, 24
  missionary work 49–50

and Newman 16–17, 26–35, 159–70
novitiate 2
ordination 26–33, 48
and Oxford 13–24
and Oxford Movement 163–4
and *Post obitum* 139–42
and Ratcliffe 47–8, 84
and Roman Question 124–5
in Rome 54–6, 138, 154
and Rosmini x–xii, 17, 55–61, 144–7, 154, 161
and Rosminian Question 56–60, 134–47
rumours of episcopate 151–3
and Sir Walter Scott 10
and Stresa 60–1
Loughborough 32–5, 38, 46, 49, 63
 Mrs Lockhart's support 69
 novitiate at 2, 45
 Sisters of Providence at 46–7, 61–2

Macwalter, Gabriel Stuart 146
Maddalena di Canossa, St 30
Manning, Cardinal Henry Edward x–xi, 68, 78, 80–1, 86
 and APUC 117
 and Mgr Capel 149–50
 conversion 43, 170
 and Ely Place 93–4, 97
 and Kingsland 93–4
 and League of the Cross 102–6
 and E Lockhart 40–4, 86–7
 and M Lockhart 38–9, 78
 and W Lockhart ix, 15, 19–20, 24, 38–9, 152–3
 and Pusey 118–19
 and Roman Question 124–5
 in Rome 55–6
 and Rosminian Question 140
Market Weighton 155

Mary Monica, Sr
 see Lockhart, Martha
Mathew, Fr Theobald 102–4
Mayo, Co 53
Melton Mowbray 49
Mendoza y Rios, Anna de 30
Meynell, Alice 128–9
Meynell, Wilfred 6, 128–9, 131–2
Milner, Bishop John 20–1
Monteith, Robert 56
Morris, John Brande 14
Mount St Bernard 45

Neale, John Mason 122–3
Newman, Blessed John Henry ix, 47, 159–70
 conversion 26, 48, 168
 death 154
 and Littlemore 23–4, 26–9, 36, 161, 165–8
 and Lockhart xii, 16–17, 28, 36, 82, 135–6, 154, 164
 and Oxford Movement 13–14, 23
 Parting of Friends x, 36, 168
 and Pusey's *Eirenikon* 120–2
 and *Tract 90* 164–5
Norfolk, Duke of 94, 97

Oakeley, Frederick 15
Oriel College, Oxford 16, 160
Oscott 32, 36, 39, 48
Osgathorpe 45, 49
Oxenham, Henry Nutcombe 116, 121, 130
Oxford Movement 13–14, 32, 41

Pagani, Gian Battista 32, 34, 36, 48, 58–9, 77
 on opposition to Rosmini's writings 58–9, 65
 receives Martha into the Church 39
 writings 39

Index

Pattison, Mark 13
Phillipps, Ambrose x, 31–2, 45, 49, 115–18
Pius VIII, Pope 57, 145
Pius IX, Pope 58, 134
Plunket, Thomas, Second Baron and Protestant Bishop of Tuam, Killaly and Achonry 53
Polding, Archbishop John 83, 151
Pope, Thomas Alder 68, 112
Post obitum 139–43, 153
Prior Park 31–2
Pugin, Augustus Welby 33, 47, 49–50, 125–6
Pugin, Edward Welby 69, 77–8, 84
Pusey, Edward Bouverie 1–2, 14, 18, 20, 28, 163
  and *Eirenikon* 118–22
  and Elizabeth Lockhart 40–1
  and Gentili 32
  and Vatican Council 123

Ratcliffe College, Oxford 30, 33, 39, 47–9, 69, 81, 84, 88
Reid, Mary 41, 44, 87
Richards, Joseph Loscombe 14, 35–6
Richardson, Richard 70, 100
Rinolfi, Angelo Maria 32, 53, 55, 85, 126
Rolfe, Frederick 130–1
Roskell, Bishop Richard 68, 151
Rosmini-Serbati, Blessed Antonio 30, 33, 46, 48–50, 62
  and Holy See 55–60, 134–44
  and Lockhart x–xii, 17, 55–61, 144–7, 161
  and Manning 65–6
  and *Maxims* 33
  and Newman 135
  and Roman Question 124
Rotelli, Archbishop Luigi 152–3

Rugby 49–50
Ruskin, John 19
Russell, Sarah 83
Ryder, Mr 74

St Audeon, Dublin 54
St Bridget's-in-the-Crypt 94
St Bridget's Mission
  see Baldwin Gardens
St Charles' School, Bayswater 81
St Etheldreda's, Ely Place ix–x, 92–106
  Irish at 98–105
  purchase and restoration 94–8
St Etheldreda's hand 96
St John's Hospice, Hackney 76
St Joseph's Press 109, 113
St Marie's Church, Rugby
  see Rugby
St Marie's College 50
St Mary's Church, Stoke Newington (Anglican) 68
St Mary's Home for Penitents (Anglican) 42
St Matthias' Church (Anglican) 68
St Monica's Priory, Hoxton 76
St Scholastica's Retreat, Clapton 76–8
St Winefride's
  see Shepshed
Saffron Hill 66, 91–5, 98–100
Scott-Murray, Charles Robert 19, 21–2, 65
Scott, Sir Gilbert 95, 97–8
Scott, Sir Walter 4, 10
Serbati, Antonio Rosmini
  see Rosmini-Serbati, Blessed Antonio
Sewell, William 14, 22
Sforza, Cardinal Tommaso Riario 45
Shepshed 45–6, 49

Signini, Fortunatus 32, 70, 85, 93, 145
Sisters of Charity of the Precious Blood, Greenwich xi, 62, 72
  move to Bayswater 86
Sisters of the Convent of Our Lady, Greenwich 61–2
Sisters of Providence 46, 61, 63, 73, 94, 100
Sisters of Wantage xi, 41, 62–3
Society for the Irish Church Missions to Roman Catholics 52
Southey, Robert 41
Spencer, Fr George 115
Stoke Newington 76
Syston 47

Tayler, Archdale Wilson 68, 112
Tayler, Mrs 72, 112
Taylor, Fanny Margaret 113
Thompson, Francis 129
Total Abstinence League of the Cross xi, 101–6

Ullathorne, Archbishop William Bernard x, 31, 60, 96, 117, 126, 140–1

Vaughan, Cardinal Herbert xii, 55, 112, 155–6

Walsh, Bishop Thomas 32, 48
Walsh, Archbishop William 101
Wantage xi, 41, 43–4, 62–3, 87
Ward, William George 28–9, 118, 121–2
Weekly Register, The 82–3
Whelan, Bernard 96, 131
White, William 33
Whitty, Robert 55, 79–80
Whitwick Mission 45–6, 49
Wilberforce, Henry 43
Wiseman, Cardinal Nicholas x, 56, 58, 79–80
  and APUC 117–18, 120
  and Kingsland 66–8, 73
  and Lockhart 36–7
  and Rosmini 65–6, 144
Wynne, Rev John 13

Lightning Source UK Ltd.
Milton Keynes UK
174795UK00003B/1/P